The Grain Traders

The Story of the Chicago Board of Trade

by William G. Ferris

Michigan State University Press
1988

Printed in the United States of America

The paper used in this publication meets the minimum requirements of
American National Standard for Information Sciences – Permanence of
paper for printed materials ANSI 239.48-1984 ∞

Michigan State University Press
East Lansing, Michigan 48823-5202

Production: Julie L. Loehr
Editing: Carol J. Bracewell
Cover Design: Lynne A. Brown
Typesetting: the Copyfitters, Ltd.

Library of Congress Cataloging-in-Publication Data

Ferris, William G.
The grain traders.

Bibliography: p.   89-B1179
Includes index.
1. Chicago Board of Trade—History.   2. Grain trade—United
States—History.   3. Commodity futures—United States—History.   I. Title.
HG6049.F47   1988   332.64'4'0977311   88-42502
ISBN 0-87013-256-3

Contents

To Dottie

Preface

M any years ago, when one of my assignments for the Associated Press was to cover the Chicago Board of Trade on a daily basis, I was astonished to find that nothing that could legitimately be called a history had been written about the Board. There was one rather curious book, a chronological year-by-year record published in 1917 and obviously derived entirely from the newspapers of each year; and just as obviously subsidized by the Board. It was the first of three volumes of Charles Taylor's *History of the Board of Trade of the City of Chicago*. The other two volumes consisted of laudatory biographies of Board members.

This absence of a realistic history on grain futures trading contrasted with the numerous books available on Wall Street and its stock market manipulators. Such colorful figures as Jay Gould, Daniel Drew, J. P. Morgan, Jim Fisk and several others had attained a place in folklore and history. But their counterparts in the futures pits—Benjamin Hutchinson, Peter McGeoch, J. Ogden Armour, Joseph Leiter, James Patten and others—remained in the deep shadows. Yet the men in the pits were dealing with a far more essential product—the basic source of the world's food supply—than were the men who speculated in stocks and bonds.

So, over the succeeding years, when I had time I delved a little into the Board's history, as well as into agricultural history. I wrote a few articles which appeared in *Nation's Business*, *Farm Quarterly* and the *Journal of the Illinois State Historical Society*. I continued to research and rather vaguely thought of putting my accumulating knowledge into book form. When I retired in 1976, a history of the Board and commodity futures trading still had not been written. I decided to expand my research and write such a history myself; further, I enlarged the scope to include limited but relevant political and economic history.

The basic theme of this book is the development of commodity futures trading, the spawning of unethical and dishonest trading practices and the efforts, initially by the Board of Trade and later by the Federal government, to eliminate these abuses. Necessarily, the reaction of producers and consumers is part of the story. I end the book with the election of President Franklin Roosevelt in 1932 because, as everyone knows, that was a major turning point in the history of free markets.

My emphasis has been on personalities—first, because I think it makes for more interesting reading; and second, because individual actions had an enormous influence on marketing and prices during the free-swinging, swash-buckling years under review.

One problem with research on such a subject as commodity futures trading is the lack of records. Speculators wanted to keep their operations secret and were notably successful in doing so. Also, businessmen in general just don't maintain diaries, memos, papers and similar memorabilia as do statesmen, military figures, politicians and other people who live much of their lives in the public eye. Consequently, one is thrown back upon contemporary newspaper accounts more than otherwise would be the case. Such accounts may exaggerate some developments but they cannot alter statistics on prices, receipts, shipments or trading volume. Newspapers do give a flavor of the times not elsewhere available, and reveal the personalities of people through direct quotations.

Research was conducted in fourteen libraries around the country. Five other libraries sent me material either directly or through the inter-library loan program. Additional material was obtained from several government agencies. I was impressed by the willingness of these institutions to aid a person they did not know for a reason which might or might not be achieved. It was an example of the greatness of a free and open society in contrast with what the inquisitive individual might encounter in totalitarian societies. I did all the research myself and consequently if there are any errors they are solely mine.

Some essential material was sent to me by Melba M. Bruno of the National Agricultural Library, Jin W. Choi of the Chicago Board of Trade, Kate Hathaway and Nicholas Memoli of the Commodity Futures

Trading Commission, Vivian Wiser of the U.S. Department of Agriculture and Robert M. Kvasnicka of the National Archives.

There were two helpful librarians whose names I cannot recall. One
was at the Ouray Public Library in the silver mining country of Colorado,
who forwarded information on Ira Munn of the famous Munn v Illinois
U.S. Supreme Court case. The other was the librarian at the Hoyt Public
Library in Saginaw, Michigan, who sent me information on Jesse Hoyt,
an almost forgotten (except in Saginaw) capitalist of the Nineteenth Century. I should also mention an unknown reader at Michigan State University whose wise comments on how the manuscript could be improved
were gratefully accepted.

I am deeply indebted to Dr. Richard E. Chapin, director of the Michigan State University Press, who had the initiative and courage to publish
a first book by a 76 year old man. Also very helpful were Julie L. Loehr,
assistant to the director, and Carol Bracewell, an editor at the Press. They
both gave me the benefit of their editorial expertise and displayed unusual
patience while I made numerous changes in my copy and notes. Most
importantly I am indebted to my wife of 48 years, Dorothy Ferris, who not
only maintained our home during my forays into research and writing, but
also read copy on the entire manuscript several times as it progressed
through various editorial stages to its final typesetting.

William G. Ferris

CHAPTER ONE

Pioneer Grain Dealers

I n the reign of Edward VI (1547–1553) in England it was enacted that, "Whoever shall buy corn or grain with intent to sell it again shall be reputed an unlawful engrosser." Various penalties were prescribed for such a person, chief of which was that he "be set in the pillory and suffer imprisonment during the King's pleasure and forfeit all his goods and chattels."[1]

In Holland early in the 17th century, time transactions took place in the products of whale fisheries. The great uncertainty of the industry and the consequent fluctuations of prices led dealers to sell the products of any particular voyage long before its results were known. In the next century such transactions extended to many commodities, including grain.

Buying grain for delivery some time in the future was not new in the new world either, at the time it started in Chicago in the early nineteenth century. A letter written in 1636 from Samuel Symonds, deputy governor of Massachusetts, to John Winthrop, governor of Connecticut, outlines a typical purchase for future delivery—and with an admonition against nullifying the deal:

> I desire you would talk with Mr. Boardman and with his help buy for me a matter of 40 bushels of good Indian corn of him or of some honest man, to be paid for now in ready money and to be delivered at any time in summer as I please to use it. I would deal with such a man as will not repent if corn rise, as I will not if it fall.[2]

Yet it was in Chicago that speculation in grain futures, as distinct from speculation in commodities stored in warehouses, developed most vigorously and became the forerunner of speculation in "futures" in various other commodities and financial instruments such as Treasury bonds and stock indices.

In the early nineteenth century, Chicago was a very small hamlet, located on an almost stagnant little river in the sparsely populated northeastern section of Illinois. It took on a burst of life in the years immediately after 1833 when the local Indian tribes were forced to sell their ancestral lands.

The immigrants left the East for the prairies as soon as the ice in the Great Lakes broke in 1834. By mid-April the vanguard had descended upon Chicago; by mid-May they jammed the town, stirring it into frenzied construction activity.

Many of the newcomers settled on the fertile soil of the Rock and Fox river valleys, an area which ran through northern Illinois and southern Wisconsin. Mostly they were New England and New York farmers, and the land they would cultivate would become, prior to the Civil War, part of the Grain Kingdom just as surely as the land along the southern Mississippi and its tributaries would become part of the Cotton Kingdom.

"Chicago is a pretty good place for men who are in business for making money," one visitor wrote, "but is a miserable place for loafers."[3]

Among the men in business to make money were those associated with the grain trade, which increased rapidly as farmers settled the lush prairie lands. These grain men were known as "forwarders"—they forwarded grain to, and brought into town manufactured goods from, the East. From the start the street south of the Chicago river, appropriately named South Water Street, was the center of the grain trade.

The leading merchant in these early years was George Dole, who had arrived in Chicago in 1831. He was a partner of Oliver Newberry of Detroit, a widely-known entrepreneur of the period. Dole fought in the Black Hawk War and became the city's first treasurer when Chicago was incorporated in 1833. He would run for mayor as a Whig in 1844 but would not win.

In 1834 Almand Walker arrived, sent by his prosperous brother Charles, from New York State with a stock of boots, shoes and leather. The next spring Charles himself came, looked around and promptly bought some town lots; then he returned to his considerable commercial interests in New York.

Two years later the Walkers opened C. & A. Walker on South Water Street, a forwarding house carrying a general line of goods. John H. Kinzie and Captain David Hunter operated similar businesses on the north side of the river, as did their neighbor John S. Wright.

Mark Beaubein, Jr., who had a store on Lake Street near La Salle offering dry goods and groceries, occasionally sought grain from the countryside, as noted in an advertisement in the *Chicago Democrat* in 1837: "OATS WANTED—At the store of M. Beaubein, Jr., for which he will pay goods at cash prices."[4]

The boom collapsed in 1837. When all the banks in New York suspended specie payments in May, the panic was on. In Chicago money simply disappeared. Business was conducted with tickets reading, "Good for 10 Cents At Our Store" or "Good For One Shave." Small boys managed to drop a great many "Good For One Drink" tickets into collection boxes at churches.

In the dreary years following the collapse, Chicago had a hint of its future. Seventy-eight bushels of wheat—a minute sum—were exported in 1838 to Black Rock, New York, the port for Buffalo. This grain was placed in 39 bags and put on board the steamer Great Western by Charles Walker. It was sent to Walker's mill at Burlington Flats, Otsego County, New York. Here Walker, who had started life as a school teacher, owned a grist mill, potash factory and tannery.

Newberry & Dole—George Dole's firm—probably shipped grain in bags to various Lake Michigan ports across from Chicago this year, and also in the preceding years. But it was not until 1839 that Newberry & Dole sent a substantial cargo of 3,678 bushels to Black Rock. The shipment differed from that of Walker in a significant way: the Newberry & Dole shipment was in bulk, not in bags.

Traditionally, at Atlantic Coast and Gulf of Mexico ports, and also at St. Louis, grain was shipped in bags. There were several disadvantages. Loading and unloading consumed much time. The bags cost 2 to 4 cents each, which, while not enormous in itself, could mount to a sizeable sum for that period on large shipments. Then, too, the bags were often stolen. Sailors had a bad reputation for this activity; it was claimed that they made clothes out of the bags.

This was the first cargo of wheat shipped from Chicago in bulk, although bulk shipments had been made previously from Detroit and Cleveland. At this time Great Lakes sail vessels could carry about 4,000 bushels of bulk grain.

By the fall of 1839, when more grain came off the prairie and more vessels arrived in which it could be shipped, forwarding houses purchased large quantities of grain daily from 30 to 40 cents a bushel, a low price in this extremely depressed period. Much of this grain was held in Chicago over the winter and shipped east when navigation opened in the spring, but a portion was turned into flour for the local and near-by inhabitants.

The *Chicago American* took note of the influx of wheat this year, coupling it with a warning: "The way wheat is pouring into our forwarding houses and store rooms is a caution to all speculating monopolists."[5]

The grain dealers were not monopolists, but they were surely speculators. They had to be. As long as wheat fluctuated in price, anyone who owned it for even a short period automatically became a speculator. He could gain or lose money by events that might happen in any far-away corner of the world, and which would be reflected in the demand for and supply of grain. When wheat was bought in the autumn with the intention of shipping it east in the spring, as was the case in Chicago, the speculation could be long and perilous. Ordinarily prices would be higher in April and May than they had been in September and October, but the forwarders could not count on this and, when calculating their profit or loss, would have to include such costs as labor, transportation, insurances and other factors.

In 1841 an economic revival got underway, spurred by increasing wheat receipts. Some of the wheat that entered Chicago in the late 1830's and early 1840's came from the Wabash Valley in Indiana. The Hoosier farmers greatly intrigued the Chicagoans of that era. Mostly, the farmers arrived in huge Pennsylvania mountain wagons—the famed "prairie schooners"—drawn by eight or ten yoke of oxen or five or six span of horses. Bells suspended from an arch, as in Russia, as well as from the horses' backs, provided a merry tinkle as the wagons lumbered down Chicago's dusty streets. In 1843 the Wabash & Erie Canal reached LaFayette, Ind., thereby diverting much of the Wabash valley wheat from Chicago to Toledo. But by then Chicago had other sources of wheat.

As a result of expanding population in the Rock and Fox river valleys, annual harvests soared. The Chicago businessmen built additional warehouses to hold grain temporarily while it awaited shipment on the lakes.

The Newberry & Dole elevator started to utilize a horse powered treadmill to move a chain of buckets carrying grain from the ground level to the upper floor. Because the tread-mill made a great deal of clatter and got in the way on the ground, it was moved to the warehouse roof. Of course, the horse went with it.

Julian S. Rumsey, who later was to become mayor, and George Rumsey (both nephews of Dole and employed by him) along with Elihu Granger, conceived the idea and worked out the problems to construct the elevating apparatus. Granger, who also built the first flour mill in Chicago, later made a specialty of manufacturing machinery for elevating grain.

The roof top tread-mill became popular, with mules sometimes replacing horses. On one occasion an enterprising mule team was said to have journeyed from the top to the bottom of a warehouse in the night, safely arriving by means of a stairway upon the lower floor.

So, as the merchants erected new warehouses in the winter of 1841–42, they chose to employ horses and mules and not human labor to supply power. Mechanization—crude and clumsy, but possessed of a vast potential—succeeded the hand labor practice of St. Louis, New Orleans, New York and other grain terminals along the Mississippi River and the Atlantic Ocean, all of which had been handling grain for a much longer period than Chicago. These other cities continued to move grain on the backs of laborers. Thus another step was taken by the Chicago businessmen away from the old, established patterns. First was the shipment of grain in bulk; now came the use of mechanical means to place the grain in warehouses.

By 1841 one W. L. Whiting had become the city's largest grain dealer and was advertising aggressively that he was "prepared to do a General Produce Business, and can furnish merchants and farmers with storage for 50,000 bushels of grain and other products on reasonable terms. CASH at all times paid for spring and winter wheat and every facility for the shipment of produce to the New York and Canadian markets."[6]

Meanwhile, Bristol & Porter, another among the rapidly expanding list of grain dealers, proclaimed: "Money—not Michigan, but good funds—advanced on Produce, upon good terms."[7]

The snide remark about "Michigan" could have referred to the "cash" Whiting was offering. Bills issued by Michigan banks under the Land Loan Banking Laws of that state, like "canal scrip," "country scrip," "St. Louis scrip," and other forms of "money" could be converted into gold or silver only at a frightful discount. A general collapse of Michigan banks had occurred in 1839 and the Michigan State Bank suspended payments. These Michigan bills had a large circulation in Chicago at that time.

Eventually, the most respected currency in Chicago would be the "certificates of deposit" illegally issued by Wisconsin Marine & Fire Insurance Co., founded in Milwaukee by George Smith in the same year that the Michigan State Bank collapsed. The company was popularly known as "Smith's Bank." It never defaulted, always paid specie on demand, provided the West with needed funds, and made a fortune for Smith and his Scotch friends. The money of "Scotch George," as he was called, came to be used extensively in the grain trade.

The original grain merchant in the country was the operator of the general store. He sold items the farmers needed and, in part payment, took commodities the farmer produced. Merchants in country towns, like Whiting in Chicago, advertised they would pay the "highest price" for grain and on occasion offered to furnish sacks and the use of corn shellers. When he had accumulated a sufficient quantity of wheat and corn, the merchant took these grains to market.

With a wagon load of grain, the trip from Galesburg to Chicago, a distance of 200 miles, consumed two weeks. Farmers living on the Rock River took five days marketing 30 bushels of wheat. The maximum load for a two horse team was about 50 bushels.

In considering where he would market his grain, the farmer had to weigh the relatively high price in Chicago against the shorter distance to his nearest terminal. In 1841 when markets in southern, central and even northern Illinois offered 50 cents a bushel for wheat, Chicago paid an average of 87 cents. But for the farmer it was a question of which gave him the most profit after deducting his transportation costs.

With the passage of time and the expansion of grain production, more merchants in the small towns began to specialize in buying and selling grain. Thus evolved the country shipper. At Ottawa one firm alone, in 1842, advertised for 50 mule teams to haul wheat to Chicago. Later, the grain might be consigned by the farmer to a merchant for sale on a commission basis, and after the rails penetrated the prairies the farmer might go with his railroad box car of grain to sell it himself.

In 1845 the grain trade in Chicago boomed under the stimulus of sharply expanding arrivals and shipments. Nearly one million bushels were exported from the bustling city. Charles Walker moved to Chicago after forming a partnership in New York State with his brother-in-law, Cyrus Clark, under the name of Walker & Clark. Once again, a speculative mania seized the inhabitants. One businessman wrote, "Our business necessities will keep us clear, but it is hard to avoid wheat, copper, stocks and land or some other operation in which most all take a chance." One house, he said, "has actually made $30,000 in wheat operations and has on hand 100,000 bushels at an average cost of 73 or 75 cents."[8]

Of this period William Ogden, the leading citizen and first mayor, was later to write in his notebook: "I purchased in 1845 property for $15,000 which, 20 years thereafter, in 1865, was worth 10 million dollars. In 1844 I purchased for $8,000 what, eight years thereafter, sold for three millions of dollars, and these cases could be extended indefinitely."[9]

In the latter half of the 1840s grain dealers who owned warehouses began storing grain not only for themselves, but for others. Thus, they became warehousemen, a group of men who before long would become very unpopular. Men called shippers bought the grain and paid the storage charges until the grain could be moved east with the opening of lake navigation in the spring. Sometimes these shippers were acting for grain merchants in the East. Warehouse receipts, certifying to the existence of the grain in warehouses, were issued to the shippers. These warehouse receipts could be used as collateral when establishing credit or borrowing money.

A typical advertisement of the period was that inserted regularly by Orrington Lunt in *The Western Citizen*, a temperance and anti-slavery newspaper, and organ of the Liberal Party. His advertisement read:

> Orrington Lunt, forwarder and commission merchant, at the new white warehouse, South Water street, near Sauganash Hotel, Chicago. Liberal advances made on produce of all kinds in store, or consigned to him for sale or shipment, to be sold in Buffalo, New York or Boston. All kinds of merchandise consigned to him will receive prompt attention.[10]

Lunt, a native of Bowdoinham, Maine, arrived in Chicago in 1842. Two years later he made a timid entrance into the grain trade by receiving a cargo of oats from Buffalo for sale in Chicago. Soon, Lunt started shipping wheat and other grains to the East. He was credited with buying all the wheat in Chicago in 1846, about 50,000 bushels, which in effect cornered the local market. All of this wheat was sold to New York dealers in one transaction, which was regarded a stupendous deal at that time. Lunt built up a considerable fortune in a long career, donating land he owned in Evanston to Northwestern University.

The Chicago market was galvanized into furious activity in 1847 by a famine in Ireland, as well as poor crops in other European countries. Grain dealers, aware of the crop shortage, expectantly awaited information from Europe on in-coming vessels. When the "Hibernia" arrived in

New York late in May, bringing news of a demand on the British Treasury for relief in Ireland, the *Chicago Weekly Democrat* said, "Since the receipt of the Hibernia's news, by the speculators, considerable quantities of wheat in store have changed hands."[11]

The *Democrat* claimed that the "speculators" had private methods of obtaining news before the local newspapers, which may have been true. "Long John" Wentworth, publisher of the *Democrat,* was a Democratic Party politician who espoused the farmers' cause and criticized Whigs in the grain trade. At one time the grain merchants combined in a plan to refrain from advertising in his newspaper. "Long John," who was 6 feet 6 inches tall and weighed 300 pounds, owned a 4,700 acre farm near Summit, Ill., southwest of the city.

Prices continued to surge ahead and in early June the *Democrat* noted "unusual excitement in the commercial world." It reported large sales of wheat at $1.25 a bushel, the highest on record for Chicago. "Several thousand dollars," the newspaper said, "were made upon one lot of wheat by several different individuals as they successively bought and sold."[12]

Canals were superior to wagons for transporting grain in this era, and the businessmen of Chicago wanted a canal to tap grain areas south and west of the city. To raise funds the canal trustees sold adjoining lots on installment—one quarter down, the balance in one, two and three years. This gave rise to the phrase "canal time" to mean buying on time. A joke of the period concerned a doctor who speculated in lots on canal time. One day he left some pills for a patient and when the patient asked, "How do I take these?," the pre-occupied doctor replied as he hurried out the door, "Oh, one quarter down, balance in one, two and three years."[13]

By 1848 the Illinois & Michigan canal, as it was called, extended 96 miles from Bridgeport to La Salle and connected the Chicago and Illinois rivers. When the first boat arrived in Chicago, all the city was there to greet it, and Charles Walker gave a speech that newspapers described as "eloquent." Walker also was present this year when the first train puffed out of Chicago on the newly constructed Galena and Chicago Union Railroad to the Des Plaines River, where a farmer met it with a wagon load of wheat in bags. Walker bought the wheat and carried it back on the train.

Also in this year, Whiting and Thomas Richmond, a warehouse owner, met in Whiting's office and decided an organization of grain men was needed.

While there has always been an official version of what thereafter happened, a newspaper of the period notes another version. It said Richmond was elected president and Whiting secretary of the Board of Trade. Rooms were rented on South Water Street as a "place of resort, to collect information in relation to commercial and other matters, and to chat away leisure time." One objective was "to settle, by arbitration among merchants, warehouses and traders, and thus do away with . . . the many law suits that ordinarily arise between men of business."[14] The interesting word is "traders"; apparently there were men around even then whose occupation was trading—that is, speculating—in grain. And they were having quarrels with the warehousemen—quarrels which would intensify in the years ahead.

This, however, is not the accepted version of the Board's start. It appears to have been inserted in a weekly newspaper, *Gem of The Prairie*, by Whiting himself as the article lauds him, a big advertiser, as the city's leading grain dealer.

The accepted, official version of the Board's founding is that it was formed after several meetings of the leading businessmen of the city. The businessmen wanted George Smith—"Scotch George," the banker—as president, but he declined. Thereupon Thomas Dyer was elected president and Charles Walker vice president. Whiting served as treasurer for the first year, but thereafter disappeared from Chicago history.

Dyer was a meat packer. The 20 or so men chosen as directors were the leading businessmen of Chicago, many of them not associated with the grain trade. For a time Richmond was a director; later he held various committee positions of moderate importance. Rooms for the Board were rented over a flour store on South Water Street.

The original announcement stated the purpose of the Board was:

> . . . to maintain a Commercial Exchange; to promote uniformity and equity in trade; to facilitate the speedy adjustment of business suits; to acquire and to disseminate valuable economic information; and generally to secure to its members the benefit of cooperation in the furtherance of their legitimate pursuits.[1]

The Board got off to a slow start. Typical was the attendance record from July 9 to July 18 in 1851. On four of those nine days, no one appeared. On four other days, only one person was present. The banner day came July 10, when three persons confronted one another—Charles Walker, J. C. Walker and J. C. White. The only other member to show up in the nine day period was Orrington Lunt.

Yet things were astir along South Water Street in these mid-century years. A sense of its impending importance pervaded the city's commercial area. Until 1848, the *Chicago Journal* said, South Water Street had been "lined on both sides with a few honorable exceptions with as rickety a row of tumble-down tenements as ever groaned under a northeaster." The street itself, said the *Journal*, was "an elongated trench, filled to a depth with a compound of most doubtful consistency." But, the *Journal* added:

> Brick blocks of stores and offices have taken the place of many monuments to human endurance—new storehouses have been built, old ones enlarged and improved—and it will ere long be rendered worthy of the great wheat market of the great Northwest.[16]

NOTES

1. George F. Stone. Board of Trade in the City of Chicago. *Annals of Political and Social Science,* vol. 38, no. 2 (September 1911): 519.
2. *The American Elevator and Grain Trade,* vol. 14, no. 9 (March 1896): 326 (hereafter cited as AEGT).
3. Caroline Kirkland. *Chicago Yesterdays* (Chicago 1919), 35.
4. *Chicago Democrat,* 8 November 1837.
5. Weston A. Goodspeed and Daniel, D. Healy, *History of Cook County, Ill.* (Chicago 1911) 1:144.
6. Elias Colbert, *Chicago: Historical and Statistical Sketch of The Garden City* (Chicago 1868), 47.
7. *Chicago Tribune,* 24 April 1841.
8. Kirkland, op. cit., 25.
9. Isaac N. Arnold, *William B. Ogden and Early Days in Chicago* (Chicago 1881), 22.
10. *The Western Citizen,* 1 February 1841.
11. *Chicago Weekly Democrat,* 29 March 1847.
12. Ibid., 14 June 1847.
13. Arnold, op. cit., 22.
14. *Gem of the Prairie,* 22 April 1848.
15. Stone, op. cit., vol. 38, no. 2, 510.
16. Charles Taylor, *History of the Board of Trade of the City of Chicago,* Chicago, vol. 1, 1917.

CHAPTER TWO

Growth of Speculation during the Civil War

An enormous change occurred in the Old Northwest in the years immediately prior to the start of the Civil War. When the first ball flew toward Fort Sumter in Charleston harbor very early on the morning of April 12, 1861, the Old Northwest was the nation's granary, made so by a mighty immigration from Europe and the eastern United States in the preceding decade. The most important contributor to the granary was Illinois.

An area stretching across the Wisconsin-Illinois border west of Chicago had become the premier wheat growing section of the country, if not the world. Both Chicago and Milwaukee competed for the exportation of this wheat to the East. Production in the 20 counties in this area— 10 in each state—exceeded the total wheat and flour exports of the United States in both 1859 and 1860. The Cincinnati Railroad Record quite correctly noted that without the Old Northwest the United States would have no surplus of grain and "the feeding power, therefore, is in the Northwest."[1]

By 1860 Illinois' pre-eminence in corn production was not challenged by any other state. Of the 23 counties in the nation producing over two million bushels of corn, 18 were in Illinois; all four counties producing three million bushels were in Illinois. It would be corn, not wheat that would propel Chicago into the country's largest futures market.

In oats, Illinois production was about half (15,290,029 bushels in 1860) of the entire 15 slave-holding states (33,210,139 bushels), although to some extent the small oats production in the South reflected the longer foraging season available in that section compared with the North.

On the Monday following the Fort Sumter bombardment, one Chicago bank took a step which would be quickly followed by other banks: it would not accept for deposit the notes of several banks backed by securities issued by states in the South.

A bank could be formed in Illinois at this time by depositing with the state treasurer a certain amount of bonds of any state as security for the notes that bank planned to issue. A specie reserve (cash or equivalent) was not required for these so-called "wild cat" banks. Such a bank might easily be without capital, or even without business, in the place of its nominal location. More than half of the banks in Illinois were of this type—simply banks that issued notes on the basis of state securities deposited with the Illinois state treasurer. Many of these states were expected to secede from the Union.

Banks could be started by borrowing the required amount of securities for deposit with the state treasurer and paying for them with the notes received from the treasurer in exchange. Thus, the banks did the miraculous: they created money without having any to start with. A report of the Secretary of the Treasury in Washington on June 30, 1860, said of Illinois: "In that state is piled debt upon debt. Funded debt forms the capital of banks and floating debt the currency . . . ."[2]

Prices of the securities of southern and border states had been declining since the election of Abraham Lincoln, carrying down with them the value of the notes issued by banks. Soon after the election, Chicago bankers and brokers refused to honor at face value the notes of seven Illinois banks that were secured by these southern bonds. In view of the uncertain situation in banking, men in the grain trade hesitated on the first Monday after Fort Sumter to buy or sell. A "wait-and-see" attitude prevailed as far as grain was concerned, although a very active demand developed for flour in the East.

Over the next day or two a dual market arose in wheat. Owners of the grain were reluctant to sell to those offering to pay with checks drawn on banks whose notes were based on southern state bonds. Wheat closed ½ to 2 cents higher for buyers offering checks drawn on these banks than for buyers with checks drawn on banks that based their notes on northern bonds.

An immediate concern over the situation in Chicago was expressed in New York where it was recognized that wheat from the Old Northwest would be needed to feed the East and gain credits via exports to Europe. In an unusually frank appraisal, *The World* (New York) said:

> The trade of the West . . . is the main source of the astonishing prosperity and growth of northern cities. It is to secure a share of this lucrative trade that every important city of the seaboard has stimulated the construction of railroads to tap the Northwest . . . . New York was a petty town 'till the genius of Clinton* gave us the Erie canal, and the astonishing growth of this city since has been owing to the fact that we have the cheapest communication with the West.[3]

By the end of the first week following the surrender of Fort Sumter, the grain market reflected a developing panic among holders of notes secured by the shaky southern bonds: they rushed into the market to convert these notes into tangible property. The *Chicago Tribune* noted, "Besides the usual speculative and shipping inquiry for breadstuffs, there was an active demand by outside parties—money brokers, dry goods merchants, grocerymen and others not usually in the market."[4]

Demand for flour became so aggressive that most holders of this commodity did not bother to open their sample bags—buyers bought sight unseen, and generally at whatever prices the sellers wanted. Immediate shipment was required, indicating concern of eastern bakers that the onrushing war might disrupt their normal channels of supply. Throughout the entire year, as well as 1862, strong buying buoyed the flour market. Volume more than doubled during the pre-war years. A large portion of the flour trade which had flourished for years in some cities and towns on the Mississippi and Ohio rivers was transferred to Chicago.

Each day farmers, country shippers and Chicago grain merchants became more apprehensive over wild cat money (or stump tail as it was sometimes called). The term "wild cat" was used because a wild cat had been imprinted on the ill-fated money issued by Michigan. "Stump tail" was derived from a picture in Frank Leslie's *Illustrated Newspaper*, published in New York. The picture, part of the magazine's crusade against milk distributed in the city, showed emaciated cows with stumps for tails. This money was either rejected or taken at widening discounts in relation to notes of banks supported by bonds of northern states.

What Chicago needed was coin and specie. On May 9 the Merchants Loan & Trust Company, the leading Chicago bank at that time, received

---

*DeWitt Clinton, New York statesman, Republican, liberal in outlook, sponsored the Erie Canal when canal commissioner from 1810-1817. He was governor from 1817 to 1821 and again from 1825 to 1829.

$200,000 in gold from the East and the event was enthusiastically noted in the newspapers. The *Tribune* attempted to shore up the confidence of Chicago's business community by quoting *The World* (New York) to the effect that banks were sending coin to the West.

Although grain prices continued to advance, the upturn stemmed primarily from further deterioration in the value of money. Another panic swept the trade on May 12, just one month after Fort Sumter, and wheat advanced to 97 cents a bushel, corn to 33½ cents and oats to 20 cents. A month earlier wheat had sold at 80 cents and corn at 27 cents. Grain merchants not only lost confidence in money, but also in banks. The merchants asserted that the banks sorted out their currency, keeping the best in their own vaults, and paying out the worst when presented with checks. It would be a natural thing to do in a classic simplification of Gresham's Law—bad money drives out good money. Large numbers of commission men simply would not offer their grain for sale at any price. On May 14 wheat hit $1, that price being paid for Northwestern Club, the top grade.

The next day the market experienced another panic, creating the most exciting scenes witnessed on the Board of Trade since its founding. The organization had come a long way from those desultory days of only ten years earlier when free cheese, cakes and ale were needed to lure grain merchants off South Water Street and into its hall. As grain was the basis of Chicago's economy, so was the Board of Trade the most important economic body in Chicago at this time. So, when a group of grain merchants met to take a position on the monetary situation, their action had an effect on all Chicago business. These merchants resolved to accept currency for grain only at the rate at which it could buy eastern exchange, plus one per cent added—that is, exchanged for money in the East, primarily New York.

Holders of southern secured notes, dismayed and frightened by this action, rushed into the grain market and bought almost regardless of price. Quotations advanced so rapidly that experienced reporters could hardly keep track of them. Wheat jumped 9 to 10 cents a bushel, No. 1 spring selling at $1.08 to $1.11½.

That evening the warehousemen met and decided that they would not take currency in payment for storage except at a reduced rate in accordance with the value of eastern exchange. Two warehousemen would meet daily and set the rate at which they would receive currency, grain or eastern exchange in payment for storage. The first day's rates were:

currency at 75 cents on the dollar, No. 1 spring wheat at 84 cents a bushel, mixed corn at 23 cents, and oats at 10 cents. Eastern exchange was accepted at a 1½ cent premium.

On the same day, Missouri bonds tumbled to 35 cents on the dollar, Virginia to 43 cents and Tennessee to 45 cents on the New York Stock Exchange. A measure of the steepness of this decline is apparent in quotations for Missouri bonds: they sold at 67 cents on the dollar on April 1 and 51 cents on April 17. Earlier in the year these bonds had been close to par ($1.00).

Behind the decline in Missouri bonds was the intention of the state legislature to appropriate funds, including money intended for July interest on these bonds, for raising an armed force. Also, a new bond issue was planned for public defense. As for the southern bonds, Virginia and North Carolina were expected to secede and default. In Tennessee the president of the Bank of Tennessee, the financial agent for the state for transmitting the half yearly interest to New York, was an ardent secessionist. So was the governor.

The debacle in Illinois currency, and a consequent blocking in the flow of grain to the East, came at the precise moment that a strong demand for American wheat surfaced in Europe, particularly in England. *The World* (New York) asserted, "The European demand for grain is increasing and is likely to continue throughout the summer. Every facility ought to be granted by the New York banks for rapid movement of grain from the West."[5]

The newspaper was fully aware of the significance of American wheat at this critical moment in history. As a result of wheat exports, the newspaper said, "Gold will flow into New York to strengthen our specie reserves and enable us to pay the immense war expenditures without deranging the currency or curtailing bank accommodations."[6]

With business in Chicago practically prostrate, the most important single activity in the Old Northwest, barring agriculture, now exerted its leadership. Railroad executives met at the Tremont Hotel and composed a list of values at which currency could be redeemed in specie, subject to daily corrections from the New York Stock Exchange (that is, price changes on southern bonds). This list was sent to all agents of the roads. At par were four Chicago banks, one in Waukegan and one in Geneva. Values placed upon notes of other banks ranged from 50 cents to 90 cents on the dollar.

Nevertheless, the grain market continued to splinter. Quotations were made in three different categories of money—gold, preferred currency and common currency. Typical were the quotations on May 19 when No. 2 spring wheat was quoted at $1.20 to $1.30 in common currency and 85 to 87 cents in preferred currency. Northwestern Club wheat, the top grade, brought 88 cents in gold. Mixed corn was 42 to 45 cents in common currency, 31 cents in preferred currency and 28 cents in gold. The market had been shattered into a shambles by the failure of southern bonds. But at this point the directors of the Board of Trade resolved that "in the opinion of the Board of Trade of the City of Chicago, all sales of property and daily quotations thereof should hereafter be made in funds equal to specie."[7]

To cheer up the distressed business world, the *Tribune* reported that coin and State of Indiana money, which was in good standing, would soon reach Chicago: "The coin will be specially welcome, for it has been a decidedly scarce article for many months past." The newspaper added, "In a few weeks or months at most, everybody will be surprised that he could ever have been deluded into the belief that 'stump tail' Illinois currency was money."[8]

Despite the resolution and the editorial optimism, there still were grain transactions in Chicago in the various types of currency. Although gold from the East entered the city at a daily rate of $100,000, much of it went right out to the surrounding country—the country shipper and the farmer. The *Tribune*, which dearly wanted the business of the city to be conducted with sound money, acknowledged that commission houses still used stump tail because "everything called money goes into the interior as fast as it arrives" in Chicago.

Nevertheless, Chicago banks would accept on deposit only gold, Indiana, Ohio and Iowa currency. Illinois paper was no longer regarded as currency and was received only as a "special deposit." One E. I. Tinkham opened a clearing house for conversion of Illinois currency into southern bonds on which the currency was based. Many brokers throughout the city, ever willing to speculate, offered to buy Illinois notes by paying coin at a rate of from 10 to 20 per cent below the rock-bottom quotations on the railroad list.

Much of the depreciated currency continued to be used throughout Illinois at various list quotations. The floating supply of money in the state underwent a startling change, accompanied by a drastic falling off in commercial activity. Out of a total of 110 banks in Illinois, 89 failed. By 1862 only 17 banks, with a circulation of $400,000, were left in the entire state.

Before the disruption, Illinois note circulation had been above $12,000,000. The loss to the public reached millions. Security of 38 banks was sold for only 60 cents on the dollar, that of 25 from 61 to 70 cents, that of 11 from 71 to 80 cents and that of 15 from 81 to 100 cents.

Despite this collapse, the business interests of Chicago enthusiastically supported Abraham Lincoln and the Union cause. Here and there some dissent existed in the commercial world—Cyrus McCormick, the reaper king, had strong sympathies for the land of his birth (Virginia)—but it remained well out of sight among those associated with the grain trade.

A new group of grain men came to the fore during the war years, successors to Dole, Lunt, Walker and the other pioneers. They operated in a new Board of Trade—a long narrow room on the second floor of a new brick building on the north side of South Water Street, hard-by the odorous river and surrounded by the hurly-burly of the market place.

There was the 30-year old Benjamin Hutchinson—"all legs and nose, with the complexion of liver sausage and weighing only 100 pounds."[9] An ex-shoe manufacturer of Lynn, Massachusetts, he came west looking for a better chance after the panic of 1857. Also present was John Lyon, who would become the foremost exponent of attempted market corners after the war; N. K. Fairbank, ready to make a fortune in cottonseed oil sold as lard; Ira Munn, president of the Board of Trade from April 1, 1860 to March 31, 1861, whom the war would propel into being the leading elevator man in the city; A. E. and Sidney Kent, destined to become prominent figures in both grain and meat packing; George Seaverns, believed to be the first western man to clean and mix farmers' grain in order to raise its grade. He made a fortune at it.

Shortly after the war started, a memorial was introduced at a meeting of the Board's membership calling for an adoption of a resolution requiring every member or applicant for membership to subscribe to an oath of allegiance. In a debate of ascending heat, opponents argued that the Board was a place of business and should not get involved in governmental affairs; several strong pro-Union men took this view as well as southern sympathizers. As a result, the resolution was softened to refusal of membership to anyone "against whom suspicions of disloyalty . . . are known to exist."[10] Those already members did not have to take an oath.

When the Union forces scored their first victory of the war at Fort Donelson in northwestern Tennessee on February 17, 1862, General U. S. Grant became an overnight hero and the Board of Trade joined with other northern institutions in a "victory celebration," throwing its doors open to all comers and staging a wildly enthusiastic party. Many of the 13,000 prisoners taken in the Donelson battle were brought to Chicago and placed in Camp Douglas, 60 acres just outside the city limits, what is now 31st to 34th streets. At this early stage, death and wounds had not hardened the lines of ideology: some Confederate officers with social contacts were wined and dined by southern sympathizers. Union sentiment was outraged.

Munn, the ex-president, offered a resolution, passed by the membership, stating that the Board "frowns upon and condemns any attempt to make 'lions' and 'distinguished citizens' of any of the prisoners."[11] Munn and two other members were appointed a committee to visit Camp Douglas and see if they could persuade the commander to give them the names of Chicago residents who were providing succor to the prisoners and perhaps encouraging them to escape. Wisely, the commander refused, saying he did not have enough evidence to arrest any citizens.

Late in 1861, Fairbank introduced a resolution barring the *Chicago Times*, a Democratic, anti-Lincoln newspaper, from the Board's reading room, and also barring the *Times'* commercial reporter from the Board itself. The resolution was adopted by the membership.

Early in 1863, Munn visited Union regiments in the field and reported that they were in need of food. The Board distributed a circular through the city asking for contributions of fruit and vegetables. Later that year on the floor of the Board, Munn eulogized Lt. Col. Joseph C. Wright, a friend killed in action.

Munn was an elevator man. He arrived in Chicago from New Jersey in the 1850s, building his first elevator in 1856 as a partner in Munn, Gill & Co. The firm became Munn & Scott in 1858 upon entry of George Scott into the business. During the war the firm grew spectacularly. When the war ended, Munn & Scott had four elevators—Munn & Scott, City, Union and Northwestern. Their total capacity at that time was 2,700,000 bushels, larger than any other elevator firm in the city and, quite possibly, the nation. Munn logically became spokesman for the elevator interests.

Movement of grain out of the Old Northwest during the Civil War followed the Chicago-Buffalo-New York axis established in the Crimean War. Elevator capacity was greatly enlarged in Chicago, Milwaukee and other Great Lakes ports. Detroit and Erie built their first elevators. New York introduced floating elevators to speed shifting grain from Erie canal boats to waiting trans-Atlantic freighters. The first elevator of this type went into use in 1861.

When the war started, many merchants in Cincinnati, St. Louis and other cities with a long-standing tradition of southern trade, shut down their firms and moved to Chicago. By the end of 1861, eight hundred members made the Board of Trade a thriving center of commerce. In his report for 1862, Seth Catlin, secretary, said, "It is generally conceded that we are the gainers by the internal troubles that affect the country."[12]

It was not only the cash grain trade that flourished; speculation in futures, started timidly in the Crimean War period, expanded enormously. It was aided by changes made shortly before the start of the Civil War in the method of storing grain and, more importantly, by an improved inspection system to assure rigid quality control.

From the earliest days, spring wheat produced a better crop in Chicago territory than winter wheat. And almost from the start, Chicago merchants mixed wheat of varying qualities. The *Quid Nunc*, a short-lived and obscure Chicago publication,* noted as early as July 12, 1842:

> We are sorry to learn that the character of Illinois wheat has suffered materially from the practice of mixing spring and winter wheat by purchasers in this market. . . . Many of our farmers neglect cleaning their wheat properly and our warehousemen do not act honestly unless they keep their good and inferior grades separate.[13]

All through the 1840s and 1850s, complaints were heard about grain quality. As the influx of grain expanded, and as more and more grain was shipped east, the elevator men began to store grain other than their own. When the grain was stored in bags, it could be designated as belonging to the person or firm which had stored it. But, as the trade grew, it became necessary to store the grain in bulk. This procedure aroused complaints from those who had stored the grain—mainly local shippers to the East— and felt that when they ordered it out of the elevators they did not get as good a quality as they had put in.

Farmers and country shippers also complained. It was the foremen of the elevators who classified the grain according to the quality whether it arrived by train, boat or team. The higher the quality, the better the price in the market; therefore farmers and country shippers pressed to achieve the top classification and often complained that the warehousemen did not grade as high as they should have. This has been the position of historians on the accepted, but not proven, theory that farmers are more honest then businessmen.

Quid Nunc was the first penny paper west of the Alleghenies. It published from July 12 to August 16, 1842. Only two copies are known to exist, both in the Library of Congress, Washington, D.C.: July 12 and July 18. Winifred Gregory. *Union List of Newspapers.*

However, the warehousemen took a different position. They asserted that a strong competition existed to secure grain in order to fill elevator space and collect storage charges. This, they contended, caused an up-grading of the grain.

Each warehouse solicited shipments from country shippers with assurances that the grain would be "justly" graded. Each tried to outbid the other with the result, it was claimed by warehousemen, that the grain was graded higher than it merited—"if they did not, the shipper would change and ship to another elevator to see where he could get the best grade," explained S. D. Foss, one of the earliest inspectors.[14]

A hazard of the inspection system was the "plugged" car—the one with good quality grain on top and inferior quality below. Foremen inspected grain by picking up handfuls from various parts of the car, but they seldom got to the bottom. In the late 1850s, the grain "Tryer" was invented. The first such instrument was made by a tinsmith who covered a broomstick with tin and cut several holes in the side to admit grain after withdrawal of the broomstick. This enabled the inspectors to pick samples from any part of the car. The "Tryer" rapidly came into general use.

In 1858, as a result of the continuing and accelerating hassle over the warehouses, directors of the Board submitted a report to members stating, "The system of grain inspection is defective inasmuch as there is no uniformity and no responsibility attached to the inspection."[15] Thereupon, a three man committee was named to review the situation.

This committee took a most dour look at all aspects of the grain trade, except trading in futures. It said it was a "common occurrence" for farmers to send damp and dirty grain to market, "calculating that under the present system of inspection it will bring about as much as it would if it were thoroughly cleaned and in good order, and consequently it will not pay for them to clean it . . . ."[16] As for the country shippers, the committee said some of them "are in the habit of mixing at times oats, rye, barley screenings or samp and unmerchantable wheat with that of sound and good quality." And the shippers from Chicago to the East, the report added, "bill rejected and standard wheat mixed as all standard or even sometimes as extra, thereby much injuring the standards of our grain abroad (i.e., in the East) and consequently at home also."[17]

The Board set up an inspection system with a chief inspector and his assistants. But this was not effective because the assistants continued to be those very warehouse foremen. As a consequence, most all grain, at least so the warehousemen contended, continued to be placed in the top grade in order to induce shipments to individual elevators. Further, the warehousemen would not have the grain inspected when going out because of fear that the out-grading would not agree with their own in-grading.

The warehousemen were accused of reserving the best quality grain in their bins for themselves and also mixing various qualities of grain while it was in their warehouses. So strong was the condemnation of this and other alleged shoddy practices that, after much criticism and agitation, the warehousemen signed an agreement saying, "We will not under any circumstances mix any grain received . . . that has not been inspected with any grain that has. . . ."[1] They also agreed not to set aside the best grain for themselves.

Nevertheless, agitation continued and in 1860 the Board took over the inspection itself and named a chief inspector with the power to choose his four assistants, none employees of elevator firms. In contrast with the former inspection by the elevator foremen, who made no charge, a fee for inspection was collected from the owners of the grain or the firm to which it had been consigned. The Board collected the fee and paid the salaries of the inspectors. Classifications were established for all grains with specific definitions as to what was required for each classification.

At last the warehousemen were obliged to deliver grain of the same quality as the warehouse receipt specified when the grain was withdrawn from the warehouses.

These reforms, enacted shortly before the start of the Civil War, set the scene for a rambunctious trade in futures during that conflict. Buyers and sellers were assured their activities would be supported by warehouse supplies of grain of the specific grade in which trading was conducted. The combination of specific grain grades and general warehouse receipts sparked the growth of speculation.

The first boom in grain prices during the war occurred in oats and reflected buying by the Army Quartermaster Corps to feed horses in the field. Oats sold within a narrow and low price range of 12 to 24 cents during 1861, being held down by a bountiful supply of corn, a competitive grain. But next year trading became more excited and the price, after starting at 16 cents, got as high as 43½ cents by the end of the year, despite the fact that receipts expanded to 4,688,722 bushels in the year ended March 31, 1863.

Farmers in territory tributary to Chicago rushed to plant oats. Large acreage expansion was recorded in Illinois, Iowa and Wisconsin.

Reducing their own need as much as possible by substituting other grains, farmers shipped what were considered enormous quantities of oats to Chicago—11,005,743 bushels in the year ended March 31, 1864. Shipments out of Chicago at 9,909,175 bushels were three times greater than in any previous year. Railroads were taxed attempting to forward oats to the Union armies. Chicago commission men, acting as either agents or principals, filled contracts let all over the United States.

Oats rose from a low of 30½ cents in August to 72 cents in the week of October 13, 1863. The boom was accompanied by a spectacular surge in wheat and corn as speculation swirled to a peak in the get-rich-quick atmosphere that gripped the city—"every third man who has a thousand dollars to spare is eager to put it up as margin to buy wheat, corn or oats,"[19] the *Tribune* asserted.

In the following year, oats receipts expanded to an incredible 16,365,440 bushels, just about 15 times what they had been in the prewar years, and the weight of this supply kept prices under control despite a very substantial demand. A high of 81 cents in July contrasted with a low of 57 cents in October, 1864. The next year the high was set in March at 55½ cents and a low at 26 cents in December, after the war ended.

The North went into the Civil War on the heels of the two gigantic corn crops (1860 and 1861) and the major problem of the grain trade in Chicago was to find the capacity to receive, store and ship this grain. In the glutted market, prices held at low levels. But this situation changed suddenly and spectacularly in 1863, when a frost on the mornings of August 29 and 30 cut down thousands of corn acres in many areas of the Old Northwest.

The corn market responded by rushing higher. As a result of speculative buying, the Chicago price was forced out of line with the Buffalo price. It became unprofitable for shippers to purchase corn at Chicago for shipment to the hungry masses in the eastern cities where corn might be sold by barefoot girls boiling corn in iron pots on street corners and offering it to passers-by in the most familiar cry of the mid-1800s: "Here's your nice hot corn, smoking hot, just from the pot!" The pipeline which carried corn from the Old Northwest's farms to the cities of the East was blocked by a speculative drive for profits in Chicago. The *Tribune* noted on October 12, "Besides the normal speculative inquiry, we observed quite a number of new faces on the Board—and the inquiry by outsiders was unusually brisk."[20]

The new faces were also noted by John Beaty, the Board's new secretary, who said that some of those present should not have been there. He posted a notice claiming, "Some people, not members, have come upon the Board of Trade and tried to transact business."[21] This was a violation of Board regulations and Beaty was quite stone-hearted about it: even those who claimed they were buying corn for a poor widow would not be admitted. "If the friends of this poor widow who desire to purchase a car of corn or potatoes will represent her case satisfactorily to the secretary," Beaty said, "he will guarantee to have either bought for her free of commission, and thus serve the poor widow without violating a rule of the Board."[22]

From a low of under 50 cents in April, the corn price soared to 98 cents in mid-November before some of the speculative steam escaped. This was the highest price on record for Chicago up to that time. But the following year the price jumped to $1.40 on November 19 in reflection of light receipts throughout the year because of the 1863 crop failure. Big crops in 1864 and 1865 pushed the price down. Wheat was not neglected for corn and oats by speculators during the war years.

The wheat crop of 1861 was in poor condition—damp, sprouted or musty—upon arrival in Chicago. As a result, agitation once again arose over wheat grading. It was claimed that wheat which could not pass inspection, and therefore could not be stored in elevators, would be carried off in bags and then blown, dried, scoured and mixed with good quality wheat. Then the bagged wheat would be smuggled into various warehouses and disappear amidst wheat stored in bulk.

In August the Board of Trade appointed a committee to investigate the situation, reflecting the Board's concern over the low repute of Chicago wheat in the New York market. Chicago wheat sold at a lower price than wheat of the same grade from Milwaukee. Henry Cooper, chief Chicago inspector, claimed, "Our best grades are sold there [New York] for Milwaukee or Racine Club, leaving only the poorer grades to represent Chicago spring, thereby detracting from the reputation of our wheat . . . giving also a false and undeserved importance to wheat from other cities."[23] Regardless of whether this was correct or not, the committee decided, and the warehousemen agreed, that warehouses should not put into storage any bagged wheat.

Wheat prices during the Civil War steadily firmed. In 1862 prices fluctuated from 60 to 90 cents, never encountering much speculative interest. The next year wheat climbed above $1, touching a peak of $1.15 on

October. In his annual report for the year, John L. Hancock, president of the Board, could look at the wheat, corn and oats markets, not to mention the demand for hay, and conclude: "We have passed through another year of great prosperity in trade and commerce, and many of the members of this association have made fortunes in the past season in their legitimate business."[24]

It was such unabashed avarice that caused the Irish in Bridgeport, along the Illinois & Michigan Canal which they had dug, to toast Confederate victories and call the hostilities, "A rich man's war and a poor man's fight."

In the speculative mania that seized the city, grain traders bought and sold from early morning until well into the night. The so-called First Board opened at 8:00 a.m. on the corner of Randolph and Clark streets, cynically referred to as "Gamblers' Corner." Then came the regular, official meeting in the Board of Trade hall at 11:00 a.m. In the early afternoon the traders were back on Gamblers' Corner. At 6:00 p.m. the striking Court House bell "cleared the sidewalks and allowed pedestrians to pass unmolested," according to the *Tribune*. But that was not all. At 7:00 p.m. the Fourth Board met at the Tremont Hotel. Dealings continued until 9:00 p.m. when the exhausted traders decided they had had enough for one day.

An extraordinary advance in price for wheat, by far the greatest ever seen in Chicago up to that time, highlighted trading in the summer of 1864. It was accompanied by a run-away market in "highwines" (whiskey) in which warehouse receipts for highwines in store boomed in price prior to placing a Federal tax on all whiskey stocks manufactured after July 1 but not on whiskey already manufactured. The evening trade in highwines and grain in the Tremont became so boisterous that on April 13 the keepers-of-the-inn told the men to leave. Undaunted, they found more hospitable accommodations at the Sherman House.

As the price of wheat rose in Chicago, a fantastic upturn occurred in gold at New York. Both were commodities into which large and small capitalists, and just plain people with a few loose dollars, rushed to convert their money. The public was spurred by fright at the possible outcome of the war. Wheat parted company with gold on June 16, advancing while gold sank into a brief decline. Such action by wheat indicated a local speculative demand in the Chicago market.

Further proof of this speculation was the fact that Chicago wheat prices were much higher than wheat prices in the East, "and there is no inducement whatever for sending produce forward," according to the *Tribune*—that is, there was no profit in sending grain to the East, so it was not sent.[25]

Of the speculative turnover, the *Tribune* noted on June 22, "We hear that much of the grain purchased here on eastern account is resold in this market, such transactions in a continuously rising market bring larger, quicker and more certain returns than by shipping it to New York." The newspaper added, "The demand is chiefly speculative and the same property changes hands sometimes half a dozen times a day—and the sales are heavier than ever before in the history of the market."[26]

On June 28, when the price was around $1.75 a bushel, the *Tribune* noted:

> Outside capitalists, afraid of constant depreciation of the currency, are investing in produce of all kinds, and merchants of all grades, stimulated by the general excitement, are taking their surplus moneys and dashing into wheat, corn or whiskey markets, seemingly regardless of the consequences.[27]

Many of the speculators continued to get rich quick the next day, when wheat soared 15 to 20 cents. At that point the bankers, apparently struck by a momentary remorse, withdrew their support. The *Tribune* said, "Our bankers today refused to advance a cent on this classification [speculation], and to men whom they had heretofore accommodated."[28]

The restraint of the bankers did not last long, nor did it have much effect, for the market continued to race ahead in the first weeks of July, along with the price of gold in New York.

With the war actually approaching a successful end for the Union cause, it seems incongruous that the northern population was less convinced of victory at mid-1864 than at any other time in the conflict. But the prices of wheat and gold, and the extreme weakness of northern currency, clearly attested to this somber fact.

News from the fighting fronts was not encouraging. In the Wilderness campaign, General Grant was suffering a frightful loss of men without appearing to be accomplishing anything against the skills of General Lee. General Sherman's famous march through Georgia was stalled even before it got to Atlanta. A Confederate raid in Maryland in early July cut telegraph wires between Washington and the North; for several days the nation could not get in touch with its own capitol. In such a situation, rumors and genuine fear must have embraced sensitive markets.

Reflecting this frightening condition, gold soared in the New York "black market" to $275 an ounce, U.S. currency reached its lowest point of the war at $35.08 compared with $100 in gold and wheat jumped above the $2.00 mark reaching a peak of $2.11½ on July 9.

Panic buying ended when the Confederates were thrown back from Maryland, wires from the capitol restored, and news arrived that the famous Confederate raider, the "Alabama," had been sunk off Cherbourg on June 19 by the "Kearsarge." By the end of July, wheat had retreated below $2.00.

All the North, farm and city, boomed during the latter years of the Civil War, but nowhere was the boom greater than in Chicago. Endless statistics, from the number of new gas mains to the number of new marriages, set records. With some awe an English visitor reported, "Chicago may be called the metropolis of corn—the favorite haunt of the American Ceres. . . . In Chicago there are great streets and rows of residences of a new Corn Exchange nobility . . . the country was bursting with its own produce and smothered in its own fruits."[29]

With the end of the war came the end of the great Civil War boom in grain prices. At that time the prices quoted by the Board of Trade were for cash—or "spot," as it was called—grain. But there can be no doubt that trading in grain futures, which had its impetus in the Crimean War period, matured during the Civil War. This is attested by the comments of Secretary Beaty in his report for the year 1864, issued in 1865:

> It is true that speculation has been too much the order of the day, and buyers on "long," "short," and "spot" have passed through all gradations of fortune, from the lower to the higher ground, and in many instances have returned to the starting point, if not a step lower, but it is to be hoped that with the return of peace this fever of speculation will abate, and trade will be conducted on a more thoroughly legitimate basis.[30]

NOTES

1. John G. Clark, *The Grain Trade In The Old Northwest* (Urbana 1966), 197.
2. George William Dowrie, *The Development of Banking in Illinois*, 1817–63. University of Illinois Studies in the Social Sciences (Urbana, December 1913) vol. 2, no. 4, 153.
3. *The World*, (New York) 16 April 1961.
4. *Chicago Tribune*, 2 April 1861.
5. Ibid., 14 May 1861.
6. Ibid., 15 May 1861.
7. Ibid., 24 May 1861.

8. Ibid.

9. *AEGT,* 15 December 1883, 103.

10. Alfred T. Andreas, *History of Chicago from the Earliest Period to the Present Time* (Chicago 1884–86) 2:338 (hereafter cited as *History of Chicago).*

11. Ibid.

12. Fifth Annual Report of the Chicago Board of Trade (Chicago 1863), VII.

13. *Quid Nunc,* 12 July 1842.

14. *AEGT,* 15 January 1894, 226.

15. Ibid.

16. Ibid.

17. Ibid.

18. Ibid., 227.

19. *Chicago Tribune,* 13 October 1863.

20. Ibid., 12 October 1863.

21. Ibid.

22. Ibid., 14 October 1863.

23. Andreas, *History of Chicago,* 2:343.

24. Sixth Annual Report of the Chicago Board of Trade (Chicago 1864), VI.

25. *Chicago Tribune,* 21 June 1864.

26. Ibid., 22 June 1864.

27. Ibid., 28 June 1864.

28. Ibid., 30 June 1864.

29. Paul M. Angle, compiler, *Prairie State, Impressions of Illinois 1673–1967 By Travelers and Other Observers* (Chicago 1968), 348.

30. Seventh Annual Report of the Chicago Board of Trade (Chicago 1865), VII.

CHAPTER THREE

First Attempts to Corner the Market

The leading businessmen of Chicago during the Civil War found the base for their activities in livestock, grains, railroads and merchandising. In the grain trade, Ira Munn became pre-eminent as an elevator man while John Lyon was the foremost shipper of grain to the East, particularly corn. The outstanding speculator was Benjamin P. Hutchinson.

Hutchinson descended from Thomas Hutchinson, Loyalist governor of Massachusetts in the years leading up to the Revolutionary War. He was born in Middleton, Massachusetts and for a while manufactured shoes in Lynn. After the panic of 1857, when his business failed, he moved to Milwaukee and briefly worked for John Plankinton, a famous Milwaukee packer. Plankinton's plant spawned several Chicago business leaders and Plankinton himself was a factor in grain speculation in both Milwaukee and Chicago for many years. Hutchinson transferred to Chicago before the Civil War and during the war built up his capital in the early flour boom. When Board of Trade Secretary Beaty issued his caustic remark about speculators, Hutchinson surely was one person he had in mind.

Hutchinson also entered the meat packing business, forming Burt, Hutchinson & Snow. In 1865, 320 acres of John Wentworth's marshland along Halstead Street was turned into the famous Union Stock Yards and when the Yards opened on Christmas Day, Burt, Hutchinson & Snow was the first packing house to move to that area.

These early businessmen had, within the commercial field, some of the qualities of Renaissance men: Hutchinson also busied himself with banks. When the First National Bank of Chicago was formed in 1863, Hutchinson and Edmund Aiken, the president, each owned 175 shares—more than any other stockholders.

Meetings leading to the formation of this bank had been held in Aiken & Norton's room at the Board of Trade building. Hutchinson was also one of the original directors of this bank. At the first annual meeting in 1864, it was disclosed that Hutchinson had become the largest stockholder. He owned 300 shares; Aiken was second with 212. But Hutchinson disposed of his shares in June, 1867 for reasons not known, but at a time when he was very actively engaged in trading in the grain market.

While much of the trading in grain during the Civil War was for future delivery, it was not until October of 1865, after the war was over, that the Board officially recognized this type of activity by setting up a minimum list of regulations for it. And it was not until 1878 that the Board's annual report began to list quotations for transactions in futures.

Delivery of the cash grain had to be made in Chicago. A seller could not hand the buyer a warehouse receipt for grain stored in Davenport, Iowa. The amount of storage space in Chicago was limited, even though it underwent almost yearly expansion. The nature of futures trading and the requirement that the grain to be delivered on the futures had to be in Chicago created a situation where the sellers of the futures might not be able to comply with the terms of the trade.

When an individual sold futures contracts, he agreed to deliver a certain amount of grain at a specific time. However, if he did not want to deliver the grain, and as time progressed this became habitual, he offset his early sale by buying an equivalent amount of futures. The offset was accomplished by "making a ring" among brokers or even within the confines of a single brokerage firm: several brokers got together and offset the buy and sell orders of their customers.

Nevertheless, it was possible for the buyer or buyers of futures contracts to push sellers into a corner. This could be accomplished if the buyer also owned all or most of the grain in store at Chicago elevators. In this case the sellers had few options, all unfavorable: he could bring grain to Chicago and store it to make delivery, but only if there was storage room (which in a well-managed corner there is not); he could buy enough futures contracts to get out of his position but only at an extortionist price set by the man or men who had bought the futures and also owned the grain in store; he could default on his contracts to deliver and permit officials of the Board, or the courts, to set a price at which his contracts with the buyers should be "settled."

Attempts at cornering sellers became a prominent trading feature after the Civil War when the Board moved to new trading facilities on the second floor of a new Chamber of Commerce building at the southwest corner of Washington and La Salle streets.

In the mechanics of the market place, no one was more astute than Hutchinson, a tall, thin fellow, somewhat morose in personality, who liked to dress in the somber style of Abraham Lincoln. He also liked to quote Shakespeare and he memorized—and compelled his bookkeepers to memorize—several of John Greenleaf Whittier's poems. He walked in long, easy strides and his deep voice carried well above the hubbub of the grain pits. As far as one could judge externally, he rarely became excited. In a day when some form of mustache or beard was sported by almost all businessmen, he was clean shaven. But the most arresting thing about him was his long, hooked nose. He must have been somewhat ashamed of the appearance it gave because there are no photographs of him, although unposed drawings abound.

Hutchinson took to the buying side of wheat in 1866 and rode along on the crest of an almost total crop failure in Illinois, Iowa and other states tributary to Chicago. In July No. 2 spring wheat sold as low as 87½ cents but by September, when it became apparent that the Illinois crop was ruined, the price soared to $2.00. The big advance came in mid-August as Hutchinson and his followers cornered the sellers who had sold for delivery during the first weeks of August. In the week ended August 4, wheat sold from 90 to 92 cents; in the week ended August 18 it sold from $1.85 to $1.88—an extraordinary surge in so brief a period and a sure sign of panic buying on the part of those who had sold but did not have the grain on hand to deliver—the short sellers, or just "shorts," as they were called.

In this same year, Burt, Hutchinson & Snow was merged with A. E. Kent & Co. to form the Chicago Packing and Provisions Co.. For many years Chicago Packing and Provisions placed a broom over its door, a symbol of the fact it had slaughtered more hogs during the previous year than any other packing firm in the city. A few years later—in 1870—Hutchinson further expanded his business activity by reentering banking, from which he had withdrawn in 1867. He organized and became first president of a new financial institution, the Corn Exchange Bank,

with the primary purpose of supplying credit to the grain trade. Through
the merger route, this bank would, many years ahead, become part of the
Continental Illinois National Bank, the largest bank in the city.

Prior to this development, however, Hutchinson was involved in a far-
cical but historically significant episode that nearly landed him in jail. In
August, 1867, trading activity on the Board of Trade was enlivened when
a deputy sheriff appeared on the floor and served summonses on several of
the more active grain men, including Hutchinson. The summonses had
been issued at the behest of Daniel Goodrich, a disgruntled former member of a grain commission firm.

This action was based upon a law passed the previous winter by the
Illinois legislature, dominated at this time by farmer interests. With the
end of the Civil War, farm product prices fell, distressing farmers and
stimulating them to search for a culprit. Their resentment converged on
the market place and particularly on those who sold grain when they did
not possess the actual commodity—in other words, short sellers.

At the same time this agrarian discontent manifested itself, the
Chicago warehousemen became embroiled in arguments with commission house brokers on the exchange. The brokers, anxious to increase
their commission business, sought to encourage speculation by forcing
the warehousemen to adhere to rigid standards of inspection and grading
of grain. As a result, the warehousemen retaliated against the brokers by
supporting the efforts of farmers to restrict "gambling" in grain futures.

The bill passed by the legislature provided for regulating the warehousemen, but it also included a provision prohibiting short selling in futures.
Violations were considered misdemeanors and the guilty could get up to
one year in prison and a fine of $1,000, half of which went to the informer.

This law was the first attempt by a government body to regulate trading
in futures on the Chicago Board of Trade. Significantly, the impetus for
the legislation came from the producers, not consumers, and it followed
upon a price decline which, of course, was viewed as harmful by producers. This pattern would be followed throughout the Board's history:
the farmer and not the urban consumer would be most effective in imposing restrictions on speculating in grains.

Hutchinson and his fellow culprits in the August, 1867 incident were
taken from the Board of Trade in horse-drawn hacks to the cheers of other
members. In court they met Goodrich and something of a burlesque took
place. Goodrich maintained that he was simply a concerned citizen
anxious to see the law enforced while the grain men insisted that the

proceedings be handled quickly as they had to get back to the trading floor, where they were received with acclamation. Goodrich failed to put up a bond needed to prosecute. The next year the sections of the legislation relating to short selling were repealed.

The possibility of cornering grain, as shown by Hutchinson in 1866 and 1867, appealed strongly to other traders. In 1868 there were corners or "squeezes," a mild corner, almost every month. A particularly large corner in wheat occurred in June and July. It was run by John Lyon in Chicago and Angus Smith in Milwaukee.

Lyon differed from Hutchinson. Lyon handled the actual grain, and in very large quantities for that period. There is no indication that Hutchinson ever shipped grain in any quantity; he simply speculated in price changes.

Like so many other early Chicago grain men, Lyon was born in the East and drifted westward to Chicago at that moment when the city was about to soar in population and wealth. A native of Canandaigua, New York, born in 1829, he moved with his parents to Ashtabula County, Ohio when he was two years old. Like other early Chicago grain men, he had little formal education. What he would eventually know—and he got to know a great deal about grain—he would learn through experience. When he was 14, he left school and became a clerk in a store. Three years later he opened his own general store and commission business in Conneqant, Ohio. After two years he came to Chicago and bought a membership on the Board of Trade for $15.

Angus Smith, a Michigan farm boy, arrived in Milwaukee in 1854. In the Crimean War wheat boom he amassed a fortune. Four years later, with the partial backing of Jesse Hoyt, a New York grain merchant with extensive interests in grain elevators, railroads and real estate, Smith built Milwaukee's first grain elevator. Subsequently, he became the leading warehouseman in Milwaukee, owning what he claimed to be the world's largest elevator.

The climax of the Lyon-Smith corner came in June in Chicago and in July in Milwaukee. In Chicago the corner was in No. 2 spring wheat, the type Lyon specified he wanted when he bought for future delivery. Ordinarily, No. 1 spring wheat, a better grade, sold higher than No. 2 by around 6 to 7 cents. But because Lyon would not accept No. 1, that grade fell as much as 10 to 12 cents under No. 2.

By June 30, the last day for making delivery on June contracts, the shorts in Chicago felt themselves in a very tight squeeze. They paid $2.18

to $2.20 a bushel in the cash market to get the grain to deliver to Lyon. At no time during the corner did the price in New York, normally considerably higher than in Chicago because of transportation costs, get above $2.02. On July 1 prices at Chicago broke sharply—a sure sign that there had been a corner. In very slow trading, small lots sold for $1.80.

In Milwaukee, Smith worked his corner in No. 1 spring wheat. On July 31 this grade sold at $2.26 while No. 2 was only $1.79—a fantastic spread of 41 cents between the two grades.

The Lyon-Smith corners, coming on top of several smaller corners and squeezes, prompted the directors of the Board to outlaw such activities. Directors solemnly approved this resolution:

> Resolved, that the practice of 'corners', of making contracts for the purchase of a commodity, and then taking measures to render it impossible for the seller to fill his contract, for the purpose of extorting money from him, has been too long tolerated by this and other commercial bodies in this country to the injury and discredit of legitimate commerce, and these transactions are essentially improper and fraudulent, and should any member of this Board hereafter engage in any such transactions, the directors should take measures for his expulsion.[1]

These noble sentiments, however, had no effect on the way commercial life was lived in this raw-knuckle age.

In 1871 the commission brokers gained a notable victory in their struggle with the warehousemen, a small group loved by no one. Farmers, country shippers, speculators, eastern buyers—all criticized the warehousemen for various infamies and all received support in their criticism from the crusading Chicago newspapers.

The *Chicago Tribune* was particularly incensed about activities in the elevator business, a feeling not ameliorated when Ira Munn became one of the founders of a competitive morning newspaper—the *Chicago Republican*. While the *Republican* initially had Charles Dana as its editor, it did not stay afloat long in the turbulent Chicago journalistic seas. It was succeeded by the *Inter Ocean*, which lasted somewhat longer as the *Tribune's* chief rival.

The peak of the antagonism against the warehousemen was reached in the Illinois Constitutional Convention in 1869, where farmers, commission brokers and speculators succeeded in convincing the delegates to enact a regulatory article—Article XIII—in the constitution, an odd place for such a matter. In April, 1871, the state legislature in three acts implemented the article, the new laws taking effect July 1, 1871.

For the most part, the acts imposed regulations which the Board of Trade had striven to apply with mixed results. The governor appointed a three man Board of Railroad and Warehouse Commissioners, consisting of Gustav Koerner, the legal member and chairman; D. S. Hammon, representing the farmers; and Col. Richard Morgan, representing business interests. Under this triumvirate, the major executive officers were a chief inspector, William Tompkins, who had power to appoint assistant inspectors, and a registrar, Stephen Clary. Both were stationed in Chicago.

The enactment of these acts, coming shortly before the Great Chicago Fire, would eventually lead to a famous U.S. Supreme Court decision which sanctioned government regulation of strictly private business.

Later in 1871—October 6—the Great Fire flamed across Chicago, consuming a vast area of hovels and mansions, factories and stores in the tinder-dry city. Included in the destruction were the Chicago Board of Trade with its books and records, the state grain warehouse registrar's office and its books, and six of the seventeen grain elevators that stood somberly along the city's narrow waterways. Approximately 2½ million bushels of storage capacity was wiped out in the flames.

A few days later, the Board appointed a committee to sell the damaged grain in store at public auction. Grain in the poorest condition was given away. A very little in the best condition brought as much as 60 cents a bushel. The total realized approximated four cents a bushel for all grain in the burned warehouses.

Chicago's major economic support, the grain trade, suffered a severe temporary blow. For a brief period railroads could bring in little or no grain, but within a few weeks were running at normal levels. During the 1871–72 winter, the reduced storage capacity was entirely filled.

An immediate problem arose because many warehouse receipts, kept in various offices throughout the commercial district, disappeared in the holocaust. The state legislature, convened in extra session, passed an act authorizing the delivery, by warehousemen, of grain stored prior to October 8, 1871, without the presentation of any warehouse receipt, upon proof, that the originally issued receipt was destroyed by fire.

It will be remembered that shortly before the Great Fire, the legislature had implemented Article XIII of the Constitution with acts limiting the activities of the warehousemen. These acts required that all public warehouses (public being warehouses where grain was stored for compensation) obtain licenses from the Circuit Court of their county, file a bond of $10,000 for the faithful discharge of their duties as public warehouses and give the registrar a report of all warehouse receipts issued and canceled as well as a report of all grain received and delivered. The acts also prescribed the maximum rates for storage.

Generally, the warehousemen were agreeable to those provisions relating to maintaining accurate records of grain in store and receipts outstanding. But, with other provisions of the law, there was a complete lack of compliance. Claiming these provisions constituted an unnecessary and unwarranted interference with their business, the warehousemen refused to take out licenses or post the $10,000 bond. They continued to charge such rates as they had been accustomed to charge.

These rates were set at the start of the year and announced in newspapers in January. In 1872 the rate for wheat received from railroad cars was 2 cents a bushel for the first 20 days, after which it became ½ cent a bushel for each succeeding 10 days. The rate applied from November 15 to April 15. A slightly higher rate prevailed for grain received from the canal. All warehouses had the same rates.

However, the warehouse acts required that the 2 cent rate apply for the first 30 days and the ½ cent rate for each succeeding 15 days. Thus the law imposed a sharp reduction in the income that the warehousemen would receive. Ostensibly, the lower rates were to benefit farmers. By the time the grain got to Chicago it was likely to be owned by various types of businessmen—shippers, millers, exporters, receivers and speculators.

In September, 1871, Charles H. Reed, the State Attorney, filed criminal charges against the warehousemen. This included Ira Munn and George Scott, the partners operating warehouses with the largest total capacity, and such other operators as George Armour, Hiram Walker, John Edenazer Buckingham and Wesley Munger. The charge—or "information," as it was called—was similar in each case; only the individual's name was changed. (An "information" is filed by a prosecutor; an "indictment" is an accusation framed by a prosecutor and found by a Grand Jury.)

Ignoring both the failure to follow the fee schedule or to post bond, the information centered on one point: the warehouses had not taken out licenses as required by the warehouse acts. The State Attorney's action was viewed as the start of a test to determine the constitutionality of the law.

As has been noted, the next month the Great Fire swept through Chicago and the information of the State Attorney in September was laid aside. But on June 29, 1872, a new information was filed in criminal court contending that on the previous day Munn and Scott's Northwestern elevator was operating without a license, contrary to a provision of the warehouse acts.*

The Northwestern was located on West Water Street and Indiana Avenue (now Grand Avenue) in an area of several other elevators. All escaped damage in the Great Fire. Built in 1862, the Northwestern had a storage capacity of 600,000 bushels. It was neither the largest nor the smallest in the city, but it was destined to become the most significant grain elevator in the country's history.

The case came before Judge Farwell in criminal court on July 6, where it was known as People vs Ira Y. Munn and George L. Scott. A motion to quash the information was overruled. The defense pleaded not guilty. A jury trial was waived on an agreed statement of facts. The court found the defendants guilty. A motion to set aside the finding and for a new trial was overruled. Munn and Scott were fined $100, the minimum penalty set by the warehouse acts for operating a public warehouse for one day without a license.

Munn and Scott appealed to the Illinois Supreme Court, which, after the usual time-consuming delays, got around to discussing the written arguments of the attorneys in 1873. Of these discussions, Chief Justice Sidney Breese was to say in his subsequent majority opinion that the Court "after much deliberation was unable to reach a satisfactory decision."[2]

In the middle of this year the Illinois court underwent a considerable transition, out of which Justice Breese emerged as Chief Justice. It is possible that he knew this upheaval was forthcoming when the deliberations on the Munn and Scott case were held; he certainly knew that in June the term of Chief Justice Lawrence was to expire. A month earlier, Justice Thorton resigned, leaving two vacancies on the seven man Court.

Chief Justice Lawrence, highly regarded by the legal fraternity, was renominated. But agrarian leaders decided to mount an aggressive assault on the State's judicial system. They nominated Alfred Craig, who, as a member of the constitutional convention of 1869–70, had favored a granger program to regulate corporations. This drive by the farm bloc was stigmatized in conservative circles as an attempt to pack the judiciary in favor of one class, but Craig won. So did the other agrarian candidate, John Scholfield, succeeding Justice Thornton.

As a result of Chief Justice Lawrence's defeat, Justice Breese became Chief Justice—and there before him was the still undecided People vs. Ira Y. Munn and George L. Scott case.

---

*Benjamin Goldstein, *Marketing: A Farmer's Problem* and Solan J. Buck, *The Granger Movement*. See the June 29 filing and subsequent July 6 hearing as a continuation of the original information filed prior to the Great Fire in October, 1871. But this is obviously incorrect as the filing and hearing applied specifically to the operation of the Northwestern on June 28, 1872.

Sidney Breese and Ira Munn were poles apart. Munn was a go-getting businessman, an immigrant to Illinois from the northeast, ardent supporter of Lincoln and the Civil War even to the extent of wanting to know the names of visitors of Confederate prisoners at Camp Douglas. But he also had been a member of a committee to clean up the Chicago River, a dumping ground for slaughter houses, tanneries, sewerage. Near the end of the war, Munn led a city-wide group of businessmen who persuaded Chicago banks to receive on deposit and to pay out at par only national bank notes and "notes of such other banks as redeem at par in Chicago," thereby halting the circulation of depreciated eastern bank notes.[3] Thus he was partly responsible for preventing what might have been, at the end of the war, a currency collapse similar to that at the war's start.

Although born in New York State, Breese migrated to Illinois and studied law in old Kaskasia, a southern Illinois city with strong emotional ties to the Confederacy. He became a Jacksonian Democrat and for many years batted around the state in various political, editorial and legal positions, but his heart and mind remained attuned to southern Illinois. During the Civil War he was a Copperhead, in contrast to Munn, a staunch Republican. In 1857 Breese was elected to the Illinois Supreme Court. When he wrote the majority opinion in the Munn and Scott case, Breese was 76 years old. That opinion came down against Munn and Scott.

Prior to rendering the opinion, Breese stated that the election had brought two new justices to the Court and explained, "to enable them to participate, a reargument was directed." He did not say by whom, but it must have been by him. He also noted, "A case of so much importance demanded, and has received, our utmost careful consideration."[4]

Curiously, some mystery surrounds the size of the vote. When the case eventually went to the U.S. Supreme Court, Justice Fine, writing the minority opinion, said the Illinois Court upheld the state by a three to two majority. In that event the majority would have consisted of Breese and the two newly-elected farm bloc justices.

But Section II of Article VI of the Illinois Constitution adopted in 1869–70 provided that the Illinois Supreme Court consist of seven justices, that four constitute a quorum and that "concurrence of four shall be necessary to every decision."[5] In this case Justice Walker, while not agreeing with all the contents of the extended opinion of Justice Breese, said he concurred. Presumably this concurrence was enough to make the decision valid even though, in Justice Fine's view, the majority was only three to two. The opinion on file in the Illinois Supreme Court is not signed.

The case moved along to the U.S. Supreme Court, where it became the famous Munn vs. Illinois. By a wide seven to two majority, the Supreme Court upheld the decision of the Illinois Court. Briefly, the Court ruled that the elevator business constituted a public use and therefore could be regulated by the government as a matter of "public interest." It was the first application of this principle, quickly followed by other so-called "Granger cases," and it paved the way for extensive government regulation of privately owned business.

Liberals have always hailed the majority opinion but for many years conservatives rejected it. One such conservative appraisal concluded, "The elevator case directly strikes at the stability of private property, at rights which lie at the very foundation of modern society and civilization."[6]

By the time the Court had rendered its decision, Munn had disappeared. The vanishing act followed a little cooperative action with Lyon, who decided in the year following the Great Fire to attempt another corner. Almost certainly he was encouraged by the reduction in storage space, which made a successful corner easier to achieve.

Along with Lyon and Munn was Hugh Maher, who at one time had been a lumber dealer, then a coal dealer, then a grain dealer, and thereafter his occupation was listed as "real estate" in the 12th and subsequent annual reports of the Board of Trade. He played politics too, at one time serving as a Democratic alderman from the second ward. Like many a good Irishman, Maher claimed an intimate friendship with Stephen Douglas. Also involved was F. J. Diamond, who over the years had been broker for Munn and Scott.

Lyon started buying wheat in late spring for delivery to him in August. Evidence of his maneuvering surfaced early in July when wheat for August delivery sold between $1.16 and $1.18 a bushel. Slowly the price climbed until it reached $1.35 by the end of the month.

Not surprisingly, wheat arrivals expanded as the Chicago price rose on the stimulation of buying from Lyon and his cohorts. Farmers hurried to clear the old crop—that of 1871—from their bins and harvest the new 1872 crop. Arrivals, which averaged less than 14,000 bushels a day prior to July 15, rose to 20,000 daily in the next week, to 25,000 in the last week of the month and to 27,000 the first week of August.

And it was during this week—on August 5—that the Iowa elevator burned down.

By some quirk of fate, the Iowa elevator had escaped the fire in the previous year, even though it was surrounded by lumber yards and coal piles in the burnt-out north division of the city. Built in 1857, the Iowa originally served as a warehouse for stoves. Additions and improvements over the years had not noticeably changed this rickety wooden structure, one of the smaller of the city's elevators, located on a corner piece of land dividing the Chicago River from the North Branch.

A blanket of legal writs disputed ownership of the Iowa, but no one doubted that Maher, the erstwhile lumber, coal and grain dealer turned real estate operator, owned the land on which it stood.

Maher had taken possession of the structure itself early in the year, moving in during the noon hour when workers for Spruance, Preston & Co., the previous occupiers, were enjoying lunch, and withstanding a call to the police to dislodge him. Thereafter, as Maher's name became prominent in the rumors circulating about Lyon's wheat deal, some Chicago banks refused to lend money on the warehouse receipts issued for grain stored in the Iowa. Apprehensive and cautious grain dealers also grew reluctant to accept Iowa warehouse receipts.

The elevator was badly damaged, but some grain was recoverable. A week previous the Iowa's management had reported to the state registrar that the elevator held 128,065 bushels of corn and 47,124 bushels of oats. It held no wheat. After the fire, holders of warehouse receipts for between 318,000 and 373,000 bushels of corn (estimates varied) came forward. Considering the fact that the Iowa's capacity was only 300,000 bushels, the number of receipts outstanding seemed very remarkable indeed.

It was not possible, at this time, for the warehousemen to over issue receipts; that is, issue receipts for grain which had not gone into the warehouse. As a result of earlier episodes of this nature, every receipt that was now issued by a warehouse had to have the signature of the state registrar, and this could be obtained only when he had a report through the state inspector that the grain had been stored in the warehouse. Without this registrar's signature, no warehouse receipt was valid for the transfer of grain.

Maher, however, found a method to circumvent the philosophy behind these regulations. He "showed it was possible to sell grain belonging to other people without calling in the receipts at all," the *Tribune* noted.[7] Furthermore, it said, when warehouse receipts were handed to Maher because grain was to be shipped out of the Iowa, Maher, instead of retiring these receipts, turned them over to a broker with instructions to sell them on the open market. Maher used the funds so obtained to support Lyon's attempted corner in August wheat.

With the duplicity of one of the elevator operators in the Lyon speculation exposed, suspicion developed against others rumored to be in the deal—that is, Munn and Scott. Grain dealers discriminated against warehouse receipts from Munn and Scott elevators when grain was delivered to them, attempting to reject Munn and Scott receipts while accepting those of other elevators. Bankers were disinclined to accept Munn and Scott warehouse receipts as collateral for loans.

When the October, 1871 fire destroyed the books of the state registrar and of the warehouse firms, all of which were kept in the central business district surrounding the Board of Trade, it created a unique problem for the grain trade. It was necessary under the warehouse acts of 1871 to compile and report receipts, shipments and the amount of grain in store for each warehouse each week. With the books destroyed, the registrar—Stephen Clary—made a guess of what he felt was in store in some elevators, while with other elevators the operators made their own guesses. It was agreed that the state inspector should move promptly to ascertain the correct amount of grain in store at each elevator.

Actually, the inspector had not moved at all; only after the Iowa disaster was he spurred to movement. All the elevator men now agreed to have their elevators inspected, but Munn and Scott put in this proviso: they asked that the warehouses operated by other warehousemen be examined first, else it would seem that the entire inspection was directed at them because of rumors involving the authenticity of their warehouse receipts. The inspector agreed.

In the market itself, bad weather, and the consequent apprehension that the new crop would mature too late for delivery to Lyon on August futures, produced a buying movement during the first few days of August. That is, those who had sold August wheat futures to Lyon had to get out of their position by buying August futures. By the 10th the price reached $1.50. By the 15th it jumped to $1.61½, the peak of the deal.

The wheat growing territories were electrified by the news from Chicago. Railroads carried carloads of lanterns to the wheat lands to enable farmers to harvest their grain at night as well as during the day. Anxious to take advantage of the advancing prices created by the attempted corner, farmers dropped all other work and dried their green grain in stoves, pots, tin cans and anything else in which it could be heated.

Farmers did not stand alone in their eagerness to take advantage of Chicago prices, highest of any primary market. Shippers who had sent their wheat to Buffalo, where prices normally were above those in Chicago because of the greater distance from the wheat belt, recalled these cargoes to get the wheat to sell to Lyon.

In the second week of August, receipts totaled 75,000 bushels daily, and on Monday, August 19, receipts soared to an astonishing 172,000 bushels. Equally distressing to Lyon and his confederates was the report that Chicago could expect to receive from 175,000 to 200,000 bushels a day for the rest of August.

Furthermore, new elevators, rushed to completion, had taken the place of those burned in the fire the previous autumn. Early in August the Air Line and the Galena, each with a 750,000 bushel capacity, started operating. Wheat could be shipped into this new storage space and delivered to Lyon in satisfaction of wheat futures he had purchased for August delivery. Later, the National and Houghs elevators were completed. Still another, the Central A, was under construction late in the year. When all these warehouses were completed, Chicago's grain storage capacity exceeded by nearly two million bushels its total prior to the fire. Russell and Oramel Hough, who up until this time had been successful in the packing industry, broke the ranks of the warehousemen by taking out a license under the state warehouse acts and announcing rates in conformity with those acts. None of the other elevatormen followed the Houghs' lead.

Grain pouring in on Lyon greatly exceeded what he had anticipated when he initiated his cornering attempt. Overcome by the avalanche, he scurried frantically among the Chicago bankers in an effort to raise more money. He found the bankers unwilling to lend an additional cent. By the rules of their charters, national banks could not loan more than 10 per cent of their capital to any one person or firm; this was the rationale for their refusal to augment Lyon's credit.

Throughout much of Monday, August 19, Lyon supported the market, buying the grain as it was offered to him, but when he learned that the banks would no longer support him, he stopped buying. Immediately, wheat collapsed, falling 25 cents a bushel. The next morning Lyon acknowledged his cornering attempt had failed, commenting ruefully that the banks had never before shown such virtue with regard to the 10 per cent rule. Wheat fell an additional 15 to 17 cents.

The collapse produced a series of brokerage house failures. F. J. Diamond, the Munn and Scott broker, simply disappeared, either destroying his books or taking them with him. Munn and Scott claimed they had had no recent dealings with Diamond.

The next day—Wednesday, August 21—the grain inspector, who had been busy with other elevators in the city, finally got around to those owned by Munn and Scott. That day Scott told a newsman, "My impression is that our elevators will come out all right but the grain may be short. You see, we started out after the fire on Clary's [the registrar's] guess and it may have been too much, you can't tell."[8] It was not the kind of remark to encourage confidence in Munn and Scott's warehouse receipts.

That same day Lyon also had something to say. He complained about the poor quality of grain receiving a No. 2 grade, thereby making it eligible for delivery on the futures contracts he had bought.

This lax grading, Lyon asserted, was occasioned by the fact that the assistant inspectors, as well as chief inspector Tompkins, were dependent for their jobs on the chairman of the Warehouse and Railroad Commission, Gustav Koerner, who was running for governor on the Liberal Republican ticket. Koerner sought the farmer's vote, Lyon contended, and one way to get it was to see that the farmer received a high price—the price Lyon was willing to pay for No. 2 grade or better—for his wheat. Lyon charged, "He [Koerner] must keep on the right side of the farmer. It was politics that let that green grain in on us."[9]

No. 2 spring wheat was defined by the Statute of Illinois as "sound, reasonably clean, and weighing not less than 56 pounds to the measured bushel." There was also a No. 3 grade, "Not good enough for No. 2, weighing less than 54 pounds." The statute also said, "All spring wheat damp, musty, grown, badly bleached or for any other cause unfit for No. 3 shall be graded as rejected."[10]

There is no doubt that the inspection was, to use a polite word, lenient. Charles Randolph, the Board's secretary and an opponent of all cornering attempts, noted in his annual report: "No such violent changes in the manner of inspecting grain as are understood to have occurred in August last [apparently to meet a contingency in the market] should ever be permitted . . . ."[11]

If the purpose of the lenient inspection was to elect Koerner, it failed; he lost to the regular Republican candidate, Richard Oglesby, riding along on a Republican tide that reelected President U. S. Grant.

Three weeks after the corner's collapse, the registrar reported on the inspector's survey of grain in store at all warehouses. The Munn and Scott elevators were listed for 340,770 bushels of wheat and 887,426 bushels of corn, more than elevators operated by any other company. This occasioned no surprise. Everyone knew that Munn and Scott was the biggest elevator firm in town. But what happened next must have shocked the grain trade: a notice appeared on the Board of Trade bulletin board stating that the Munn and Scott elevators had been transferred to the elevator firm of George Armour & Co.

What had happened?

Testifying before a committee of the Board of Trade in December, Armour said that on September 23 Munn had got in touch with him and urgently asked for a meeting. That evening Munn and Armour met at the home of Hiram Wheeler, another elevator man. Munn told Armour and Wheeler that he had obtained loans secured by warehouse receipts for grain, but there was not sufficient grain in his elevators to redeem the outstanding warehouse receipts. He added that his affairs were in such a condition that he could no longer go on with his business.

Munn conveyed his interest in the Munn and Scott elevators to Armour for $10. Armour was to continue operating the business and to honor the outstanding warehouse receipts, even though they admittedly were in excess of the grain in store.

Armour must have been startled at what he found. After checking the grain in store, he reported that in the week ended November 10, the bins contained only 53,473 bushels of wheat and only 370,800 bushels of corn. But the registrar's report for the same week placed the storage at 169,734 bushels of wheat and 479,448 bushels of corn. This was based on the August inspection of Munn and Scott elevators, announced September 13, minus the movement out of the elevators since that date.

Because of the large and ominous discrepancy in the figures, it was decided that the inspector should make another check of the Munn and Scott elevators. On this reinspection an employee of the firm revealed that the delay Munn and Scott had asked for and obtained before their elevators were inspected had been used to floor over several bins of the Northwestern elevator near the top. Upon this floor was sprinkled some wheat and corn. Thus it appeared that the bins were filled with grain, and the initial inspection so recorded them. (This was the same elevator cited in the State Attorney's case against Munn and Scott for violation of the warehouse act.)

This little trick made it possible for Munn and Scott to claim that they had more than 100,000 bushels of wheat and 100,000 bushels of corn in store than they actually had. Underneath the flooring, where the additional 200,000 plus bushels should have been, was air.

On October 19, two banks filed bankruptcy claims against Munn, Scott and three other men comprising the firm of Munn, Norton and Scott: Charles Munn, son of Ira, and John and Warren Norton. Replying to questions of attorneys in this matter, Ira Munn revealed an interlocking ownership among many of the elevators. The elevator men had made a secret agreement in 1862, renewed in 1866, pooled their interests and formed an Elevator Association.

Attorney: Which elevators were in the association?
Munn: Three north side and four west side elevators.
Attorney: Who kept the books?
Munn: The north side elevators kept their books, and those of the west side were kept by us—Munn and Scott.
Attorney: Did you have any losses?
Munn: No.
Attorney: How much did you make?
Munn: My interest was worth about $100,000 a year.
Attorney: Why are you bankrupt?
Munn: Outside the elevator business I incurred losses—very heavy losses.
Attorney: How?
Munn: Paying more for property than it was worth, and getting less than I paid.[12]

(This is a reference to his dealings in grain futures, of which the collapse of the Lyon corner was one example.)

Ten days later Munn, Scott and both Nortons were adjudged bankrupts. A report of the District Court of the Northern District of Illinois listed more than 150 creditors of the various principals, ranging all the way from little grain dealers in obscure towns of the Midwest to Jesse Hoyt* of New York who was owed $350,000 by Munn and Scott, the elevator firm.

This $350,000 indebtedness grew out of large shipments of grain by Munn and Scott to Hoyt during the autumn of 1868. Seven promissory notes were executed, each of $50,000 carrying a 10 per cent interest rate and maturing in six to forty-two months. They were secured by about one million bushels of wheat and corn.

---

*Besides his numerous commercial activities, Hoyt was instrumental in founding the city of Saginaw, Michigan. He was a good friend of George Bancroft, the historian, and when he built a hotel for Saginaw he named it the Bancroft House.

But the price of the grain fell to a point where the grain's value no longer covered Hoyt's loan. He held a meeting with Munn, at which time Munn offered to mortgage Munn and Scott real estate and elevators in Chicago. Munn asked that the mortgage not be recorded, lest it injure his credit. Hoyt complied, but by April 12, 1871, he felt differently about the situation: he recorded the mortgage in Cook County.

Munn and Scott's troubles started with the formation in 1865 of Munn, Norton and Scott, the commission firm. The commission firm became the vehicle for the elevatormen's flyers in the futures market. Munn estimated that the elevator firm had a net worth of about $1 million in 1868; but by spring of 1869 the firm was no better than even. Munn told Hoyt he could pay off the mortgage in time, but 1869 was not the time.

Hoyt held the agreement for the operations of the Elevator Association, although Wheeler had a copy. There was a total of 400 shares in the association, divided among the various members. Munn and Scott were the operating heads. All the accounts of the elevators were turned over to Wheeler, who struck the balances and distributed the dividends. Each member of the agreement received dividends several times a year and no member had any losses in the elevator business. Not all Chicago elevators were part of the combine.

Munn disclosed a multiple ownership of many of the city's elevators. For example, the City and Union elevators, while ostensibly owned by Munn and Scott, were actually owned in the following ratio: Munn and Scott five-sixteenths; Armour two-sixteenths; Albert Munger two-sixteenths; James McKay two-sixteenths; Wheeler three-sixteenths; and Percy Smith and George Dunlap two-sixteenths.

When built, the Northwestern elevator was owned by Munn and Scott. As a condition for building the Northwestern, Munn and Scott made a contract with the Chicago and North Western Railway providing that the railway deliver grain to Munn and Scott elevators—an example of the interlocking relationship between railroads and elevators which infuriated farmers. Later, Dunlap and Smith, officials of the railroad, obtained a one-fourth interest in the Northwestern elevator. In the Illinois River elevator, one-fourth interests were held by: Munn and Scott; Armour and Munger; Hiram Wheeler; and the Buckinghams. All these interlocking relationships had been suspected, but it was Munn's testimony that confirmed the suspicion and detailed the situation.

Ownership fluctuated over the years but it remained in the hands of a very small number of people. In 1874 there were 14 warehouses owned by about 30 people, but actually 9 business firms controlled them. In the Munn vs. Illinois case, the majority opinion of the U.S. Supreme Court asserted this interlocking relationship "may be a virtual monopoly."

Commission brokers on the Board, following their traditional hostility to the warehousemen, saw an opportunity to exert their influence and, perhaps, sustain the reputation of the Board. Acting on a petition from some members, the Board's directors investigated the case and decided that Munn and Scott had moved grain out of their elevators without calling in an equivalent amount of warehouse receipts and, in addition, when warehouse receipts were returned to Munn and Scott for grain moved out of store, the elevatormen reissued these receipts upon the market through a broker, F. J. Diamond, instead of canceling them.

The directors discovered that Munn, Norton and Scott—the commission firm operating at the same address as the elevator firm—owned many warehouse receipts that had been deposited as security for credit at local banks. Armour said Scott told him this firm had taken much wheat out of store at Munn and Scott elevators, promising to return the warehouse receipts; but they had not been returned. Armour added that Scott said as far as he knew all the warehouse receipts represented grain properly stored initially in the warehouses, and were duly registered with the registrar.

The directors called a meeting of the entire Board to consider a proposal to expel the discredited leaders of the warehouse business. By a 100 to 13 vote, Munn, the former president, was expelled. Scott met the same fate, 96 to 10. When the decision was announced, someone in the gathering of grain men called, "Next!," and a slight flurry of nervous laughter rippled over the group.

Hoyt was not satisfied. At his prompting, the assignees in the bankruptcy contended that the testimony of Munn and Scott was indispensable in many matters relating to their bankrupt estates; therefore, the assignees argued, action should be taken to assure the continued presence of the broken warehousemen in Chicago. The judge thereupon directed the U.S. Marshall to arrest them.

Scott, arrested, put up bail of $5,000 supplied by a friend, Orville Cronkite. But Munn skipped the city before the Marshall could catch him. Munn, his wife and two sons, both Civil War veterans, went west. They were among the first settlers in the town of Uncompahgre, now known as Ouray, in the mountains of western Colorado. For a time they ran a boarding house for silver miners. When the town was incorporated in 1876, Munn became a member of the Board of Trustees. In the same

month and year he was discharged from bankruptcy in the Munn and
Scott affair. Conducting his business under the name of "George Wilder
and Co.," he owned the local saw mill and ore sampling works. He died in
1882 and was buried in Ouray as, much later, were his wife and two bache-
lor sons.

As far as Chicago history is concerned, Munn became a "non-person."
The history books of the period, largely devoted to eulogy, do not give his
biography although presenting full biographies of less important men. But
his name is indelibly a part of American history, linked forever with
Illinois in Munn vs. Illinois.

The Northwestern elevator was operated by George Armour & Co.
until 1874, when the firm dissolved and its elevator properties were
absorbed by Munger & Wheeler, another firm. In 1889 the Munger &
Wheeler elevators, including the Northwestern, were purchased by an
English syndicate. Next year this syndicate, named the City of Chicago
Grain Elevator Co., Ltd., took out licenses on seven of the eight elevators
it purchased. The exception was the old Northwestern. Instead of being
an elevator in which grain was stored, it was turned into a cleaner—that
is, one where grain was cleaned for all other elevators in the group.

The Northwestern lacked the pneumatic sweepers of newer elevators to
convey the screenings, dust and sweepings from all parts of the house to a
dust collector immediately over the furnace, in which debris was burned.
Instead, over the years the fine dust settled on every beam and made its
way through every crevice of the old Northwestern.

Then, in the late afternoon of August 5, 1897, a little fire broke out in
the elevator's cupola. It was soon discovered and the fire department
called, but the fire could not be controlled. It gathered headway and soon
enveloped the structure. Chicagoans, on their way home from work, gathered in the streets to watch the spectacular blaze. Before long, Illinois
Street was lined from curb to curb from the North Branch to Lake
Michigan with spectators. After half an hour, a great lateral explosion
ripped the aged structure. Hundreds of windows in buildings within a mile
of the blast were broken. Fifty spectators and firemen were injured and
five firemen were killed.

With that, the old Northwestern passed into history.

NOTES

1. Federal Trade Commission, "Report on the Grain Trade," (Washington, D.C., 1920–26) 5:323.
2. Benjamin Goldstein, *Marketing: A Farmer's Problem* (New York 1928), 72.
3. Andreas, *History of Chicago,* 2:359.
4. *Chicago Tribune,* 4 February 1874.
5. Goldstein, *Marketing,* 77.
6. Charles Warren, *The Supreme Court in the United States History* (Boston 1925), 583
7. *Chicago Tribune,* 23 August 1872.
8. *Chicago InterOcean,* 22 August 1872.
9. Ibid., and 23 August 1872.
10. Statute of Illinois, Fifteenth Annual Report of the Chicago Board of Trade (Chicago 1873), 146.
11. Fifteenth Annual Report the Chicago Board of Trade (Chicago 1873), VI.
12. *Chicago Tribune,* 26 November 1872, 2 November and 28 November, 1873.

CHAPTER FOUR

Is There a Device to Curb Manipulation?

The breakdown of Munn and Scott did not suppress the desire to use the market to achieve unwarranted profits. With the passing years, a struggle developed between speculators, who preferred an uninhibited market place, and critics, who wished to surround the market with regulations to maintain order and protect both producers and consumers. Regulation was a natural consequence of excessive price manipulation, but, in these early years of grain futures trading, the swashbucklers paid little heed to the reformers. Yet we can see the reforming impulse developing as speculators became more daring, more greedy, and more disdainful of restraint.

Among the late nineteenth century speculators who were daring, greedy and disdainful was one "Black Jack" or "King Jack" Sturgis, a sartorial oddity in his day. Refusing to wear the customary suit jacket, he often appeared on the Board's floor in a flannel shirt, pants and a vest of blue, and battered old shoes which gave the impression that he had just come from the stockyards.

Sturgis' interest centered in corn. Before long cynics referred to the corn crowd on the floor as "Sturgis' Dairy" because of the "milking" process—that is, the financial squeezing of the unsophisticated—going on there. Despite the fact that the Illinois legislature had passed a law against corners, scheduled to go into effect July 1, 1874, Sturgis attempted a corner in corn for delivery by July 31 of that year.

In the days immediately prior to July 31, the last day for delivery of grain on July futures, corn sold between 62½ and 65½ cents a bushel. On July 31 it opened at 67 cents and then fell to 62. From there it started to climb, going steadily higher until it reached 70 cents shortly before the closing bell. It hung there until the last minute, when Sturgis' voice sang out a bid of 80 cents. He ostentatiously purchased 250,000 bushels at that price from a broker friendly to him.

It was to Sturgis' advantage to have a high closing price because, under the rules then in effect, this would become the price at which those who had sold short to him, and failed to make delivery, would be required to settle. Because of Sturgis' last purchase, the shorts settled at 80 cents a bushel rather than the 62 to 70 cents that had prevailed throughout the day—that is, they would have to pay Sturgis 80 cents a bushel for grain they had sold to him at a lower price for future delivery.

Following the close of trading in futures, those who were short had until 3:00 p.m. to deliver the warehouse receipts for grain stored in Chicago elevators. As the 3:00 p.m. deadline approached, the business area took on an appearance of disaster. Sturgis' office was located in the Kent Building at 153 Monroe Street, near La Salle. Both La Salle and Washington streets leading to his office were crowded with brokers and curious on-lookers. Brokers seeking to make delivery jammed the doorways, corridors and stairways of the building.

A requirement of the delivery regulations was that the broker making the delivery not only be in the office at 3:00 p.m. or before, but also have the warehouse receipt on the counter. One broker, G. P. Comstock, with 35,000 bushels to deliver, got inside the Sturgis office at 2:58 p.m. But he couldn't push his way through the crowd, some members of which may well have been purposely blocking his passage, in the next two minutes. Officially, he defaulted and had to settle at 80 cents a bushel.

When Sturgis' clock showed 3:00 p.m., the doors to his office were promptly closed. This infuriated many brokers who, insisting that the clock was wrong, broke down the door.

There appeared to be another little trick. Some brokers in league with Sturgis delivered warehouse receipts so late to brokers who were short in relation to Sturgis that the latter brokers were not able to pass the receipts along to Sturgis before the 3:00 p.m. deadline. Lyon was one of the men caught in this woeful predicament. He had 15,000 bushels delivered to him at one minute before 3:00 p.m. and, of course, could not get to Sturgis' office in the remaining minute.

Eventually the Board would establish a clearing house, which would act as a buyer to all sellers and a seller to all buyers. Grain is delivered to a clearing house by means of a warehouse receipt. The clearing house then delivers this grain to the broker who has the oldest "long" position with the clearing house. When the broker notifies his customer of this delivery, the latter either accepts the grain or "re-tenders" it. When the grain is retendered, the clearing house recirculates the warehouse receipt until it lodges with someone who wants it. While the creation of the clearing house eliminated some of the more absurd visible aspects of grain delivery, it did not suppress or even diminish speculation.

The actual amount of grain delivered always has been very small in comparison with the amount of futures bought and sold—usually much less than 10 per cent. Whenever an individual wishes to withdraw from his position in a futures contract, he enters the opposite side of another contract for the same quantity of grain. Through the clearing house mechanism his two contracts cancel each other. He's out of the market. His broker credits or debits his account a sum of money equal to the difference in the prices of the two contracts.

After his tricks to block delivery of corn on July contracts, Sturgis took to the opposite side of the market: he sold September corn short. By the time September 30 arrived he was short several hundred thousand bushels. And he did not deliver a single bushel of corn to those to whom he had sold, nor did he show any disposition to settle at the settlement price.

For the protection of those who had bought from him, Sturgis claimed he had deposited money at the Cook County National Bank—the place he had put up "margin" (money) to cover his operations. But, according to a report of a committee set up by the Board to investigate Sturgis' manner of trading, Sturgis had refused to release any of this deposited money. Furthermore, the committee insisted that Sturgis' purchase of 250,000 bushels at 80 cents on July 31 had been a fraud—it had been a pretend transaction with no grain or money changing hands.

A movement grew to throw Sturgis off the Board for unethical conduct, not because he had attempted a corner but because he obviously had not played the game according to the brokers' rules. Nevertheless, Sturgis had friends on the Board and when a meeting was held to vote his expulsion these friends created a rumpus, shouting down those in favor of the expulsion. The Sturgis crowd was noisy, undemocratic and anti-establishment.

Late in November one of the aggrieved brokers, Murry Nelson, began a lawsuit against the Cook County National Bank. Nelson demanded that the bank distribute the money that Sturgis said he had deposited as margin. Moreover, the suit charged that the bank, or some of its principal officers, used bank funds for supporting Sturgis' operations and controlled him in his refusal to turn over the money owed brokers. Nelson wanted the bank to pay for the loss he had sustained as a result of this situation.

Nelson was right. Early in 1875 the bank's president, B. F. Allan, posted a notice on the door saying that the bank had suspended operations. The Cook County National Bank was not very large, and in this era bank suspensions and failures were almost routine. Allan and a partner had bought control of the bank in 1873, two years after its establishment. Allan had come to Chicago from Iowa where he had set up several banks after passage of the National Banking Act. Sturgis had acted as a "front" for Allan in the latter's speculations in corn. Because these speculations proved unprofitable, the bank underwent voluntary liquidation.

As for Sturgis, he was expelled from the Board in a vote of the full membership, despite heroic electioneering on the part of his friends. He took his case to the courts, initiating a spectacular legal fight which lasted until 1885. In that year a compromise was reached, one result of which was that he was readmitted as a member. A year later he died.

While Chicago had become the center for grain speculation, its neighbor to the north, Milwaukee, housed a group of nervy adventurers who played the market with a strong tendency to hang together when one of their members got into financial trouble. This group became a potent influence in both the Milwaukee and Chicago grain and provisions markets.

The nucleus of the Milwaukee Crowd was John Plankinton, whose packing plant spawned several Chicago packers. Plankinton, born in Pennsylvania in 1820, arrived in Milwaukee in 1844 after serving an apprenticeship as a butcher's helper. It was said of him that upon arrival he opened a store, bought a cow and rented a pasture. Whether this was or was not the chronological order of his entrepreneurship, he quickly became the city's leading packer.

In 1863 Plankinton met up with Philip Danforth Armour. He was impressed by Armour's commercial sagacity and took him into the business, which became Plankinton and Armour. Armour was born in Stockbridge, New York in 1832, not far from Oneida, home of one of the better-known pre-Civil War communal efforts. He was not the type to be attracted by socialist experiments. Later, he was to explain, "Oneida is for those whose dream did not come true. Mine has."[1]

He attended Caznovia Academy where his greatest achievement was getting expelled for taking a buggy ride with a young lady in the moonlight. He wasn't much for education, at least of the book variety.

In 1875 Armour moved to Chicago where he set himself up in an unpretentious, dreary house on fashionable Prairie Avenue with his wife and children. He was 43 at the time and undoubtedly a millionaire several times over. The story is that he collected his first million near the end of the Civil War when, seeing a forthcoming Union victory, he sold pork to Wallace & Wicks of New York at $40 a barrel. It was specified a delivery should be made several months after the sale—a typical short selling maneuver on Armour's part. In the interim, the Union forces made substantial military gains and pork fell to $18 a barrel. Armour bought it and sent it east to the chagrined New Yorkers. Eventually, Armour would become the biggest meat packer in the city of big meat packers.

Armour was thick-set, bull-necked, red-haired and strong. He rose every work day at 5:00 a.m., an old farm boy habit, breakfasted at 6:00 and arrived at his office in his buggy at 7:00. He explained he liked to get to work "before the boys with the polished nails show up." He remained at his desk until 6:00 p.m., went home, ate dinner, and retired at 9:00. This left him little time for what was known as "the finer things in life." "I have no interest in life but my business," he said. "My culture is mostly in my wife's name."[2]

Another member of the Milwaukee Crowd, although somewhat in the background because of his occupation, was Alexander Mitchell. Mitchell, born in Aberdeen, Scotland in 1817, arrived in Milwaukee in 1839 where he met "Scotch George" Smith. Smith put Mitchell to work in the Wisconsin Marine & Fire Insurance Company. There were times when Mitchell rode a horse carrying gold and silver back and forth between Smith's office in Milwaukee and his office in Chicago. In 1852 Smith sold his interest in the firm to Mitchell and retired to Scotland. Mitchell was head of the company, which soon became the Wisconsin Marine & Fire Insurance Bank, the largest bank in the city and usually referred to simply as "Mitchell's Bank."

A little off to the side as far as speculation in futures was concerned, but definitely a leader in the Milwaukee business world and a friend of packers, bankers and grain dealers was Daniel Wells. Wells was Milwaukee's first Justice of the Peace. In 1839 he prepared the charter for "Scotch George" Smith's firm and secured its passage in the Territorial Council, before

Wisconsin became a state. Wells was named a director of the firm. From 1852 to 1856 he served as a member of the U.S. Congress from Wisconsin. Over the years, Wells acquired much property; he had interests in the grain and wool businesses, hotels, lumber, storage and shipping, among others.

Peter McGeoch was another member of this Milwaukee Crowd, and its least stable personality. Born in London of Scottish parents, McGeoch moved with his family to Waterloo, Wisconsin, where he grew up. He started shipping grain to Milwaukee and eventually became a well-known commission merchant. He moved to Milwaukee, continued to prosper and by 1878 had become a power in the city: proprietor of one of its largest packing plants, owner of a farm which sold more milk than any other in the city, and a big dealer and speculator in provisions on the Milwaukee Chamber of Commerce.

Like Armour, McGeoch was a heavy-set man, weighing just under 200 pounds, but he was nervous and suspicious, possessed of a bad temper. He sported a black beard and mustache. He usually had a tooth pick or oat straw in the left corner of his mouth. The coat cuff of his right sleeve was often drawn back. Sometimes he would remind fellow traders on the Milwaukee exchange, "I can sow, and reap and thresh, which none of you fellows can."[3] But for the most part he was a rather quiet person, speaking only when spoken to.

Besides its production of the Milwaukee Crowd, the Wisconsin city gave another gift to the speculative trade: the famous trading "pit." Before its invention, traders had gathered in small groups or wandered about the exchange floor. One of the first efforts to improve this situation in Milwaukee was the construction of a circular table with a hole in the middle. Traders stood around the table. This innovation failed and the table was sold to a Milwaukee beer garden where it found useful employment as a bar. In 1870 William J. Langson, secretary of the Milwaukee Chamber of Commerce, conceived the first trading pit—an octagonal pit with steps on the inside and outside. Chairs were placed on the top rung, but have long since disappeared. Langson was modest enough to say, "The principle was very old—it is the Roman amphitheatre over again, but on a smaller scale."[4]

McGeoch in Milwaukee and Armour in Chicago teamed up, probably with the aid of Mitchell's bank, to run a corner in July, 1878 wheat. McGeoch bought more than two million bushels of wheat as it arrived in Milwaukee, shipping it east so that those who had gone short in futures could not get the wheat and deliver it to him. One of these shorts was

John Lyon, who sent around 65,000 bushels from Chicago elevators to Milwaukee.

This grain failed to pass inspection as No. 2 spring wheat, the grade deliverable on futures contracts, and C. J. Kershaw & Co., to whom it had been consigned, appealed to the Committee on Inspection of the Chamber of Commerce. The Committee inspected the wheat as it lay on the steam barge and tow in Milwaukee harbor. They pronounced it No. 2 spring wheat and ordered the inspector to pass it. With that McGeoch raised a strong protest and the Committee visited the barge the next day and discovered the wheat wasn't No. 2 spring after all. They told the inspector not to pass it.

Lyon raced up from Chicago to find out what was going on. He decided to have the grain cleaned and mixed with No. 1 spring wheat. Mixers specializing in this operation were located on the south side of Milwaukee. After they finished with it, the grain was carted to the elevator "hospitals" of Angus Smith and the Chicago and North Western Railway. These were the only elevators in the city that could take wheat from wagons, and therefore the only ones that could accept this "doctored" wheat. Lyon upgraded his wheat to No. 2 spring at a rate of about 10,000 bushels a day, delivering it to McGeoch.

Wheat rose steadily in July at both Milwaukee and Chicago, but Milwaukee set the pace. Normally, Milwaukee wheat sold 1 1/4 to 1 1/2 cents above the same grade in Chicago, but in mid-July buyers paid 97 cents in Milwaukee for wheat that brought 89 1/2 cents in Chicago. Ordinarily the difference would have moved wheat out of Chicago elevators and into those of Milwaukee, but wheat was also needed in Chicago.

Chicago Board of Trade regulations required that wheat deliverable on futures contracts should be No. 2 spring. This produced a confusing situation as the corner progressed. Because the shorts became eager buyers of the cash grain to deliver it on futures contracts, No. 2 spring wheat in the cash market advanced above the price of No. 2 hard winter wheat, a better grade which normally sold at a higher price.

In grading wheat, the Board had a rule that, if different grades were mixed, the resultant product took the grade of the lowest part of the mixture. Therefore, the shorts, when delivering grain to Armour and his followers, mixed winter with spring wheat. Cars of winter wheat arrived in Chicago with a little spring wheat carelessly tossed on top. Some enterprising shorts loaded a canal boat with winter wheat from an elevator, towed the boat around the river a few minutes, sprinkled some spring wheat amidst the winter grade, and then brought the boat back to the elevator where the grain was graded No. 2 spring wheat, and therefore deliverable on futures contracts.

Winter wheat was cheaper than spring as a result of the corner, but spring wheat was of poorer quality. When the two were mixed, the result was spring wheat—deliverable on futures contracts.

Toward the end of July, however, the warehousemen, who may well have been partial to Armour, refused to issue regular warehouse receipts for this mixed grain. All receipts had the phrase "Special Bin" stamped on them. One short tendered one of those "Special Bin" receipts to Armour, who refused it. The case came before the directors. Under Board rules when grain was mixed to raise it from a lower to a higher grade, it had to be stored in a separate bin, warehouse receipts had to state it was so stored, and these receipts could be delivered on contracts only by agreement between the deliverer and the receiver; if the holder of the futures contracts—the "long"—refused to accept the grain, it could not be delivered.

But, argued the "shorts," the grain they wished to deliver to Armour had not been raised in grade by mixing; its quality had, instead, been lowered. Therefore, it could be delivered on futures contracts without agreement between the parties involved, the "shorts" contended. The directors did not accept the argument, thereby siding with Armour: "Special Bin" wheat was declared not deliverable on futures contracts.

In part because of the agreeable attitude of the directors, prices continued to advance at both Chicago and Milwaukee. A few minutes before the close on July 31, final day for making deliveries, McGeoch instructed his brokers to bid $1.30 for all the July wheat offered. This established $1.30 as the price at which defaulters had to settle. Armour displayed greater restraint. The Chicago closing price was $1.10. This absurd difference of 20 cents between the two markets on the same grade of wheat aroused more than a bit of personal antagonism toward McGeoch because it meant the shorts would have to settle with McGeoch at a much higher price than with Armour.

Up to this time, the "July Wheat Deal," as it became known, was the most successful ever attempted and completed.

Hardly had Armour and McGeoch finished their deal than one of Wall Street's famous characters, James Keene, descended upon Chicago. He would find no opposition from the Board's leadership to stay his operations, but he did eventually succumb to economics.

On December 3, 1878, Keene wired 1.5 million dollars to several Chicago brokers, headed by J. K. Fisher & Co. and told them to buy wheat. They immediately picked up about two million bushels, approximately half the wheat in store in Chicago. The money arrived in the morning and Keene in the evening. He had wanted to arrive simultaneously with the money, which would have been a nice touch, but a railroad tie-up delayed him. The next morning he was at Fisher's office, which became his Chicago headquarters during an extensive campaign.

Keene's entry into Chicago aroused a storm of interest and perturbation among the grain men. Keene was a man to reckon with. Known as the "Silver Fox," he moved in the Jay Gould crowd. When J. P. Morgan merged several steel companies into United States Steel in 1901, he called upon Keene to manage the market for the new company's stock. Keene was considered an expert on market trading techniques.

A Londoner by birth, Keene had grown to maturity in California. There he started his business career peddling milk on the streets of San Francisco. Eventually he accumulated his first fortune by dabbling in mine and railroad stocks, plus a flyer in Western Union Telegraph. He was something of a loner. In his New York office he kept his door locked. One had to identify oneself to a guard before gaining admittance. Inside, one large room revealed Keene's sporting interest—pictures of thoroughbred horses decorated the walls.

In this office one might find Keene sitting before a roll top desk and a stock market ticker. He often wore a silk hat tilted back on his head, held an unlighted cigar in his mouth and kept his hands deep in his pockets as he sat watching the ticker. The office contained a copper brazier. Every night before he left for his uptown residence (at No. 17 West 10th Street), Keene piled the brazier full of all correspondence, memoranda, instructions and general evidence of the day's work. Then he applied a match.

Keene was a small, thin man whose hair turned grey at an early age, thus giving him his nickname. At the time he attempted to corner wheat he was 42 years old. He had dark features, heavy eyebrows, a twisted mustache and a well-trimmed beard. His appearance was more like that of a Spaniard than an Englishman. Actually, his family came originally from the west coast of Ireland, where, long previous, many a Spanish sailor from the defeated "Invincible Armada" had been stranded. For centuries the area had carried on a commercial trade with Spain, and Spanish-looking Irishmen were not unheard of along that coast.

It would eventually turn out that Keene, despite his reputation, was no loner in this wheat deal. He was part of a combine, in which he held a one-half interest. Jesse Hoyt of New York held one quarter. Others in the combine, holding altogether only a quarter interest, included two old Chicago and North Western Railway officials who liked to dabble in grains from the days of Munn and Scott—George L. Dunlap and Perry E. Smith.

Keene kept buying throughout the 1878–79 winter and it became clear that he was not indulging in any ordinary attempt to squeeze a few short sellers in any specific delivery month in Chicago. Soon, he owned a substantial amount (some said all) of the No. 2 spring wheat in Chicago and Milwaukee, as well as a good quantity in New York. The design was that of a grand corner of cash wheat at crucial markets.

On March 7, Archibald Fisher, second in command of J. K. Fisher & Co., received a telephone message at the Chicago Club saying an important night dispatch had been received at his office. It read: "Sell whatever wheat March or April market will take without declining more than three cents—Keene."[5] Fisher hurried to the Board of Trade and started selling, at the same time messaging Keene as the wheat was sold.

The market broke more than 3 cents under this pressure. Starting at 96⅜ cents, April wheat sank to 90⅞. Then it rallied a few cents. With Keene in his New York office as the messages from Fisher arrived was William Taylor Baker, another of Keene's brokers. Both Keene and Baker were dumbfounded by the news from Chicago, or professed to be. Keene told Baker to buy the wheat Fisher was selling. Baker did. Almost 3 million bushels changed hands.

Keene promptly posted a reward of $25,000 for information disclosing the author of the telegram. It had been sent from a New York office of the Atlantic & Pacific Telegraph Company, but no one at the office could identify the sender. Author of the bogus telegram never was discovered. Baker's son, Charles, in a biography of his father, said that after this incident Keene shifted his business from the Fisher firm to that of Baker.

By July, the 1880 wheat crop was making fine progress; indications were there would be an excellent harvest.

When autumn arrived, Keene was able to dispose of some of his increasingly burdensome hoard to exporters, but he again accumulated more cash wheat as the 1880 crop came to market. Because Keene's group was holding back wheat, it was reported that numerous vessels lay idle at Atlantic Coast ports. The visible supply of wheat by mid-January 1880 reached a figure nearly twice as large as a year earlier; this was grain held in warehouses at major terminal markets. In May a minor squeeze developed in May wheat at New York, the shorts settling with Jesse Hoyt & Co. at $1.45 a bushel.

But such minor squeezes were of little relevance against the huge hoard of wheat that the Keene combine had collected. One major problem in running a corner was that, after accepting the grain, the buyer had to dispose of this grain. It had to be sold at a price that would still enable the cornering group to keep a portion of the profit it had squeezed from the shorts in the futures market. This was known as "burying the corpse." Keene had a frightful corpse to bury.

He did not succeed. He had to sell his cash wheat at a loss, estimated at $1.75 million. Whether a correct estimate or not, one thing is certain: he left the grain market alone thereafter, returning to Wall Street.*

The Keene collapse did not daunt Armour, McGeoch and others of the Milwaukee Crowd. By this time Armour & Company had become the leading packing firm in Chicago, ousting Hutchinson's and A. E. Kent's Chicago Packing and Provisions Co. from that desired position.

Hutchinson and Armour held to different operating techniques. Hutchinson spent most of his time on the floor of the Board of Trade or in his office at the Corn Exchange Bank. Armour seldom visited the Board, preferring to operate through his brokers. He spent his own day at his packing plant where he contended for supremacy with Gustavus Swift, founder of Swift & Co. Swift had no interest at all in grains. Armour paid a tribute to Swift with the statement, "I have ordered a rule posted in our house [that is, Armour & Co.] that anyone who refers to business in the future, and says we ought to do so-and-so because Swift is doing so-and-so, will be shot."[6]

Armour and the Milwaukee Crowd, now sarcastically referred to as "The Scottish Chiefs," came back to the grain market in 1882, centering their attention on wheat for delivery in April. They bought at prices ranging from $1.17 to $1.40, averaging $1.27. It was a good spring for buying wheat, particularly for buying No. 2 spring wheat—the type deliverable on futures contracts. The wheat crop of the previous year—1881— had been a lamentable failure in all states from Ohio to Minnesota. Nationally, production totaled only 380,280,000 bushels compared with 498,549,000 bushels in 1880. In Illinois the wheat turnout fell more than 50 per cent between the two years—from 60,959,000 bushels to 26,822,000. Spring wheat was hit hardest in this crop failure, so there was not much wheat available when the April, 1882 corner was run.

Receipts of No. 2 spring wheat at Chicago in the first half of 1882

---

*Henry Clews, *Fifty Years in Wall Street*, (New York 1908) says Keene became bankrupt at this time and several other books on Wall Street financiers of this period have also made this statement, obviously based upon Clews. However, there is no report or indication of a Keene bankruptcy in the daily press of the period. Not until 1884, five years after the famous wheat deal, did Keene fail to meet his financial obligations. See *New York Times*, 1 May 1884.

totaled only half a million bushels. Armour and the Milwaukee Crowd held title to all the wheat there was in store, estimated at 3½ million bushels. The price ran up quickly toward the end of April as some, but not all, the shorts canceled out their positions on a rising market. The final quotation on April 30 was $1.40. Holders of about a half million bushels defaulted. Among them were A. N. ("Charlie") Wright and William Taylor Baker, who had been involved in the Keene caper. Both Wright and Baker would become presidents of the Board, Baker holding that position four times, a record. He also would be president of the Columbian Exposition, Chicago's fabulous World's Fair of 1893.

Armour insisted upon $1.40 as a settlement price, but Wright, Baker and others in a like position demurred. They noted that on the day following April 30 both cash wheat and wheat for May delivery sold from $1.28 to $1.29, very considerably less than what Armour was demanding. Hence, the defaulting shorts contended, Armour had run an illegal corner and his request for a $1.40 settlement price was exorbitant.

The Board of Trade appointed a committee to hear arguments from the contending parties. Armour did not appear before it, leaving that task to his grain representative, George Bryan. After considerable argument, the committee set $1.31 as a settlement price. Armour called the decision "disgraceful" but the shorts were elated, asserting with a new found morality that this meant "good-bye to corners."

While this committee was holding hearings, the shorts came up with a resolution that would in effect make winter wheat deliverable on futures contracts, heretofore limited to spring wheat of No. 2 grade. What worried the shorts was not only the April corner, now past, but the indication that Armour and the Milwaukee Crowd would continue to corner the market in July. Considering the fact that the Armour group owned all the spring wheat in store, there was no way they could fail unless the specification on what type of grain could be delivered was changed. This the shorts hoped to do.

There had been a good planting of winter wheat in the previous autumn, particularly in Illinois, and the shorts knew it would be possible for them to obtain this grain as it was harvested and sent to market. All they needed was to be allowed to deliver it, a better quality grain, on futures contracts. In a hectic campaign, membership adopted a resolution declaring that, beginning June 1, all contracts made for future delivery of wheat should be understood as for No. 2 wheat, either spring or winter, or for a higher grade than No. 2.

Once this rule was adopted, the shorts started to bring in winter wheat. Receipts of winter wheat in July far exceeded that of any other July in Chicago's history, and nearly 2.5 million bushels of this grain was a superior quality to red winter wheat—now eligible for delivery on futures contracts (but not on such contracts if made before June 1).

Armour bitterly opposed tendering of winter wheat on July futures. He noted the newly adopted rule read, "On contracts for future delivery, the tender of a higher grade of the same kind of grain than the one contracted for shall be deemed sufficient . . . ."[7] Armour claimed winter wheat was not the "same kind of grain" as spring wheat.

"The best class of men won't tender winter wheat," Armour said. "I met a man a while ago who had done it, and he had never done such a thing before, and he was going down to take a sewer bath to get clean."[8]

July wheat closed at $1.36. Again, several leading shorts, including Baker and Wright, did not deliver grain to Armour; again, a committee was appointed to determine a fair settlement price. Baker appeared before this committee and testified under oath that Armour had informed him that Armour's group had bought July wheat with millions of dollars in back of them; that they had borrowed more money than had ever been borrowed in Chicago to carry the deal through successfully; that they intended to run the price up to $1.50; and that Armour had $2 million in cash in the banks ready to meet any call for margin.

This time Armour had more influence with the committee. They put the settlement price at $1.35, only one cent under the final July futures price on July 31. It was the turn of Baker and Wright to indulge in pitiful protests, and they were joined by several other shorts, including Perry E. Smith of the Chicago and North Western Railway and George M. Pullman, whose name was familiar to railroad travelers as the manufacturer of Pullman Cars.

Finally the dispute went to the courts. Armour noted that he had been tendered winter wheat when he believed, based on the Board's regulation in the matter, that he should have obtained spring wheat. The shorts argued that Armour was engaged in running an illegal corner and, therefore, did not have any rights at all. Various law suits worked their way through the courts, grievously dividing the Board's membership for more than a decade, but eventually resulting in establishment of more rigid regulations governing settlements and delivery of grain.

The game was getting rougher each year and the Board was experiencing difficulty in enforcing its own rules against squeezes and corners;

furthermore, even the officers could not easily define what constituted legitimate trading and what were illegal attempts at manipulation. Thus, Charles Randolph, the Board's secretary, in his annual report to members, said:

> It seems difficult, or perhaps impossible, to surround this immense business with safeguards so that no undue advantage shall accrue to either of the sides to the ceaseless contest between those who desire to operate with the expectation of a decline in prices, and those whose views are adverse.[9]

Not that Randolph was against speculation. He opined, "there could scarcely be a more unfortunate general result to the agricultural interests of this country than would be produced by the elimination of the speculative element from the market in which their products are sold." It was excessive speculation that bothered Randolph, although he did not define what that was; "any device which will tend to hold speculative operations in reasonable check should be hailed as a most beneficent and wise measure . . . ."[10] The search for that "device" would proceed for many years.

NOTES

1. Wayne Andrews, *Battle for Chicago* (New York 1946), 88.
2. Ibid., 87.
3. *New York Times*, 16 July 1878.
4. John G. Gregory, *History of Milwaukee, Wisconsin* (Milwaukee 1931) 1:464.
5. Charles Baker, *Life and Character of William Taylor Baker* (New York 1920), 60–61.
6. Andrews, *Battle for Chicago*, 92.
7. *New York Times*, 1 August 1882.
8. Ibid.
9. Twenty-fifth Annual Report of the Chicago Board of Trade (Chicago 1883), XII.
10. Ibid.

CHAPTER FIVE

Actions by Board
Break Two Corners

The "device" which Secretary Randolph felt was needed was also sought by the leadership of the Board of Trade in the years immediately following Randolph's comment.

In these years there were two major attempted manipulations that caused severe losses for thousands of innocent victims, created highly unfavorable publicity for organized futures trading, and proved that commodity speculation had an influence far beyond the confines of Chicago.

One manipulation was attempted by Peter McGeoch and the other by a Cincinnati banker, E. L. Harper. Let us first look at the glory days of Peter McGeoch.

After his successful wheat corner in Milwaukee in 1878, McGeoch ran a little deal in pork futures in 1880. At one point he ran out of funds and pleaded with Alexander Mitchell, his friend the banker, for money. Mitchell refused. Then McGeoch approached Daniel Wells, another Milwaukean, who agreed to lend support. On Wells' credit, Mitchell lent McGeoch $3 million and the corner was carried through to a successful conclusion—successful to McGeoch, Wells and Mitchell, that is.

Shortly thereafter McGeoch headed a group that bought the Milwaukee Railway Company, one of the city's horse drawn trolley systems. He had become a very big man in Milwaukee.

In 1882 McGeoch joined others of the Milwaukee Crowd in Armour's spectacular and controversial corner in April and July wheat. Flushed with victory and money, McGeoch decided later that year to engineer a little corner of his own in lard. He invited several others to join in the frolic, including Robert and Anderson Fowler, brothers who operated the Anglo-American Packing Company. Anglo-American ranked second to Armour & Co. in the manufacture of hog products and cured meats. But the Fowler brothers turned down McGeoch's invitation, a move that would have singular significance for McGeoch.

Wells joined with McGeoch, although he later claimed that he did not enter until April, 1883. McGeoch was able to borrow money from Mitchell's bank by putting up real estate and his Milwaukee City Railway Company stock as collateral.

McGeoch was not one to hide what he was doing; he had a following in the country and he wanted those unknown country cousins to support him in his buying. For several months he moved in and out of the market, attempting to take profits on short term trades. In March, 1883, he started buying in large quantities, concentrating on the May delivery. The price rose to $12.10 per hundred pounds on May 7, the highest, but no corner developed. McGeoch accepted delivery of cash lard and switched his efforts to the June and July contracts.

McGeoch became such a dominant figure in the market that newspapers dubbed him "The Lord of Lard." The price of June and July contracts rose above that of August, a reversal of the normal relationship. On May 31, June closed at $11.60 per hundred pounds, July at $11.75 and August at $11.40. As the price rose, it appeared as though Chicago had become the destination of every hog in the country. McGeoch had counted on very few hogs coming in before autumn but the high hog prices (which resulted from the high price of lard caused by McGeoch's buying) brought them in at an exceptionally heavy rate. Hogs actually were shipped west from Cincinnati to Chicago, an unprecedented directional flow. Furthermore, these were good, fat animals, estimated to be 20 pounds heavier than a year earlier.

By June 1 McGeoch was credited with owning 200,000 tierces of cash lard and being long 600,000 tierces of lard futures. (A tierce was an old measure of capacity used for packing lard. One tierce contained approximately 320 pounds.) On this date of June 1, the Fowler brothers—who had refused to join the cornering group—delivered a relatively small quantity of cash lard on June futures contracts to McGeoch. Shockingly, McGeoch refused to accept it even though it had received a certificate of inspection as pure lard from the Board of Trade's inspector.

McGeoch explained, "I received last month 10,000 tierces of Fowler brothers lard and upon examination I found it generally unmerchantable and worthless. I paid over $350,000 for the 10,000 tierces."[1]

The Board's rules on lard required that the commodity delivered on futures contracts be "pure" lard, consisting of nothing but hog fat. Refiners in Chicago also produced what was known as "refined lard," which consisted not only of hog fat but also tallow (the harder fat of sheep and cattle, used to make candles and soap) and, it was sometimes charged, cottonseed oil. Some refiners reportedly also put in grease or stearin in their refined lard.

Refined lard was considerably cheaper than prime steam lard and it was claimed that the export trade wanted the lower-priced lard. One dealer asserted, "This adulteration is no new thing. It has been done for years. Dealers in foreign ports knowingly order the adulterated article because the price of pure lard is too high."[2]

The Monday after this startling action, McGeoch, having had time to think of the consequences, changed his position. A Board of Trade regulation specified that a certificate of inspection, which the Fowler lard had, could not be ignored by a party to a trade. So McGeoch accepted the lard, but he filed a complaint with the Board's directors.

McGeoch claimed that the lard that had been delivered to him in May was adulterated with tallow and vegetable oil. The Fowlers, he contended, were guilty of bad faith and he therefore asked that the firm be disciplined by the directors and that the provisions stored in their warehouse be declared "irregular." If the warehouse and its provisions were not "regular," the lard could not be delivered on futures contracts. With the lard in the Fowler warehouse removed from the market, it would be much easier for McGeoch to run a successful corner.

The directors decided to hold secret hearings on McGeoch's charges. As had happened before and has since, the proceedings were "leaked" each day to the newspapers.

This was an era of little government. Somnolent Washington, stirring only slightly under reformist winds, made practically no effort to regulate business. Markets were free. Investigations of possible irregularities were left to commercial bodies themselves; transgressors were tried by their peers. So the press followed this Board of Trade investigation with the avidity of news media hard on the heels of a Congressional investigation of a later era.

McGeoch produced a series of witnesses to testify concerning the activity at the Fowlers' Anglo-American plant. One, a steamfitter, stated that in order to render lard all that was needed was simple machinery, but at the Anglo-American plant he had installed "intricate and complicated" machinery not necessary unless the company intended to use tallow and cottonseed oil in the product. Another witness, a laborer, testified that he had seen bones, tallow, cottonseed oil and canning scraps thrown into the vat to make lard.

A professor, M. de La Fontaine, described as "a well known chemist," claimed he had investigated the lard and found it adulterated "with beef or sheep fat, commonly called tallow, and in at least two instances with cottonseed oil."[3] He placed the quantity of adulterants at 10 per cent. M. de La Fontaine was employed by P. D. Armour, McGeoch's friend, and could hardly be considered an objective analyst.

These revelations created an uproar in newspapers. One letter writer told editors about "Fisher's Stock," which he said was the product of hogs that die in transit—"the hog goes into the tank whole, bristle, hide and all; nice stuff for pie crust."[4] He called attention to "Canada Clay" or "Missouri Clay," a pigment imported from Denmark and used to bleach such stuff as "Fisher's Stock." While these comments, and others like them, may have been exaggerations, their surfacing in print compounded public distrust of the purity of lard and other foods as well.

As the investigation continued, heavy cash lard deliveries were being made to McGeoch and he either had to accept and pay for them or acknowledge his failure to complete the corner.

By June 12 trouble started brewing. McGeoch needed more money. His confederate, Wells, went to see Mitchell, the banker, and asked for $500,000. Mitchell refused. Wells lowered his request to a quarter of a million but still got no specific answer from Mitchell.

On Friday, June 15, some signs of weakness developed in lard in the morning trading, but nothing that could be described as a panic. In trade circles, the shipping demand for lard was said to be reduced because of the adulteration investigation scheduled for resumption three days later. Obviously, McGeoch had made a serious mistake. It was he who had asked for the investigation, and it was his witnesses who supported his contention of adulteration. But the widespread publicity given the hearing had made the consuming public, both domestic and foreign, suspicious of lard. And McGeoch owned most of the lard, both that in store and that which would be delivered in the future.

In the afternoon that Friday, trading became much more nervous than it had been in the morning. Late in the day some lots changed hands as low as $11.00 for July, and the close at $11.17½ was down 42½ cents from May 31. Rumors started to circulate that McGeoch had reached the end of his resources and that the Chicago banks, concerned with the quality of lard as a result of the Board's investigation, had scaled down the advances, secured by lard, that they had made to brokerage houses. This, in turn, meant the brokerage houses had to obtain more cash from customers. To one market observer it seemed as though "holders were simply letting the stuff [lard] drop as fast as they could find somebody to take it."[5]

In Milwaukee, Wells and Mitchell held an emergency meeting at McGeoch's home. McGeoch told them the total loss if the deal failed would be 3 to 3.5 million dollars, but he appears to have been conservative. A few days later Mitchell recalled that he would have gladly lent a quarter million—the amount requested by Wells—that night, if it could have averted the collapse—"but when it came to shouldering the monster load that was necessary to prevent the crash, and without security, it is what I or any other businessman would not do."[6]

After this meeting McGeoch left for Chicago, where he sought out his old friend P. D. Armour. All night long McGeoch and Armour remained at the telegraph desk in Armour's office and tried to work out a plan to save McGeoch. At the Milwaukee end of the wire sat Wells, Mitchell and Plankinton, now drawn into the maelstrom in a desperate effort to rescue their fellow Milwaukean. Armour offered to put up one million dollars, but it was not enough. Finally, Mitchell confronted the others with the hard reality that even if McGeoch accepted and paid for all the lard delivered to him, he would be in an untenable position: he would own all the high-priced lard on the market and there would be few, if any, buyers. It was all over.

In Chicago on Saturday morning, McGeoch sent a note to all his brokers stating that he could not meet their margin demands. They hurried to the Board to sell lard. At the opening, prices crashed. June lard, which had closed Friday at $11.11½ per hundred pounds, plunged to $9.05 before the sickening spin halted. At that point Hutchinson started buying. Quite possibly he was covering previous short sales, turning a profit on the price break. Armour also stepped into the market on the buying side, taking large quantities.

"I bought in order to save a panic and for the good of the Board," Armour said later, "although, of course, I expect to get my money back."[7]

June lard closed at $9.66, July at $9.80 and August at $9.92½—the three contracts returning to their normal price relationships.

McGeoch was crushed. Ominously, and almost prophetically, considering what was to happen later, the *Milwaukee Sentinel* reported, "Those who know him best are fearful that he will do himself harm."[8]

McGeoch proclaimed, with a touch of paranoia not unusual among speculators in those days, "There was a conspiracy to ruin me, and it has succeeded."[9]

Editors were shocked by the catastrophe. The *New York Times* concluded there was "no simple remedy" for what it termed "reckless speculation." It added, ". . . when the general sense of the community permits it [speculation] there is little use in trying to restrict it by legal enactments."[10]

The *Milwaukee Sentinel* thought everything was the fault of the "system":

> With the provisions market in the hands of moneyed cliques, with the combinations among mining companies and coal dealers, with the whole system of contracting reduced to a system of plunder, with combinations of undertakers even, the average American who isn't able to enter a combination is promised an expensive time of it while he lives and his entire estate promises [to] go to pay his funeral expenses when he dies.[11]

The extent of the financial loss is not accurately measurable, and in addition, the frightful depreciation of the dollar since 1883 tends to make the sums involved appear small. However, when P. D. Armour was asked why his offer of one million dollars in the hectic conference between Chicago and Milwaukee the night before the crash was not sufficient, he replied, "Well, he [McGeoch] would have required $6,200,000. . . . consequently you see that $1,000,000 would not have saved him."[12]

Of course, there were other losses than those of McGeoch. Several small brokerage houses failed. The small-time speculators in the city, as well as the country cousins who followed McGeoch, undoubtedly took very heavy but never to be known losses.

Over the weekend the chastened Milwaukee Crowd worked out a deal to appease McGeoch's creditors. With the aid of P. D. Armour, Plankinton and Mitchell, McGeoch offered, and his creditors eventually accepted, to pay immediately 25 cents on each dollar he owed. He obligated himself to pay an additional 25 cents in three months and to give long term notes for the residue.

With the wreckage more or less cleared, P. D. Armour took off for a hunting and fishing trip to the northwest with N. K. Fairbank, Sidney Kent and Marshall Field. Mitchell left for Europe, but before doing so, sent a telegram to The *New York Times* denying he was a member of the cornering group and adding, "I have never had any personal interest in the grain or provisions markets, and I have always condemned combinations to corner them."[13] Earlier he had said of McGeoch and Wells: "I am exceedingly sorry that the trouble has come upon the gentlemen, much as I detest what brought it about."[14]

Mitchell's bank had made substantial credit available to the "gentlemen," secured by McGeoch's Milwaukee City Railway stock and his and Wells' real estate. Mitchell apparently could not, or would not, connect the credit with the speculation.

"I am now about as poor as a man can be," McGeoch lamented shortly after the collapse. "If my best friend were in need I don't think that in the present circumstances I could raise $500 for him."[15]

He exaggerated. While he probably did not have much ready cash, he still had his stock in the Milwaukee City Railway. It was lodged with Mitchell's bank, but the bank did not take over the railway. Instead, it decided to let McGeoch redeem the pledged stock from the earnings of the line. In other words, the public transportation riders of Milwaukee were to pay for McGeoch's unsuccessful flyer in lard.

The Board's directors resumed hearings in the lard adulteration case immediately after the price break. Professor de La Fontaine was recalled and he once again testified, on the basis of four new chemical examinations, that he had found at least 10 per cent tallow, stearin and cottonseed oil in samples of the Fowler brothers' prime steam lard.

Thereafter, the defense put its witnesses on the stand. Both the Fowlers denied all the charges. So did Robert Neil, the superintendent of the plant, who also claimed that the prosecution witnesses had not been in jobs which would have given them the knowledge they claimed to have about adulteration at the plant. Furthermore, he contended that the "intricate and complicated" machinery that the steamfitter had previously testified to installing had been put into place to conduct an experiment and was used only once.

Two days later the workers in the rendering room, who had previously testified that they were required to throw tallow into one of the kettles rendering prime steam lard, now asserted that they had been given $30 by McGeoch's attorney to testify as they did. They had expected more. Both repudiated their previous testimony. Another employee said he was induced to go to McGeoch's office where he was offered $1,500 to make a statement, prepared by McGeoch and his attorney, pertaining to the method of lard adulteration. Despite what must have appeared as a liberal sum, he claimed he refused.

By coincidence, manufacturers of cottonseed oil were gathered in Chicago at this time for a national convention. Chicago was the major cottonseed oil consuming city in the nation. Asked about the effect of mixing cottonseed oil with lard, one manufacturer said, "It don't hurt the lard any. But the lard spoils the oil."[16] Another predicted, with considerable clairvoyance, "Oil is going to take the place of the best lard ever made."[17]

The Fowlers countered Professor de La Fontaine with a group of their own professors. Heading the list was Professor Bellfield of Rush Medical College. He said he had examined several specimens of prime steam lard and refined lard from the Anglo-American plant and had discovered no traces of cottonseed oil or tallow stearin in the prime lard but traces did appear in refined lard.

After the defense rested, the prosecution placed the former foreman for Fowler Brothers on the stand. He corroborated the statements made by other witnesses to the effect that tallow and beef bones were mixed with the hog fat and put in the lard rendering tank, from which was drawn the Fowler brothers' prime steam lard. He said he knew this positively because he had entire charge of the rendering.

In late August the Board's directors ruled, 7 to 4, that the charges against the Fowler brothers had not been sustained. But the directors added sufficient gratuitous comments to indicate they felt the charges might be true, after all. They said they:

> . . . could not refrain from expressing their unqualified disapproval of and censure upon defendants for the remarkable methods of conducting the business of manufacturing lard in their establishment, as developed by the evidence in this case.[18]

The directors added that it was possible that the "system of intricate machinery and pipes" at the plant could cause "by accident or design upon the part of employees" the adulteration of prime steam lard with "beef product, cottonseed oil and other unknown substances used in the manufacture of so-called refined lard."[19] The directors recommended that the intricate machinery and pipes be removed.

The case became a cause celebre. It had gone far beyond the attempt of Peter McGeoch to run a corner in Chicago lard.

Several states passed laws prohibiting adulteration of lard. Canada and Mexico banned American lard. So did some European countries. The Butchers National Protective Association petitioned Congress for a law requiring that refined lard be labeled as "lardine." The New York Produce Exchange complained to Congress about lard adulteration and asked for legislation to compel manufacturers to label their products in such a way that buyers would know what they were buying. McGeoch's attempted corner, and the subsequent adulteration revelations, had come at a time of reformist agitation against adulterated foods, but it was not until 1907 that a Pure Food and Drug Act became effective. It prohibited adulteration or misbranding of foods and drugs.

What of McGeoch?

He did not have to give up his home. He and Mitchell continued as very good friends, Mitchell often visiting the McGeoch residence. The two men owned a large cattle ranch in Wyoming. In 1890 a group led by Henry Villard bought and merged the Milwaukee trolley lines. Among the securities purchased was McGeoch's stock in the Milwaukee City Railway Company. McGeoch sold at a nice profit and built a new, handsome brick home on his 12 acre "farm." This property contained a little park with an artificial lake, an ornamental bridge and several grottos.

After his first wife died, McGeoch remarried. But the marriage did not go well. McGeoch had never been very popular and his personality traits—nervousness, hot-temper, unhappiness, suspiciousness—seemed to intensify as he grew older. His second wife left him and sent her attorneys to discuss the terms of a divorce settlement.

In 1895, on the morning after the conference with his wife's attorneys, the long forgotten warning in the *Milwaukee Sentinel* of 1883 was fulfilled. McGeoch, after breakfast, entered one of the bathrooms of his home, put a 38-calibre Colt revolver in his mouth and pulled the trigger. He died covered with blood, but with a large diamond in his cravat.

Four years after McGeoch's lard corner collapsed, another spectacular attempt to manipulate prices on a grand scale was engineered; this time by the president of the largest bank in Ohio.

The Fidelity National Bank of Cincinnati, founded in 1884, achieved success from the start. Its first day's deposits amounted to nearly $1.5 million. It began paying dividends six months after it was organized and its capital was soon increased to $2 million from an original $1 million.

Assets soared to more than $7 million by early 1887 when the bank was located on the ground floor of the city's tallest structure (nine stories), and its luxurious appointments gave the impression of a very solid institution—"a better, or rather more elegantly managed, institution of its kind did not exist anywhere in the United States," proclaimed a local weekly with only the normal parochial exaggeration for the period.[20]

In newspapers throughout the state the Fidelity advertised its own eminence (and its generosity):

The Largest Bank In Ohio
Invites Accounts Subject To The Best Terms
And Conditions

Depositors Have Free Use of Fire And Burglar Proof
Boxes In One of The Finest Safe Deposit
Vaults In The United States[21]

Briggs Swift, a 76 year old gentleman, the most respected and wealthiest citizen in the city, presided as president of the Fidelity. But at his age, Swift could not be expected to busy himself with the daily chores of bank management, a task left for E. L. Harper, the aggressive bank vice president. Harper was a man of considerable means who had obtained banking experience at the Third National Bank, a much older Cincinnati bank than the Fidelity. He had done a little speculating, picking up between $700,000 and $1,200,000 in a wheat corner run on the Chicago Board of Trade some years previous by a fellow Cincinnatian, Truman Handy.

At the Third National, Harper had been a major stockholder, a director and a big depositor. He and two of the bank's lesser officers, Ammi Baldwin, cashier, and Benjamin Hopkins, assistant cashier, had left that bank to form the Fidelity. In Cincinnati banking circles there was talk that the three men had been asked to leave.

Persistently, all through March and April of 1887, while the Fidelity shown so splendidly in Cincinnati, buying orders entered the wheat pit on the Chicago Board of Trade. Steadily, the price advanced. Traders, worried and mystified by the buying, dubbed the buyers the "clique." Houses through which the buying was accomplished were termed the "clique's brokers."

The price of wheat in Chicago advanced far above other cities, acting as a magnet; the city's warehouses filled with wheat. Wheat-laden railroad cars arrived in the city and found no room; for miles around Chicago these cars stood on rail sidings.

The directors of the Board took action to ease the tight situation by declaring two additional grain elevators "regular." This meant that grain stored in these elevators (300,000 bushels of wheat) could be delivered on futures contracts.

The clique's brokers in Chicago were Charles Kershaw, David Irwin and Maurice Rosenfeld, three well known grain men. Still, these were only the Chicago brokers; it could not be said in public print who was behind them, although it must have been quite well known to traders who knew the money was coming from Cincinnati. A Cincinnati grainhouse, Wilshire, Eckert & Co., gave the Chicago brokers direction in the campaign.

"We have 10,000,000 bushels of wheat, we have bought 3,000,000 more for June and we have sufficient funds to carry the deal through to the end of July," the clique brokers announced on May 17.[22] They seemed confident.

Chicago flour mills went on part-time operations or shut down, throwing men out of work. "Wheat is entirely too high for us to grind into flour for export," said Senator Eckhart of Eckhart & Swan, millers.[23]

Z. T. Cole, secretary of the Star and Crescent Milling Company, explained: "Chicago is today without question the highest wheat market in the world, and it is the money power of the clique which has stopped business. They have bought all the wheat, and we cannot expect to bring grain from distant points to grind it here and compete with other markets."[24]

The shorts gathered their forces and hit the clique with heavy sales on May 24. The clique bent, but did not break. July wheat dropped 2 cents and June 1½ cents. But the next day, $2,000,000 arrived from Cincinnati to purchase sufficient wheat to hold the June future at 88 cents.

On the first day of June, the shorts delivered large quantities of cash grain on June futures. Kershaw and Company took 3.4 million bushels. Irwin, Green & Co. took 1.7 million. The clique had made arrangements to accept, and pay for 8 million bushels. The clique had money—plenty of money. Wheat for June delivery advanced to 91¼ cents, but the clique stopped buying and the price receded to 88½.

On June 2 there was a rumor that the shorts had quit, surrendering to the clique. It was claimed they had made a private settlement. June wheat went to 93½ and July to 94¾. The clique was in control, but the directors declared three additional warehouses, containing nearly one million bushels of wheat, "regular." That added nearly one million bushels that could be delivered on futures contracts—one million more bushels that the clique had to accept if it was to run a successful corner.

An owner of corn was paid a cent a bushel by the shorts to move his grain out of store. Demand for steamer transportation on the Great Lakes expanded and freight rates doubled. The Illinois and Michigan Canal was practically blocked by the glut of wheat—canal boats were loaded with grain and had no place to unload it. An elevator shipped out two million bushels of other grains, making room for wheat. Three thousand wheat-loaded railroad cars stood on tracks around Chicago with no place to put their wheat.

Actually, it was not a good year to attempt to corner wheat in Chicago. Bitter class strife polarized the city into warring factions. One year before, a bomb had exploded at a radical labor rally in the Haymarket on West Randolph Street, killing 7 policemen and wounding 67 people. Because of this, 7 men were sentenced to death. (Four were eventually hung.) During the summer, as the clique attempted its corner in wheat, Chicago seethed with hostility and fear between those who believed the 7 had been unfairly convicted and those who insisted they deserved the death penalty. Class antagonism was not ameliorated by knowledge that wheat was piling up in warehouses, railroad boxcars and canal boats around the city and not being turned into flour and bread.

From the standpoint of wheat production and supply, the times did not encourage a corner. The wheat crop of 1886 had been a big one (513,540,000 bushels) and even though exports from this crop were unusually large, (102 million bushels in the fiscal year ending June 30, 1887) there still was no shortage of wheat. Furthermore, in this spring of 1887, the outlook for wheat production was considered quite satisfactory. Eventually, 1887 production totaled an adequate 490,761,000 bushels.

The *Chicago InterOcean* estimated that $25 million was "locked up" in the wheat deal. Of this, it asserted, four-fifths was borrowed from Chicago banks. Possibly, but actually most of the money seemed to be coming from Cincinnati, not Chicago. But its estimate gave the *InterOcean* a foundation upon which to moralize: "Bankers owe a duty to themselves and to the business community. For a little extra profit they should not lend themselves to such illegitimate business ventures."[25]

On Saturday, June 11, the clique brokers announced they intended to peg July wheat at 85½ cents. It was an invitation to the bears. They concentrated on July, throwing huge quantities on the market. The price cracked, hitting 85½, and paused there for a time. Then selling orders swept over the clique—85, 84½, 84. July wheat dropped to 82½. It was a sign of weakness. It was the first sign of weakness the clique had shown.

Robert Lindblom, one of the shorts, said, "Everybody who had a speaking acquaintance with anybody connected with a clique house was told this morning that July wheat would not sell below 85½. The whole pit knew it and acted upon it. . . . We will have a panic in July wheat."[26]

Directors of the Board of Trade were scheduled to hold a regular meeting on Tuesday, June 14. Prior to the meeting, reports circulated that they would do all that was possible to prevent a corner by declaring wheat stored in still more tumble-down warehouses "regular." This was expected to add another million bushels to the "regular" wheat, all of which could be delivered to the clique to fulfill June contracts.

Moreover, and most important, it was claimed that the directors had been informed by the Board's consul that they had the power to declare wheat held in vessels and railroad cars "regular." This would further, and very substantially, increase the supply that shorts could deliver to the clique. (A few weeks later, George Stone, secretary of the Board, sent a letter to the Chicago Chamber of Commerce in which he said that the directors never considered making the railroad cars regular.)

At the opening bell on Tuesday, a vast hoard of wheat was thrown on the market. Rosenfeld had his men in the pit, supporting June. But no one was supporting July, which opened at 83¾ and quickly started to fall.

Rosenfeld's men had gone into the pit with instructions to buy up to five million bushels of June wheat if necessary. The wheat poured down on them. They took five million bushels, then another million. Rosenfeld watched incredulously as July plunged below 80 and his men were overwhelmed with June wheat. Something was wrong. The wheat was coming not only from the shorts, but also from Charles Kershaw. Kershaw was selling the clique's wheat—one clique house dumping on another clique house. These were not "wash" sales. Rosenfeld bought 3.3 million bushels of June wheat and would buy no more. All his men were withdrawn from the pit. The clique was busted.

Rosenfeld's failure was announced by the Board's secretary. Two other houses failed before the day was over. Directors held their meeting but did not get a quorum. No matter; the storage question was unimportant now that the clique was broken. July wheat dropped to 74 and then closed at 75. June closed at 74¾.

The *Cincinnati Enquirer* began its front page story the next morning: "Yesterday witnessed the greatest panic in wheat ever known in America."[27]

The *Enquirer*, like the officials of the Fidelity Bank, was annoyed by circulars that had been sent to the Fidelity's correspondent banks in the country intimating that the Fidelity was connected with the Chicago wheat deal as well as telegrams received by the Cincinnati Police from several cities asking if it were true that there was a "run" on the Fidelity. In the exaggerated language of the period, the *Enquirer* said:

> Could the desperation of the damned be exhibited to a greater extent than by these circulars and telegrams? The Fidelity National Bank is stronger today than ever by reason of these cowardly attacks. Its friends are convinced that it is well named Fidelity and Cincinnati is proud of its enterprise.[28]

The *Cincinnati Commercial Gazette* said the Fidelity believed it had traced the circulars to the Third National Bank, erstwhile home of Harper, Baldwin and Hopkins.

From the ruins, F. E. Johnson of Rosenfeld and Company philosophically looked about him:

> The clique had figured the total storage capacity of the Chicago elevators at about 15,000,000 bushels of graded wheat. But there seemed to be endless room over and above that amount. The directory of the Board have shown a decided tendency to make every available home and shed regular.[29]

The *Chicago Tribune's* man in Cincinnati reported, "E. L. Harper declares that he was not in the deal. He says that he knows nothing about it, but is very indignant at the attempt to cause a run on the Fidelity Bank."[30]

Nevertheless, Swift, the Fidelity president, was upset over the mounting rumors concerning Harper and the wheat deal. He had heard them before, and had asked Harper about them. Each time, Harper denied the rumor. Swift then brought Richard Smith, editor of the *Commercial Gazette*, to visit Harper. Again, the question was put forth concerning the rumors. Again, Harper denied them. Smith responded by writing an editorial defending the Fidelity.

The price collapse, and its revelation of wild speculation, produced an outcry in the press. The *InterOcean* branded the incident, "A crime against society for which its promoters should be punished."[31] The *New York Tribune* was more philosophical: "In time a wiser public opinion will prevail, holding speculation in food products hostile to public welfare and the gambler in grain an enemy of the American producer."[32] The *Buffalo Commercial Advertiser* said, "Certain little speculative games, much in vogue in American commercial centers. . . have made the exchanges of our large cities huge gambling clubs."[33]

General Eugene Powell, the U.S. bank examiner for the western district of Ohio, descended upon the Fidelity on Monday, June 20. Harper begged Powell to pass the examination—that is, not perform it. Powell refused. He found only about $125,000 in the bank's vaults. In the cashier's drawer he uncovered notes—actually I.O.U.s—for $600,000. The notes represented cash withdrawn by Harper at various times, but they were counted by Baldwin and Hopkins as cash in the bank.

Powell promptly called a meeting of directors. He told them that Harper, Baldwin and Hopkins must resign. Unless they did, the bank would not open the next day. Harper refused to resign. Powell then said that if the bank could raise $500,000 in cash before 9:00 a.m. next morning he would permit it to open.

Next morning at 7:00, two hours before the bank might open, Fidelity directors met again at the bank. There was no $500,000. At 9:00 a.m. the bank did not open. At 3:00 p.m., after a hectic day of crowds trying futilely to get their money out, Harper was served by a U.S. Marshall with a warrant. He confessed, lamenting:

> It would have been all right except for the Board of Trade in Chicago and I would have come out $2,000,000 ahead, but the Chicago Board of Trade committed murder by changing the rules on me. They did something contrary to all precedent when they made all the wheat "regular." It killed the Fidelity, it killed me, and everybody else. It was a monstrous, atrocious thing to do.[34]

In its story the next day, the *Cincinnati Enquirer* proclaimed: "The glorious Fidelity, the pride of the city, the surprise of the country, is gone."[35]

Harper was placed in jail, where he remained until his trial in November. On the first day of the trial, Wilshire, the Cincinnati broker, took the stand.

Attorney: How much wheat did you buy?
Wilshire: Nearly 25,000,000 bushels. Some of it was bought and sold again without being carried long.
Attorney: What was the amount when the crash came?

Wilshire: About 14,000,000 bushels of cash wheat and 6,000,000 bushels of options [futures].

Attorney: For whom were you carrying this 20,000,000 bushels of wheat?

Wilshire: For E. L. Harper. He was to furnish the money and it was carried on margin.[36]

Wilshire testified he deposited checks drawn on various Cincinnati banks in the Fidelity. These ranged in sum from $16,000 to $25,000 and there was not one cent to meet them. He said he did this at the instruction of Harper.

On June 20, Wilshire, Eckert and Company's ledger at the Fidelity showed a balance of $239,260. Actually, the firm was overdrawn to the extent of $1,146,000.

In his testimony, Harper placed the blame on Wilshire, who, he noted, was a stockholder in the Fidelity. Also, Harper said, Wilshire owed the bank money. Harper claimed Wilshire sustained large losses in Chicago wheat, came to Harper and asked for money—"the matter kept growing worse and worse until we had to furnish him money or we would lose large amounts of money. It is the old story of putting good money after bad."[37] Harper simply denied that he had ever given Wilshire any order to buy wheat.

The jury did not believe him. It quickly returned a verdict of guilty. He was sentenced to 10 years in the Ohio Penitentiary and started for Columbus, where the penitentiary was located, immediately after the verdict. When he arrived that evening a large, curious crowd had gathered at Union Station and police officers had to clear a path for him. He had dinner in the station with his family and entered the prison.

The Fidelity remained closed. Over the years, as some assets were salvaged from the debris, a few payments were made to the thousands of depositors. Correspondent banks in Ohio suffered too, but there is no record that any of them were forced to close. It was obvious that the Fidelity's generous offer to depositors and country banks was simply a means to attract money to enable Harper to attempt to corner the wheat market.

Newspapers showed no sympathy for Harper, and not much more for the unfortunate depositors. The *New York Times* proclaimed:

As to the depositors. . . the most that the Government can do is to guarantee that the business of the bank shall be conducted on sound general principles and shall conform to such conditions as can be laid down by law and enforced by the ordinary forces of government action. The government can do no more.[38]

The *Commercial and Financial Chronicle,* leading financial periodical of the day, reviewed the case and concluded, "Under these circumstances no one can lament greatly over the miserable failure of the largest bank in Ohio; it is a welcome lesson in banking, the public will say."[39]

Harper did not suffer in prison. Ironically, he was assigned to keeping books in the secretary's office. His cell, in a new building, was adorned by pictures of his wife and family, an assortment of knick-knacks and five astrakhan rugs. After six years he was pardoned by President Harrison because of kidney trouble. He left the prison April 30, 1893.*

Hopkins was tried for his part of the crime, found guilty and sent to prison. Subsequently, he was pardoned because of poor health; he died the day after he arrived home. Baldwin died before he could be tried.

Up to its time, the Harper deal was the most disastrous collapse in Chicago Board of Trade history. In both the McGeoch and Harper cases, gigantic attempts to corner basic food supplies were broken by the directors of the Board of Trade. But in neither case was the result entirely satisfactory. In the Harper case, financial losses were sustained by innocent bank depositors who had no personal involvement in the deal. With McGeoch, the deep suspicions aroused concerning the quality of American lard hurt the demand for that product abroad and consequently injured American hog producers.

Clearly, the problem was not to break the corner after it had become a full-blown market maneuver, but to prevent it from developing in the first place while at the same time maintaining a free and open market. That was a problem which would occupy the minds of marketing experts for many decades.

---

*Harper Leech and John Charles Carroll. *Armour And His Times,* (New York and London 1938) say that Harper died the day after he was released from prison. They have him confused with Hopkins. Actually, Harper went to New York, obtained a position with the United States Steel Corporation and lived on Central Park West. He continued to insist that Wilshire was the culprit in the wheat deal.

NOTES

1. *Milwaukee Sentinel*, 2 June 1883.
2. *Chicago Tribune*, 3 June 1883.
3. Ibid., 12 June 1883.
4. Ibid., 10 June 1883.
5. Ibid., 16 June 1883.
6. Ibid., 18 June 1883.
7. *Milwaukee Sentinel*, 18 June 1883.
8. Ibid.
9. Ibid.
10. *New York Times*, 17 June 1883.
11. *Milwaukee Sentinel*, 20 June 1883
12. *New York Times*, 18 June 1883.
13. Ibid., 21 June 1883.
14. Ibid.
15. Ibid., 23 June 1883.
16. Ibid., 27 June 1883.
17. Ibid.
18. Ibid.,23 August 1883.
19. Ibid.
20. *Illustrated Graphic News* (Cincinnati) 2 July 1883.
21. *Cincinnati Gazette*, 1 June 1887.
22. *Chicago Tribune*, 18 May 1887.
23. *New York Times*, 22 May 1887.
24. Ibid.
25. *Chicago InterOcean*, 4 June 1887.
26. *New York Times*, 12 June 1887.
27. *Cincinnati Enquirer*, 15 June 1887.
28. Ibid.
29. *Chicago Tribune*, 15 June 1887.
30. Ibid.
31. *Chicago InterOcean*, 16 June 1887.
32. Albert Stevens, "Futures in Wheat," *Quarterly Journal of Economics* (2 October 1887), 37.
33. Ibid.
34. *Chicago Tribune*, 22 June 1887.
35. *Cincinnati Enquirer*, 22 June 1887.
36. *Chicago Tribune*, 1 December 1887.
37. *New York Times*, 10 December 1887.
38. *New York Times*, 13 December 1887.
39. *Commercial & Financial Chronicle*, 25 June 1887.

CHAPTER SIX

Urban and Rural Discontent

The flamboyant activities on the Board of Trade, well publicized nationally by the press, stirred up antagonism in both urban and rural areas. Starvation wages and 10 to 12 hour work days in the cities as well as low prices and oppressive debt in the country provided the background for this antagonism. Armour, Hutchinson, Keene, Harper, McGeoch and other famous speculators became personal symbols for what the laborer and farmer viewed as an unfair system.

A pattern of criticism of grain dealers could be traced to the earliest days in Chicago, even before development of futures trading. "Long John" Wentworth's *Democrat* stoutly defended the farmers in their dealings with the commission merchants. Following the Great Fire, The *Chicago Tribune* urged the Board:

> . . . to purge itself as fast as possible of the gambling spirit that has character- ized no inconsiderable proportion of its members during the past two or three years. Gambling in grain was scarcely known till since the war, and provisions options are of even more recent date. It will be comparatively easy now to expurgate this excrescence and keep it banished forever . . . .[1]

In 1874 A. C. Hesing, editor of the *Chicago Stats Zeitung*, in a largely Germanic protest against prohibition of selling beer on Sundays (it severely hurt the German beer gardens) asserted:

. . . if anyone gets drunk on Sunday, or any other day, he should be arrested
and punished, but I cannot admire or agree with the man who goes to
church on Sunday, and prays, and goes the next day on the Board of Trade
and swindles his colleagues there out of so many bushels of grain.[2]

In an article in the *North American Review* in 1883, Henry Demarest
Lloyd, a noted reformer who lived in Chicago, asserted:

Carlyle has handed down Louis XV to us as "the great regrater of bread." The
sweetest epitaph on any tomb is on the stone to the memory of Sir Robert
Peel: "He gave the poor cheap bread." The Carlyle who hunts through the
newspapers of this generation, for the history of its people, will dig the
regraters of our Boards of Trade and Produce Exchanges out of their obscu-
rity, to write against their names: "They made bread dear."[3]

It was obvious that a latent hostility existed against the grain traders in
the 1880s. It was exploited by a relatively small group named the International Working People's Party, ambivalently defined in the press as "anarchists" or "communists." The group sought to channel the justifiable
efforts of laboring men to improve their sad lot into a violent overthrow
of the established order. Its leader was an inflammatory and combative
individual named Alan Parsons.

As a boy of 13, Parsons had joined the Confederate Army; he fought
with it for four bloody years. Later in Texas, he edited a weekly newspaper
pledged to equal rights for black people. He had to leave the state. Some
years later he turned up as a typesetter on the *Chicago Times*, married to a
black woman. It was natural that he would view the Board of Trade as the
headquarters of the oppressive rich he so ardently hated.

The Board, something of a gentlemen's club as well as a commercial institution, had in its membership numerous men who were not traders in grain.
Of course, many of the local bank presidents were members; banks found
many good customers in the grain trade. Cyrus H. McCormick was a member
to his death in 1884. His son continued as a member. Marshall Field, the
great merchant, was a member, as was his former partner, Levi Leiter, by this
time living in Washington. Among other well known Chicago members was
Charles Hutchinson (son of Benjamin "Old Hutch" Hutchinson), president
of the Chicago Art Institute and chairman of the committee on finance and
investments at the University of Chicago.

The urban dissent against the Board of Trade got an opportunity to
express itself as a result of the Board's decision to forsake its outgrown

quarters for a new and more impressive home. The site chosen was at Jackson Boulevard and La Salle Street, marking a step still further away from the river which had spawned the city's grain trade. The area was vacant or occupied by dilapidated rookeries, but in order for the new building to straddle La Salle Street it was necessary to get approval of the city's aldermen to block off that street for one block. With P. D. Armour on a committee of three, the aldermen were approached and proved agreeable. They were noted for their agreeableness in this period.

The cornerstone was laid in 1882 but the building was not finished until 1885. It was, of course, a very conspicuous construction job and the city's radical group used the Board repeatedly as a butt for invective during these years.

When April of 1885 arrived, the new building was undergoing final touches for its grand opening, and several meetings of the radicals were held. At one such street gathering in mid-April, a speaker thundered that means should be devised for blowing up the "robbers' roost"—the new building.

After trading concluded on the second floor of the Chamber of Commerce building on April 28, a procession formed behind a band and a crowd of about 1,000 men, mostly members and employees, marched down La Salle Street to the new building. Crowds jammed sidewalks and friendly people waved from office windows. That evening came the grand promenade.

The doors were open at 7:30—but only one set of doors, on the northwest side of the building. This precaution was taken because earlier that evening the radicals had gathered at Market and Randolph streets. Parsons had issued a call, asserting that the group would march against "the grand temple of usury, gamblers and cut-throatism where they will serenade the high priests and officers of King Mannon."[4] On a hastily improvised stand, to which was nailed a huge black banner symbolizing starvation, one of the speakers roared, "One of the Board of Trade thieves went on the Board and came off in 24 hours with one million dollars. Where did he get it?"

"Stole it from us!" the crowd replied.[5]

The neighborhood of the new Board of Trade building shown with light. Calcium burners gleamed along the Jackson Boulevard approaches over a seemingly endless stream of carriages, bringing members and their ladies, as well as invited guests and their ladies, to the gala event. Thousands of pedestrians walked up La Salle Street to the light from windows on each side. An air of festivity, achievement and pride enveloped the night.

Once inside the building, however, the dignitaries found little to do beyond watching each other mill around the Great Hall, as the trading floor was called. Some sat down in the pits. Others viewed the congested scene from the visitors gallery. Twenty arc lights suspended from the ceiling helped light the hall, as did four huge "sunburners" in the ceiling. It was estimated that 6,000 people surrounded or entered the building during the evening. But Alan Parsons and the little band of International Working People's Party stalwarts were not among them. Before their march reached the building, a National Guard detachment shunted them down a side street. The revolution would have to wait.

Parsons, however, said of the Guard in a later speech:

> They're Marshall Field's boys. If we would achieve our liberation from economic bondage and acquire our natural right to life and liberty, every man must lay down a part of his wages and buy a Colt's Navy revolver, a Winchester rifle and ten pounds of dynamite![6]

The building itself was a solid structure of granite, squatting somewhat ominously astride La Salle Street. Beyond doubt, it was the most impressive edifice in the city. Its main feature would be—it was not yet completed—a tower of masonry and iron rising 312 feet from the ground, the tallest structure in the city. A light from this tower would be visible for dozens of miles across the city and into the receding prairie.

The urban revolt sputtered out down a side street, achieving nothing against futures trading because it had no program beyond wanton destruction. Meanwhile, a much more serious revolt erupted in the farm communities.

By 1890 the grain growing country, moving ever westward, reached the Great Plains, that land which only a few years earlier had been called "The Great American Desert." Free or cheap land was the lure that filled the plains. The Homestead Act of 1862 and the Pre-Emption Act of 1841 promoted pioneering. In addition, land could be bought from one of the land grant railroads or from any state at very low prices.

The plains beckoned not only to Americans but also to immigrants. One immigrant group, German-speaking Mennonites from the southern Russian steppes, brought with them to Kansas a hearty strain of wheat called "Turkey Red." This hard winter wheat grew well in Kansas, which would eventually become the premier winter wheat state of the nation. Cultivation of Turkey Red spread to other areas in surrounding states—

Nebraska, Oklahoma, the Texas panhandle, western Iowa and Missouri, and eastern Colorado.

In 1917 the agriculture experiment station in Kansas developed Tamarq, a cross between Turkey Red and Marquis, but it was not released to the public until 1932. Meanwhile, it was used in crosses to develop, among others, a group of Papoose wheats—Comanche, Pawnee and Wichita. Released to the public in the early 1940s, these wheats accounted for a sensational increase in production during World War II.

To the North, the spring wheat territory swept westward from its stronghold in the Fox and Rock river valleys, just as it once had moved to the Illinois-Wisconsin line from the Genesee Valley in New York. Soon, the home of spring wheat would be in Minnesota and the Dakotas. The vast hard red spring wheat industry developed from a few seeds saved from a single plant by David Fife of Otonabee, Ontario. The plant was sent to him from a friend in Glasgow, Scotland. From this came Red Fife, parent of Marquis. (Marquis was cut down by stem rust in 1935 and 1937 and superseded by Thatcher.)

There were no forests and no wood in the Great Plains. All the world stretched away in a sea of short grass. The log cabin of pioneering fame in the lands to the east was replaced by the dug-out and the sod house on the plains.

Most of the immigrants were poor. It is from them, much more than from the settlers of the Old Northwest or Pacific states, that the nation derives its tradition of poor folks populating the frontier. They needed money. After the 1873–78 depression, they got it—on loan. Between 1880 and 1890, the volume of currency in circulation increased by nearly 50 per cent—from slightly under $1 billion to $1.5 billion. Gold mining, a favorable balance of trade, and European investment in American securities combined to stimulate a great expansion in business activity. Despite this, prices tended downward, an unusual phenomenon harmful to producers of raw materials—the farm community.

The East, rollicking in good times, poured its surplus funds into the Great Plains. Mortgage companies sprang up overnight; money was everywhere. Enterprising agents drove over the plains, seeking borrowers. Farmers could not resist. In all settlements, the towns which hoped to be cities and the cities which hoped to be metropolises, land values soared. Speculators won fortunes. Settlements vied with one another, and each town developed a notable tendency to see its competitors experiencing an "unhealthy boom" while viewing its own development as "legitimate growth." Farmers fenced in their land, cutting the cattle trails which led the Texas longhorns into the plains states. Rains fell, grains grew, mankind flourished.

Then came the summer of 1887, and with it the first of eight out of ten years of drought. Week after week of red hot sun baked down on the prairies, shriveling both grain and land values. Overnight, the boom collapsed. Profits disappeared, hopes died, money ran away, and so did some settlers. They packed themselves into their prairie schooners and headed eastward, with the canvas bearing such legends as, "In God We Trusted, In Kansas We Busted."[7] Half the population moved out of some western counties. Gaunt ghost towns stood naked against the summer sky.

The farmer had grievances. A barren world surrounded him. Automobiles existed only in the wild dreams of visionaries, and a distance that could be traveled by a wagon team over rutted roads limited the rural man to a narrow, tediously familiar area. No telephone wires stretched across the country landscapes, no television introduced a wide, new world— none of the modern inventions were available then, and the farmer moved through a dull, monotonous routine in the great silence of open spaces. The farmer was a lonely man.

Men who had left the farm and gone to the city had made great fortunes. The Board of Trade was filled with former farm boys. The farmer rose early and worked hard, but the return on his labor gave him none of the sparkle which city men might attain. An energetic man who chose to go to the city became a millionaire; a man with equal energy who remained on the farm became a pauper. The farmer did not see why hard work on the land should not give him a reasonable share of those benefits gained by hard work in the city.

With the railroads, the grain elevators, the Board of Trade "gamblers" and the eastern bankers as enemies, the farmers organized into the Populist Party and won some astonishing victories in the South and West in the 1890 election. While these victories were shocking the eastern establishment, a strong attack on grain futures trading erupted in Congress. The Populists found an unusual ally in William Drew Washburn, Republican senator from Minnesota.

Aristocratic, reserved, wealthy, a lawyer and a businessman, it is doubtful if Washburn ever permitted any farm soil to get under his fingernails. He had founded the flour milling firm of W. D. Washburn & Company in 1878, which was merged into the Pillsbury-Washburn Flour Mills Company in 1889 when several milling companies were purchased and consolidated by an English syndicate.

Washburn entered national politics in 1878 when he was elected to the House in a contest which pitted farmers against millers. Ten years later he was elected to the Senate. At that time he dropped all his business activities, which were considerable, except that as director of Pillsbury-Washburn Flour Mills Company.

Nothing in his background could have led one to believe that in December, 1891, Senator Washburn would introduce a bill which he claimed would certainly stabilize, and possibly raise, farm prices by eliminating trading in grain futures. Asserting, "I do not believe the people of this country realize the disastrous results arising from gambling in wheat and other farm products," he set upon a campaign to teach them.[8]

Washburn's bill provided that dealers should pay annually a tax of $1,000 and a transfer of 5 cents a pound on cotton and hog products and 20 cents a bushel on grains. Its fundamental purpose was to eliminate trading in commodity futures and "puts" and "calls" (options).

Over in the House a somewhat similar bill was being written in the agriculture committee, of which William Henry Hatch of Missouri was chairman. Hatch was a true friend of the farmer. In 1884, he had pushed through Congress an act creating the Bureau of Animal Husbandry and, in 1889, the act which elevated the Department of Agriculture to the status of an executive department in the Cabinet.

Hatch, along with Representative Sydenham Alexander of North Carolina and Representative Marriott Brosius of Pennsylvania, introduced bills aimed at eliminating trading in what Hatch's bill termed "fictitious futures." These were defined as sales in which the seller had no cash grain to deliver and no means of getting it. The bills would have eliminated a form of short selling which Hatch and other farm congressmen felt drove down prices—particularly at harvest time. They were basically similar to the Illinois legislation of 1867, which had created such discomfort to "Old Hutch" and several other traders, but, of course, they appeared more menacing to the Board of Trade because they represented potential Federal legislation.

The bills, when consolidated, were referred to in the press as the "Anti-Option Bill," a misleading term because in market terminology "options" meant "puts" and "calls" (the right of holders to buy or sell futures at a specific price over a stated period of time), not futures.

H. H. Aldrich, a member of the Board who testified before the House agriculture committee, expressed the opinion of many—probably most—members when he said he heartily favored the elimination of options but not of futures. A more accurate term for the Hatch-Washburn proposals is Anti-Futures Bill.

Some arresting testimony, ranging from the hysterical to the informative, developed in the House agriculture committee hearing. One witness, John Whitaker, described as a large pork packer from St. Louis and Wichita, declared, "The short seller is the anarchist of America."[9]

More knowledgeable was A. J. Sawyer of Minneapolis, a grain merchant who owned a string of elevators in the Northwest, bought wheat as it came to these elevators and sold the grain to millers and others in the United States and Europe. Sawyer explained that often he had to buy more grain on any day than he could sell in world markets—and on such occasions he would sell in the futures market.

Representative Henry Youmans of Michigan asked, "Then the sale of these options would be the only way that would help you out in this business under that condition of things?"

"We would close the elevators but for that," Sawyer replied.[10]

Charles A. Pillsbury, managing director of the Pillsbury-Washburn Mills, testified in favor of the Hatch bill, asserting that "one effect of this short selling of wheat has been that millers of the country have come to the conclusion that it is hardly safe for a man to be long a bushel of wheat overnight."[11]

Pillsbury criticized short selling and showed a rather remarkable lack of knowledge of markets when he added, "Now, they say the short seller has to buy this wheat [that he has sold short]; to be sure he does, but he buys it back generally from another short seller . . ."[12] Pillsbury insisted that the millers had lost money in their operations for the previous 10 years.

But Pillsbury may inadvertently have revealed his real reason for objection to short selling when he was asked by Representative Charles Moses, "Can you make more money with high price wheat than with low price wheat?"

"Yes sir," Pillsbury replied. "Say we make 10 per cent on flour, or 5 per cent, which is perhaps near the average, our percentage of profit has always been very much larger when breadstuffs are high than when they are low."[13]

The higher the price of wheat, the more the profit for millers; no wonder Pillsbury did not like to see speculators sell short.

W. E. Brown, president of Isaac Harter Company, a winter wheat miller, was asked to describe his operation in the wheat market and he replied:

> The way we do is, we buy the wheat at any time it is offered. As soon as we
> buy it we sell futures against it. . . . Then it makes no difference whether the
> price of wheat goes up or down. The mill is absolutely protected and we do
> not gamble in grain.[14]

There is no use of the word "hedging" in this testimony, but that is the
operation described. Less than 50 years after trading in futures made its
timid start, the futures market was being used to pass along the risk of
price changes from exporters, warehouses, millers and others to
speculators.

Brown was closely questioned by Representative Alexander, producing
this interesting exchange:

Alexander:	You state you would have lost $60,000 if it had not been for these futures?
Brown:	Yes sir.
Alexander:	That acts in the nature of insurance?
Brown:	Yes sir.
Alexander:	Who pays the $60,000 you would have lost?
Brown:	That I am not able to say, just who pays for it.
Alexander:	Do you get it out of the actual crop of the country?
Brown:	No sir. I do not think it comes from that.
Alexander:	Well, who pays for it?
Brown:	Well, that probably would be rather intricate to find out just who pays for it.
Alexander:	Well, somebody must pay for it?
Brown:	Yes sir. It is paid by someone.
Alexander:	By the producer or the consumer?
Brown:	No. It would not be paid by the producer.
Alexander:	You are satisfied it would not be paid by the miller?
Brown:	It would be but for the use of futures.
Alexander:	Call it insurance, because it is actually that in your business. The miller would not pay the $60,000?
Brown:	Not if he was protected; nor would the producer pay it, because we had paid him his price at the time of purchase.

Alexander:	Who is it that pays that?
E. P. Bacon:	The speculator.
(interrupting)	(President of the Milwaukee Chamber of Commerce.)
Chairman Hatch:	We do not permit any interruptions by any gentleman outside the committee.
Brown:	I would consider the man who bought the wheat would pay for it.
Rep. Moses:	The lambs would pay it.[15]

The bill received the unanimous approval of the agriculture committee and was brought up on the floor of the full House by Hatch on "suspension day," a day when the strict—some would say dictatorial—House rules were suspended to enable the Congressmen to vote on a variety of bills.

Despite the Hatch bill's importance, only 15 minutes was allotted each side of the debate. Hatch himself received only one minute to discuss his bill.

The bill passed 168 to 46, a relatively small number of Congressmen voting (the House membership totaled 335). One reason was the fact that the Republican National Convention was in session in Minneapolis and many Republican Congressmen were in that city rather than in Washington. Another reason was the heat—it was June 6 and Washington was experiencing an early mid-summer heat wave. And a third reason may have been that the Congressmen just did not want to vote on so controversial a measure with an election coming up in November.

Hatch's decision to bring the bill before the House on "suspension day," and when the Republican Convention was meeting, led one opponent, Representative Cummings (D–New York) to remark it was fit that the measure should be put through at the dead of night "when churchyards yawn and Hell itself breathes out contagion to this world."[16] (Hamlet, III, ii)

More opposition developed in the Senate, largely stressing the old "state's rights" arguments and declaring the bill "unconstitutional." Probably the most effective attack came from a newly elected Louisiana senator, who later would become Chief Justice of the U.S. Supreme Court—Edward White. In his maiden speech, White spoke over a two day period in the usual florid language of that era.

In his most telling argument, White quoted Pillsbury's statement before the House agriculture committee that for the last 10 years the millers had paid more for their wheat than they had obtained from the flour made from that wheat. If that was true, White asked, what became of the argument that under the futures system the farmers did not receive for their wheat what they otherwise would have?

The Republicans were anxious to avoid any decision on the anti-futures bill before the November election. They saw the bill as a trap: President Benjamin Harrison would have to either approve or veto, and would lose votes in either case. Senator Washburn objected to the idea of having the bill go over to a post-election Congress, but agreed to that maneuver when the president nominated Soren Histon, a prominent Scandinavian editor of Minnesota, as consul to Dusseldorf.

The Senate reconvened in December, after Harrison had lost the election to Grover Cleveland, and passed the anti-futures bill, 40 to 29, on January 31, to the delight of Senator Washburn, who exulted, "Passage of the bill will destroy some of the worst gambling places in the country . . . . The Board of Trade in Chicago is the heart center of all the deviltry because it sends out tips to different cities as to the condition of the produce market."[17]

However, there were some differences between the bill passed by the Senate and that passed by the House; therefore, the bill had to go back to the House for approval. The House agriculture committee accepted the Senate amendments and Hatch attempted to bring the bill before the full House for passage. To his disgust he discovered the Congressmen embroiled in a discussion on an Indian appropriations bill, which seemed to arouse the interest of members not heretofore notably concerned with Indians.

With time running out on the 52nd Congress—its life would end on March 4—on March 1 Hatch asked for a suspension of the House rules in order to take up the bill. To obtain a rules suspension, a two-thirds majority was necessary. Hatch did not get it. Although a majority favored the bill, 172 to 124, that nevertheless fell a substantial 26 votes short of the required two-thirds.

This was the high water mark of the agrarian attack in the late nineteenth century upon futures trading, although several bills designed to eliminate such activity were introduced in the House and Senate in the immediately succeeding years. None ever passed the Senate.

The victory of Grover Cleveland in the 1892 election was, at least in part, attributed to the Populist revolt, which drew enough votes away from Harrison in the plains states to swing the election to the Democrats. But the political change produced no economic improvement. Prosperity eluded both parties.

In May, 1893, the New York Stock Market went into one of its traditional tailspins. Fall of the nation's gold reserve below the custom established minimum of $100 million scared investors. The panic was on. Before it was over, 74 railroads tumbled into receivership, 573 banks closed their doors and 12,040 businesses failed. By July the price of wheat in Chicago had dropped to 54¾ cents a bushel, the lowest price since the Civil War.

Rumors of business failures mounted even higher than the failures themselves. One such concerned Swift & Company, the giant meat packing firm. A note on the ticker carried the rumor and Gustavus Swift, founder and chairman, heard of it. Hopping into a carriage at the Union Stockyards, he sped as fast as he could to the Board of Trade. Striding through the door, he walked to a cash grain table and pounded on it.

"Attention, attention!" the packer cried.

The traders stopped to look at the infuriated Yankee.

"It is reported that Swift & Company has failed. Swift & Company has not failed. Swift & Company cannot fail!"[18]

With that he strode heroically out the door.

Not so fortunate was John Cudahy, victor in many a previous struggle on the Board. In the spring of 1893, Cudahy thought that mess pork would be a good buy and he began making purchases for September delivery. He also bought large quantities of lard. A. M. Wright was another big buyer while N. K. Fairbank took a smaller position on the same side of the market. Mess pork rose to $23 a barrel and optimists felt it would rise to $25 or $30. However, with the crash in the New York Stock Market and the general economic collapse, heavy pressure developed against all commodities.

Cudahy's money ran out late in July. On the last day of that month, September pork closed at $19 per hundred pounds. It opened the next day at $18.75 and immediately plunged, losing 50 cents and $1 between trades. J. Ogden Armour, son of P. D., rallied the other packers and they stopped the decline at $10.50. Slowly, the price got back to $12. But then, shortly after noon, the Board's secretary announced the failure of John Cudahy and several other firms and individuals, including Wright. Fairbank escaped. Pork promptly plunged to a close at $6.30.

Lard did a little better. Throughout the morning Cudahy's brokers held prices at $9 per hundred pounds. But after the failure announcement, it dropped immediately to $6.

All told, there were 11 failures, and Cudahy's was the largest of the lot. Charles Hutchinson was made trustee of the Cudahy estate. John Cudahy sold some of his real estate and his three brothers helped out with payments to Hutchinson. Edward, Patrick, Michael and John Cudahy were all involved in meat packing in the Midwest, but only John drifted into speculation on the Board of Trade. John appeared on the floor of the Board daily, directing the operations of the corps of brokers. Initially as successful in speculation as in packing, he lived on Michigan Avenue in one of those ostentatious stone fortresses so favored by the very rich of that period.

Because the Cudahy brothers rallied 'round, John's indebtedness was paid off and he remained on the Board but later returned to real estate. An interesting point about the Cudahy failure was that on the day it happened Benjamin "Old Hutch" Hutchinson turned up on the floor, possibly happy to see an old rival defeated.

Hard times forced a band of 3,000 workers to march through the financial district, demanding work. Memberships on the Board of Trade were offered for sale at $850. Newspapers headlined that Armour & Company received one half million dollars in gold to pay wages. Members felt the Board of Trade building was about to collapse and hired an engineering firm to give a report. Eventually, the building's tower was torn down. Then, on September 27, 1893, Cassius Belden, a carriage painter and former mental patient, fired five random revolver shots from the visitors gallery. Three people were hit—a trader, an operator in the telegraph office and a woman from Titusville, PA who was in Chicago to see the World's Columbian Exhibition. All recovered.

In politics there came to the fore one William Jennings Bryan who had been elected Congressman from Nebraska during the Populist uprising in 1890. At 36 he was tall, black-haired, magnetic, full of a great energy and able to pour out charm while shaking hands for votes. He was the greatest orator of his time, and in a period when oratory was held high in public esteem. On the night of July 9, 1896, at the Democratic National Convention, Bryan rose to close the debate on the free silver plank in the party's platform. From that moment until the election of Woodrow Wilson, Bryan controlled the Democratic party.

Bryan's voice swelled over that hot, tired audience of desperate men and lifted them from their seats, filling them with determined hope. In a winging spellbinder which would become known as the "Cross of Gold Speech," Bryan could not afford not to mention the Board of Trade:

We say to you that you have made the definition of a businessman too limited in its application. The man who is employed for wages is as much a
businessman as his employer. The attorney in a country town is as much a
businessman as the corporation counsel in a great metropolis. The merchant
at the crossroads store is as much a businessman as the merchants of New
York. The farmer who goes forth in the morning and toils all day—who
begins in the spring and toils all summer—and who, by the application of
brain and muscle to the natural resources of the country, creates wealth, is as
much a businessman as the man who goes upon the Board of Trade and bets
upon the price of grain.[19]

The Democrats nominated Bryan for the presidency on the fourth bal-
lot. When the Populists met at their convention, they, too, nominated
Bryan.

Bryan did not mention legislation to outlaw futures trading, nor did
the Democratic platform. Nor did the Populist platform. That grievance
had been submerged by the realization that tight money was the real
culprit in keeping the rural areas in distress. In passing, it should be noted
that both Senator Washburn and Congressman Hatch were defeated in
their attempts at reelection.

Throughout early 1896 prices sank to sickening levels, aided only temporarily by the death of Edwin Pardridge, the greatest "bear" in Board of
Trade history. A former dry goods merchant, he gained a fortune by selling short in the years of post-Civil War agricultural depression.

There was a slight upturn in prices following Pardridge's death, although
it did not reflect an unseemly celebration by the bulls. It grew out of the
market's technical condition. Pardridge died as he had lived—a bear. His
short line had to be closed out after his death, and it was this buying which
caused a temporary advance. Nevertheless, cash wheat soon dropped to 53
cents a bushel, not much above the 48⅞ cents low in the previous year.

While the wheat crop fell short, bumper crops of feed grain were harvested. Corn and oats prices tumbled to the lowest levels ever recorded at
Chicago, as did rye prices. These were lows not reached in the Great
Depression of 1930–33. Lows for the contract grades—grades which could
be delivered on futures contracts—were 19½ cents for corn, 14¾ cents for
oats and 28 cents for rye. The bottom for corn was made September 8, for
oats September 5 and for rye August 12.

Out in the country, of course, prices fell even lower. Contract grade
corn sold on track at Onawa, Iowa at 15½ cents and oats at 9½ cents.
Corn was 11½ cents and oats 7 cents in South Dakota.

The low prices did not aid Bryan as much as might have been expected. Bryan lost the Old Northwest states, and with them the election. He also lost the northeast states, as expected, but he carried the south (except Kentucky) and the Great Plains (except North Dakota).

Bryan's defeat has been attributed in part to an advance in the price of wheat based upon a smaller domestic crop, poor European harvests (especially in Russia) and a crop failure and resultant famine in India. Between the time Bryan was nominated and election day, cash wheat at Chicago advanced from 54¾ cents a bushel to 79 cents a bushel and the December wheat future from 57½–58⅛ to 78¾–80¾ cents a bushel.

The 1896 corn crop at 2,283,875,165 bushels was, at that time, the largest on record. The cash price on the day Bryan was nominated was 26¼ to 26⅝ cents a bushel, and on election day it was 24¾ to 25½ cents. The December future showed the same pattern: 27 to 27⅛ on nomination day, 25½ to 25⅞ cents on election day. Oats gained a few cents a bushel for both cash and futures between the two dates.

The great popular uprisings of the 1880s and 90s ended with the repulse of Bryan by the business community and its middle class supporters. Both the urban agitators and the rural reformers who had hoped to eliminate or place governmental restrictions upon futures trading would have to wait for another depressed economy before they could try again.

Meanwhile, an extraordinary increase in the world's gold supply and an expanded volume of money in circulation, along with the washing out of heavily mortgaged farm properties, would restore sufficiently prosperous conditions to quiet rural discontent in the early decades of the twentieth century.

NOTES

1. *Chicago Tribune,* 15 October 1871.
2. M. L. Ahern, *The Great Rebellion: A History of the Rise and Progress of the People's Party in the City of Chicago and Cook County* (Chicago 1874), 97.
3. "Making Bread Dear," *North American Review* (August 1893), 124.
4. Harper Leech and John C. Carroll, *Armour and His Times* (New York 1938), 227.
5. Wayne Andrews, *Battle for Chicago,* 130.
6. Ibid.
7. John D. Hicks, *The Populist Revolt: A History of the Farmers' Alliance and the People's Party* (Lincoln, Nebraska 1961), 2.
8. *New York Times,* 15 December 1891.
9. Ibid., 6 February 1892.

10. *Fictitious Dealings in Agricultural Products,* Testimony of witnesses before the Committee on Agriculture, House of Representatives (52nd Congress, 2 sess, Washington, D.C. 1892), 32.
11. Ibid., 188.
12. Ibid., 192.
13. Ibid.
14. Ibid., 213.
15. Ibid., 215.
16. *New York Times,* 7 June 1892.
17. Ibid., 5 February 1892.
18. Louis F. Swift and Arthur Van Vlissingen, Jr. *The Yankee of the Yards: The Biography of Gustavus Swift* (New York and Chicago 1927), 36.
19. William Jennings Bryan, *The First Battle: A Story of the Campaign of 1896* (Chicago 1897), 200.

CHAPTER SEVEN

The Professional and the Amateur

T here were two types of corners—first, a technical corner in one delivery month in Chicago which created no response in other markets; second, a combination of a corner in a Chicago delivery month and an accumulation of cash grain which resulted in higher market prices in consuming areas, both in this country and abroad, for that grain and the various products derived from it.

An example of the first type of corner was one run by Benjamin Hutchinson in 1888, the same year that Washburn and Hatch introduced their Anti-Futures bills. For the second type, a cornering attempt in 1897–98 by Joseph Leiter, an extremely wealthy and naive young man, is an outstanding example. It was notable that in neither case did the leadership of the Board of Trade make any attempt to prevent or break the corners.

By the latter half of the 1880s, Hutchinson was referred to as Old Hutch to distinguish him from his son Charles, who had attained a great personal popularity and in January, 1888 was elected president of the Board. Old Hutch still had his deep voice and still walked in long, easy strides—but he did not dominate the Chicago business and financial worlds as he once had.

While he had started out as a businessman, dealing in meats and flour in the pre-Civil War days, eventually trading in grain futures became his whole life. He was the major force behind establishment of a "Call

Board" in grain in Gamblers Alley in 1880. He always sat up in front where he could be quickly recognized by the caller, Charles Stiles. (The caller called out his bids and offers, completing trades when these calls were matched by those in attendance.) This trading was conducted during periods when the Board of Trade was not in session. Old Hutch often traded at the Tremont, Sherman or any other place where off-hours trading was conducted. But only on the Board itself could he trade in large quantities, a place where his big orders could be matched by other traders.

In the spring of 1888, Old Hutch began to talk bullish on wheat and to accumulate the grain for September delivery. He spent most of the day sitting on a chair—referred to as "the Throne" by other traders—on the Board's floor. He wore the same old-fashioned, square cut clothes which had been in vogue 30 years earlier. His coat, buttoned at the top, was described as "a criss-cross between a cutaway, sack and frock." The color was "dingy looking brown or faded black."[1] To the spectators he was something left over from the Civil War years, but to other traders he was a menace who might cause them great financial harm.

Prices slowly rose during the late summer and early autumn. It was believed that Old Hutch had accumulated his contracts at an average price of around 87 or 88 cents.

Selling came in part from a group of professional traders who followed a policy termed "percentage short selling." These traders sold at the start of each crop year and kept on selling in the hope that prices would decline sufficiently to enable them to cover their short positions at a profit. In these years of depression for agriculture, the technique usually rewarded its operators.

Among these men were John Cudahy, the County Kilkenny Irishman who had several run-ins with Old Hutch and would meet with disaster in pork and lard in 1893. And Nat Jones, who in 1890 was to sell his palatial home on North Shore Drive and move to New York; he lost heavily in the stock market and died practically penniless. And Norman Ream, who, on being accused of being a chronic bear, denied it and asserted, "I am in the market to make money and I go on the side that makes me the most money with the least trouble."[2]

But the most famous of all these short sellers was a little, stoop-shouldered man, weighing only slightly more than 100 pounds, awkward of speech and of gait. This was Edwin Pardridge, former dry goods merchant turned speculator. Pardridge, born on a farm near Durhamville, New York, operated dry goods businesses in several cities with his brother before they came to Chicago in 1869. They opened a strictly cash store on the premises on State Street occupied by the famous merchant Potter Palmer at the start of the Civil War. Pardridge began to dabble in grain and little by little, not unlike Old Hutch, he was drawn deeper into the whirling speculation. Eventually he gave up his dry goods business and concentrated exclusively on grain trading.

In late summer Old Hutch got an ally. A frost swept over the Red River Valley of the northwest, ruining a large part of the spring wheat crop. The reports came down to the grain trade in dribbles, but they were all emphatic in telling one story—the wheat crop north of the Northern Pacific Railroad had been disastrously damaged. At the same time reports from Europe were pessimistic. Crop failures on the continent created a wheat deficiency estimated at 140 million bushels. Europe needed wheat and the northwest crop was ruined—and there was Old Hutch sitting on his long line of September wheat!

On September 22 one lot of cash wheat changed hands at the magical figure of $1. The news of dollar wheat for the first time in five years filled the country people with joy and hope. Nevertheless, the bears kept hitting the market, selling in the belief that Old Hutch would retreat and cause prices to break when—and if—he was forced to dump his wheat. Their selling angered him.

"I'm not after the lame ducks," he said. "I hope everyone of them will make money. The chaps I'm gunning for are those smart guys who have been trying to down me, and I'm going to get them. Lord, how I'll make them howl!"[3]

On Thursday, September 27, three trading days before the end of the month, September wheat opened at $1.05. It rose steadily throughout the day, reaching $1.28. At that figure the small-time traders—the "lame ducks" to Old Hutch—who were caught on the short side of the market moved out of the pit, surrounded Old Hutch's throne and begged him to sell wheat.

"Let them have what they want at $1.25," Old Hutch told one of his brokers, John Brine.[4] The shorts stood in line before Brine, who handed out 125,000 bushels at $1.25.

When a reporter asked Old Hutch what he intended to do the next day, the trader replied, "Do you think this is high? It will go higher before Saturday."[5]

Old Hutch owned much of the wheat in Chicago elevators and was still long several million bushels of September wheat. In their fury at being cornered, Cudahy, Jones and Ream threatened to withdraw their accounts at Hutchinson's Corn Exchange Bank; Old Hutch had founded it but it was run at this time by his son Charles. Nothing came of the threat.

On September 28 Old Hutch set the price at $1.50. He explained, "It was never my intention to put the price above $1.10. But the boys won't settle. Tomorrow the price will go to $2."[6]

And so it did.

Old Hutch remarked, "Wheat's worth it. I get up in the morning and read four or five papers before the rest of these men are out of bed, and I know what is going on."[7]

He had a sense of the drama of the situation. When reporters crowded around him he talked of Shakespeare and Longfellow. At one point he replied to a query: "Have you heard of my last purchase? No? Well I bought an old history of the Hutchinson who was governor of the colony of Massachusetts before the Revolution. It's valuable."[8]

Eager visitors crowded the gallery to get a glimpse of the famed speculator. When he arose from his chair to walk around the floor, other traders trailed him, hoping he would hand them a few lots of September wheat. As Old Hutch walked off the floor on that final trading day for September wheat, traders sang after him

> I see Old Hutch start for the club
> Goodbye, my money, goodbye,
> He's given us a pretty rough rub,
> Goodbye, my money, goodbye.

A little more than a million bushels of cash wheat were delivered to Old Hutch; at the final bell there were one million bushels of September wheat in default.

Old Hutch explained that he had not meant to do what he did:

> I first got stirred up about 10 days ago. I thought wheat was worth the money and was buying it on its merits. Then Cudahy, Ream, and Singer and some of the smaller operators thought they could down the old man apparently. They had run the market pretty much their own way for several years and I made up my mind that it was time to show them that they couldn't rule it to all eternity.[9]

Many people were incensed by Old Hutch's action, and not only those caught short in the market. Grand Master Worker T. V. Powderly, head of the Knights of Labor, wrote sourly in the Journal of United Labor:

> Congress is in session quarrelling over a tariff bill to regulate the price of articles that come to our shores in ships, and Hutchinson is raising the price of wheat which is native to our soil and which every working man is most in need of, but no steps are taken by Congress to put an end to Hutchinson and his methods. Can we put an end to this system of robbery without revolution? . . . Write to the President of the United States to send a message to Congress demanding that these institutions that gamble in food be abolished.[10]

Actually, the price advance in the last few days of September, the period in which the corner became effective, was purely local; there was no reflection in cash wheat prices anywhere else. Within a week Old Hutch arbitrarily caused the price of September wheat to jump from about $1 to $2, but the price of wheat did not double in other markets. This was a localized technical corner in one specific futures contract at one market.

In contrast, there was the corner of Joseph Leiter, the son of Levi Leiter, one time retail merchandising partner of the legendary Marshall Field. Leiter made millions from merchandising and real estate and shared his profits with the Chicago Art Institute, the Chicago Historical Society and the Chicago Public Library. Retiring to Washington he built up a substantial collection of Americana. His son Joseph was one of four children, the only boy.

It was an era when rich men's sons were sent to the proper prep schools and the proper colleges; Joseph attended St. Paul's and Harvard. At Harvard he joined a proper fraternity: Delta Kappa Epsilon. Upon graduation, his father gave Joseph a generous cash reward and put him in charge of some Leiter holdings, which included coal and copper mining.

Part of the Leiter legend holds that, in the spring of 1897, he was undecided whether to buy control of the Atchinson, Topeka and Sante Fe Railroad, which had been wrecked by poor management, or to corner wheat. He tossed a coin and wheat won. The story is probably apocryphal, but nevertheless reveals the grain community's feeling that Leiter embarked upon his heroic venture on little more than a rich boy's whim. He was 28 years old.

From a statistical standpoint, it was not a bad year to buy wheat. Substantially less wheat was in store at Chicago at the start of the year than a year earlier (14,349,981 bushels vs. 21,212,561) and the visible supply in the United States (except California) and Canada fell below the previous year (54,651,000 bushels vs. 69,842,000.) While the American crop outlook was favorable, forecasts of significant reductions from the previous year were made for Europe.

Writing scathingly about early cornering episodes, Henry Demarest Lloyd prophesied in 1883, "The great corner is yet to come."[11] But even the clairvoyant Lloyd could not have foreseen that the responsible person would be a young man who, during the summer of 1897, should have been up in Lake Geneva, Wisconsin, enjoying himself with the rest of the Chicago social set.

During April, May, June and July, persistent buying entered wheat. The price inched ahead as interest in the market expanded. By July it became known that Levi Leiter's son was behind the buying move, and the traders speculated that he had rolled up an enormous paper profit. Joseph Leiter himself was to say after it was all over, "Once, in July, I could have got out and cleared 10 million dollars. But that seemed too small an operation in comparison with what might be done, if all the wheat in the world could be controlled, so I didn't stop but went on with the scheme."[12]

In the hot days of August, many a farmer saw relief from his financial troubles not in Washington, as he hoped, but in Chicago. At the end of the session in those pre-air conditioning days brokers left the pits in a state of exhaustion, their clothes dripping with sweat. Rural visitors to the city sought out the Board of Trade as a mandatory tourist attraction. The December wheat future hit $1 on August 21, to the accompaniment of cheers from the galleries, filled with the largest crowd in the Board's history.

Leiter was not only buying wheat for future delivery but buying cash wheat and moving it out of Chicago at a staggering pace. By August 1 wheat of contract grade in Chicago—that is, wheat qualified for delivery on futures contracts—had dropped to just above 3 million bushels; it had never gone below 11 million in the previous year, nor below 13 million in 1895, nor below 17 million in 1894.

On August 23 the Hungarian government issued its annual estimate of world wheat crops. Importing countries were expected to have a deficit of 539,976,000 bushels and exporting countries a surplus of 348,445,000 bushels, leaving a wide gap between need and capacity to fill that need.* Wheat prices responded to this estimate, as well as to continued heavy shipments by Leiter of cash grain out of Chicago. The cash grain reached $1 for the first time on August 26 while the December future hit $1.03½ on the same day.

---

*Among major producers, only Spain had a larger wheat crop in 1897 than in 1896. The crops were: Russia and Poland 248 million bushels vs 319.5 million in the previous year; France 243,616,000 vs. 329,408,000; India 188 million vs. 200 million; Germany 107,744,000 vs. 110,704,000; Spain 95,736,000 vs. 87,760,000; Hungary 92 million vs. 142.4 million; Italy 83,264,000 vs. 140.8 million; and Great Britain and Ireland 56 million vs. 58,240,000—from the 40th Annual Report, Chicago Board of Trade, 1898, p189, 208.

By September 1 there were only 852,076 bushels of contract wheat left in Chicago; by October that figure dropped to an incredibly low 382,962 bushels. Leiter explained, "My plan is to ship my property away. I can get a great deal cheaper storage rate at Buffalo, New York or Boston than I can here."[13]

Someone asked Old Hutch, who had undergone a painful financial and emotional decline since his 1888 corner, for his opinion on Leiter's activities. The old man replied, "Mankind will always dig out some hidden stores of wheat if the price is high enough. The young fellow had better look out."[14]

One of the men who had sold wheat for December delivery to Leiter was P. D. Armour. His elevators were virtually empty. Fearful that he was about to be cornered by the brash young man, Armour is reputed to have responded that ambition and pride keep a man at work when money is merely a by-product. He showed what he meant.

Armour sent emissaries to scour the country for wheat. They stopped at every country elevator in the Northwest, buying wheat. They urged farmers to sweep grain out of their barns, meeting joyful cooperation. Armour found wheat in Duluth, Minneapolis and Canada. The *Chicago Journal* reported that Armour borrowed wheat from Frank Peavey of Minneapolis, known as the elevator king, guaranteeing to repay it later.

In addition to elevators at major terminals, Peavey owned or controlled more than 200 elevators in country towns in the Midwest and Northwest. Armour got wheat from Peavey in December in time to deliver it on December futures to Leiter, and then repaid Peavey with wheat gathered off farms during the winter. During January and February, Armour's men were still scouring the country for wheat and sending it to Peavey.

To bring wheat down from the Northwest, Armour chartered the biggest lake carriers and sent them to Duluth. He had his tugs plow through the harbor ice, keeping open water for the ships. He also chartered tugs to keep the Soo Canal open, and more tugs to cut the ice in Thunder Bay where he sent ships for wheat stored in Fort William, Ontario. He brought down hundreds of thousands of bushels by rail. At his massive elevators, freight trains were backed up for miles while steamships in the blocked river fought for space to unload.

Armour escaped from the corner. By December the contract grade wheat in store in Chicago had expanded to 2,530,534 bushels. Armour, satisfied if not triumphant, handed over the warehouse receipts to Leiter. The young man took the grain with aplomb. "I am confident that the price of wheat will go up," he said, "and we will sell our wheat at much higher prices than now quoted for cash wheat. It has been bought cheap, and in general conditions of supply and demand are in our favor."[15]

Mills, of course, needed a steady influx of wheat to keep running, and bakers needed flour to keep baking. But the millers, long accustomed to cheap wheat, refused to pay Leiter's price. Some bakers reduced the size of the loaf of bread and there were reports of serious deterioration in quality. Talk spread about the possibility of "dark bread," a phrase derived from the Middle Ages when Europe ate a bitter, dark and soggy bread made from rye.

In response to criticism, Leiter said:

> The millers can buy all the wheat they want from us—but at our price. They won't pay what we ask, and are putting a poor grade in their flour. But they make no difference in their charge. The price of flour is right up with that of wheat. The millers are fooling the people.[16]

Flour is adulterated by using poorer qualities of wheat. Sometimes a substitute grain—such as rye—can be used. By such substitutions the millers could stretch out their supplies, not buying from Leiter, until the 1898 winter wheat crop came in. Newspapers charged millers were mixing corn with wheat to produce flour.

Leiter, sitting on a substantial paper profit, was nevertheless having trouble. Not only did the mills refuse to buy his wheat; he also found that, in order to support the market for cash wheat, he had to buy the May 1898 and July 1898 futures. Furthermore, he had to buy additional cash wheat as it arrived in Chicago. While Leiter had attempted the usual technical corner in the December wheat futures, he was involved in a much more fundamental effort: he was actually trying to corner the nation's visible wheat supply.

How much did he own?

Leiter was to say later, "During my experience in trying to corner wheat, I at one time owned two-thirds of all the wheat in America and every bushel that there was in England. During that time I shipped over 30 million bushels from this country."[17]*

While Leiter held onto his huge store of wheat, events over which he had no control, and which he could not have foreseen, were about to lend him unexpected support. The battleship Maine, on a good-will tour, blew

---

*The reference is obviously to the visible wheat supply in the United States, not the entire wheat crop.

up in Havana Harbor, Cuba, on February 15, killing 266 Americans. Leiter was about to have a war—a short and glorious war as it turned out.

Wheat reacted to the Maine explosion by rising above $1. On February 17 May wheat advanced to $1.06½. For the rest of the month cash wheat did not fall below $1.00½ and May wheat not below $1.01½. Things looked pretty good for Leiter.

Rivalry between Armour and Leiter was stressed by local newspapers, anxious for a little personal drama in their grain reports. It was claimed that Leiter was shipping grain from Armour's elevators first, leaving supplies in other elevators. This, of course, would reduce Armour's income from storage charges.

The market action of March 10 heightened the Armour-Leiter battle rumors. Armour's brokers overwhelmed the market with sales, a raid to see if Leiter's forces would hold up under the deluge. They did. Leiter took one million bushels of May wheat from Armour at $1.04 a bushel.

Attacks upon Leiter's credit spread. Gossips said he would not be able to accept May deliveries—that he would not be able to put up the money needed. Leiter was said to have received a letter from Francis Wells Praag, who described himself as a 14 year old boy who had heard Leiter needed money and was therefore enclosing $100. Traders who saw the letter said it was remarkably well written for a 14 year old boy, not to mention the unique event of a 14 year old boy willingly parting with $100. Leiter's brokers wrote letters to newspapers denying rumors that Leiter was borrowing money in New York because he was unable to obtain it in Chicago.

At this point Levi Leiter left his Americana collection to revisit Chicago. Like other Chicago business leaders, the elder Leiter was a member of the Board of Trade. He quickly realized, if he did not already know, that Armour, although possibly not a direct antagonist of son Joe, was at least a man who had much to say about the price of wheat. On March 18, eight days after Armour's bear raid in May wheat, we find him writing to the wife of P. D. Armour Jr.:

> Papa Leiter and I have become great chums. We have had our arms around one another for the last few days, and we are a loving couple. I feel sorry for the old man to get into such a deal at his time of life. But he is a pretty strong character, and perhaps it is just as well if he don't have so much money to hand down to the next generation. But I guess you will not hear much more about Armour and Leiter crossing swords.[18]

Seven days after writing this letter, Armour sold about 2 million bushels of cash wheat to Joseph Leiter. Leiter explained:

> I wanted the cash wheat to ship and preferred it now rather than in May. Mr. Armour had the wheat, with a profit in it. He bought it to sell. He made a concession on the storage and instead of delivering the cash wheat in May, I took it now and he secured his profits.[19]

With a vast pretension of innocence, Armour said:

> I have never assumed a belligerent attitude toward Mr. Leiter and there is no basis for all the fight rumors. We simply buy grain in the West and ship it here to fill the storage room in our elevators. Our position in the market is simply that of shipping grain.[20]

In April Leiter started to liquidate his futures. On the fifteenth, with the country racing toward war with Spain, he sold several million bushels of July wheat, cleaning out all his holdings in that month. It was a large transaction but the price retreated only 3 cents because of buying support based upon war hysteria. The *Chicago InterOcean* noted, "Leiter's sales of cash and July wheat have been so large in the past three weeks, over 10 million bushels, that his holdings have been greatly reduced."[21]

By getting out of July futures, Leiter served notice that he had no intention of carrying his deal into the new winter wheat crop, which would be available for delivery on July futures. But he still had some cash wheat and was long May wheat, upon which little if any new crop wheat would be available for delivery. The corner he had tried to run the previous December, only to have Armour extricate himself, he would now try to run in the May futures. First, though, there was something important to take care of.

Leiter went to Minneapolis in April and held a meeting with Peavey and C. A. Pillsbury—the same Pillsbury who had wanted to outlaw short selling and testified in favor of the Hatch-Washburn bills. He had admitted at that time that his mills earned more money when wheat prices were high than when they were low.

Peavey, the elevator king, could not have had much feeling of rapport with Leiter. At nine Peavey lost his father; at 14 he had gone to Chicago, where an uncle had found him a messenger boy job for a grain firm. Later, he moved to Sioux City, Iowa, where he organized a firm to sell agricultural implements. The firm began handling grain in 1873 and erected a warehouse on the Missouri River at Sioux City. From there he built up his vast elevator empire. Fatherless, lacking formal education, hardworking, self-made success, Peavey could not have easily understood the wealthy playboy dabbling in wheat.

What happened at this meeting? Leiter was to say, many years later in court, that he, Peavey and Pillsbury agreed to form a pool. Peavey and Pillsbury were to keep cash wheat in the Northwest, thus assuring success of the corner of May wheat in Chicago. Leiter wanted to prevent in May what had happened in December—Armour's transporting of wheat, some of it borrowed from Peavey, to break Leiter's corner.

Said Leiter after the deal was over:

> I told them I wanted it understood that no wheat was to be shipped to Chicago, as I had my May corner on. This was agreed to. I said I didn't want the "shorts" to get the wheat we had so they could deliver it to me in Chicago. I told them that I wanted to squeeze the "shorts" and get all I could.[22]

When the United States formally declared war on Spain on April 25, wheat responded with its usual enthusiasm to the clash of arms. Cash wheat reached $1.23½ on April 28. May wheat went to $1.25. The pace of the upturn quickened in early May. On May 5 the cash price hit $1.50. On May 10 it reached $1.85, high point of the entire Leiter deal and up more than 60 cents in 15 wildly exciting days.

"When I got wheat to $1.75, I found there was a great decrease in demand," Leiter later said. "The people in this country and other countries turned to corn meal and those of certain European countries to rye and other cereals."[23]

At this point Leiter's capital gain was estimated by the grain trade at $4 million—but it was still largely a "paper" profit; he still had wheat to sell and would have more after the May deliveries, of which there would certainly be some from various "shorts" despite the agreement with Peavey and Pillsbury.

In fact, the price upturn was obscuring a fateful, fundamental development: cash wheat arrivals in Chicago were not diminishing, as they should have been if the northwestern grain was being held back, but instead were increasing at what must have been to Leiter a frightening rate. A comparison table of wheat receipts at Chicago for the first six months of 1898 and 1897 tells the story:

Chicago Wheat Receipts

	1898	1897
January	1,006,844 bu.	564,397 bu.
February	1,093,265	418,732
March	2,434,228	383,407
April	1,841,414	160,033
May	4,363,414	293,523
June	988,958	178,076

The rate of weekly receipts in May, the month of prime importance to Leiter, when of all times it was essential that receipts fall off, is particularly arresting:

Chicago Wheat Receipts

Week ended	1898	1897
May 7 (8)	1,152,295	28,381
May 14 (15)	946,395	96,752
May 21 (22)	1,319,438	115,050
May 28 (29)	811,084	34,021
Total	4,229,212	274,204

Late in the month, prices cracked. From the high of $1.85, May wheat slipped to $1.75 on May 28. When it became obvious there would be no corner, and that Leiter was again licked, May wheat crashed 50 cents to $1.25 on May 31. And once more Leiter had to accept cash wheat on his expiring long position on futures.

"There has been no squeezing and everyone has been treated with the greatest consideration," Armour pontificated. "Mr. Leiter's campaign has been a great help to the farmers."[24]

Leiter had more cash wheat than he wanted and he was confronted with the monumental task of marketing it—burying the corpse—before the 1898 harvest. And on June 2 came an ominous development. The first car of 1898 crop wheat arrived in Chicago from Texas. This was 20 days earlier than the earliest recorded arrival. Obviously, there would be an early harvest in the winter wheat territory, and probably a big one. Leiter's time was running out. Two days earlier the government had forecast a 1898 combined spring and winter wheat crop of 650 million bushels. If realized, it would be a record.

Meanwhile, the war with Spain moved rapidly. Dewey sank the Spanish fleet at Manila on May 1 and on Sunday, June 12, American newspapers headlined, "Marines Land On Cuban Soil." It looked like a big crop and a short war—wheat prices dropped.

Once again Levi Leiter was called to the rescue. He arrived on the day the newspapers headlined the Marines' landing. Joseph Leiter was running up fantastic storage charges on his wheat and interest charges on money borrowed from the banks to carry this wheat.

A hurried consultation was held at the Auditorium Annex Hotel. Both Leiters attended. So, too, did representatives of Peavey and Pillsbury. What they decided became clear the next day. Levi Leiter would not pull his son out of a jam again; Levi and Joe surrendered. At the insistence of the bankers, Leiter turned all his wheat over to Armour Grain Company to dispose of it world-wide.

"The treatment I have received at the hands of Mr. Armour is in the highest degree considerate, courteous and complimentary," Joseph Leiter said.[25]

The next day wheat sold below $1 at all major markets.

While the news that "dollar wheat" was gone—and no one knew for how long this time—depressed the farm communities, half a world away there was joy, plus moral preaching. Said the *London Star*: "If the prime mover in this war against mankind is beggared by his greed the retribution is well merited. Nothing can atone for the awful suffering Leiter and his accomplices have caused."[26]

The wheat assigned to Armour for marketing was estimated at around 15 million bushels. Included in the stock was wheat owned by Pillsbury. But not that owned by Peavey—"he [Peavey] will have to shift for himself," the *Chicago Tribune* said.[27] Why was Peavey left out? During the day of Monday, June 13, Leiter said:

> . . . a great deal of gossip has come to me on the subject of the alleged treacherous conduct on the part of northwestern interests which I have always heretofore considered friendly to me in a personal and business way. I have nothing whatever to say on this subject. If in the history of today's doings there have been events to which the public is entitled, it is more than likely the facts will come out in due time, but not from me.[28]

Leiter made another cryptic reference to his northwestern associates—Peavey and Pillsbury—in 1901, when he visited his mining properties in Montana. A reporter for the *Butte Miner* asked him why his corner had failed and Leiter replied:

> Well, you might say that it was brought about by my not being able to control all the wheat in the world. There were those associated with me in the deal who became alarmed and backed out of the undertaking—but that is another story.[29]

Thirteen years later, long after most of the other principals in the cornering attempt had died, Leiter appeared in court to defend himself against a suit brought by the Interior and Monarch elevator companies of Minneapolis for the recovery of $380,935. In 1898 Peavey had been president and majority stockholder of both companies.

The suit grew out of the May 1898 wheat deal. Leiter's defense was that the deal had been an attempted corner, an illegal conspiracy, and therefore he was not liable. In testimony before the court Leiter explained his version of what had happened. When the Leiters, father and son, held their conference in Chicago with representatives of Peavey and Pillsbury, Leiter senior tried to get the northwestern pair to bind themselves in writing to the agreement which Joseph Leiter believed he had negotiated back in April in Minneapolis. Peavey refused. At that Leiter called off the operation and turned his son's wheat over to Armour to sell.

The jury believed Leiter and returned a "Not Guilty" verdict.

Leiter commented, "Well, I finally got justice."[30]

And then he showed that the years had not widened his mind to embrace the social significance of his actions, nor blunted the naked financial acquisitiveness by which he judged success or failure:

> I would like to correct the impression that Pillsbury had anything to do with the Judas play against me. He did not. He was in the pool, but he was straight as a die. It was Peavey who double-crossed me.
>
> If Peavey hadn't sold me out, I would have got out all right and made a lot of money. There is no doubt about that. You see, Peavey had the warehouse receipts owned by Pillsbury and myself.
>
> It was he who 'busted the market wide open,' as he expressed it. He sold our wheat, of which he was custodian.
>
> Oh, Peavey was a dandy! He made a pile of money. He had his life insured for $1 million and six months later died of pneumonia.[31]*

Even Leiter did not know how much he had lost. When the end came, he had wheat scattered throughout this country and Europe. It took many months for Armour to sell the wheat and years for Leiter to settle his accounts. Leiter reminisced:

> I have turned over millions and millions of dollars due to the Illinois Trust & Savings Bank since 1898. These sums were to cover all property and collateral put up by me as guarantees against margins. I owed between $10 and $12 million to the bank.[32]

---

*Peavey had a $1 million life insurance policy payable to his estate so that his death might cause no embarrassment to his business interests.

While the Hutchinson and Leiter corners differed both in method and results, trends of similarity ran through them.

First, there was the feeling of the participants that they were playing a game, that their actions were not significant beyond the confines of the trading pit, or if they were that was of no consequence to the participants. Thus Hutchinson said he was out to get some traders who had downed him—"Lord, how I'll make them howl!" Leiter saw Peavey's selling of wheat as a "Judas play against me." Both statements reveal an amazingly parochial outlook.

Second, luck proved a compelling factor in both campaigns. When Old Hutch started buying wheat in the spring of 1888, he could not have known that a late summer frost would decimate a large part of the spring wheat crop in the Red River Valley of the Northwest. When Leiter began his campaign, the statistical outlook appeared attractive; he could not have known the extraordinary lengths to which P. D. Armour would go to rescue himself, nor did he know that the 1898 winter wheat crop would be very large and ready for an early harvest.

Third, there was no condemnation of, not to mention positive actions to restrain, the cornering activities by the Board of Trade hierarchy. This contrasted with the Board's responses to the Harper and McGeoch cornering attempts and probably reflected a more tolerant (or less socially conscious) administration. Neither Harper nor McGeoch were members of the Board; both Hutchinson and Leiter were, and this may have been a factor in the official immobility.

Fourth, while the escapade infuriated the spokesmen of labor—the Knights of Labor in New York condemned it—there was no similar outcry from conservative ranks. The old "supply and demand" credo held firm. Thus the *New York Times* pontificated editorially:

> . . . it ought to be clear that any attempt to check such operations as his [Leiter's] by law will be needless, since the laws of human nature check them when they become excessive, and such an attempt may be exceedingly mischievous since it is by such operation, freely undertaken, that the true relationship of supply and demand and the 'fair' price of any stable commodity are fixed.[33]

After his successful corner, the career of Old Hutch careened downward. He made several faulty speculative moves, finally having to sell his seat on the Board—purchased for $5 in the pre-Civil War years—for $900 to P. D. Armour, who bought it for an employee. Hutchinson left

Chicago, visited New England for a time and then turned up one morning on the Produce Exchange in New York. After some small scale speculating, he leased the ground floor of a building in the shadow of the Brooklyn Bridge, announcing he would open a grocery. His family brought him back to Chicago and placed him in a sanitarium in Lake Geneva, Wisconsin where he died in 1899.

Following the 1898 plunge, Leiter never again attempted to corner wheat and no evidence exists that he ever again put so much as a dime into the market. While managing his inheritance, he lived a comfortable life, mostly in Washington. In 1908, when he was 39, he married Juliette Williams, daughter of an Army colonel, and built a lavish home, known as the Crystal Palace, across the Potomac from Washington in Virginia. For recreation he took to big game hunting, fishing and cruising on his yacht.

While attending the races in New Orleans in 1932, Leiter caught a cold, returned to Chicago, and died of pneumonia on April 11. He left his wife, a son Thomas, and a daughter Mary.

NOTES

1. *Chicago Tribune*, 23 September 1888.
2. *AEGT*, vol. 4, 15 January 1886, 86.
3. *Chicago Tribune*, 23 September 1888.
4. Ibid., 28 September 1888.
5. Ibid.
6. Ibid., 29 September 1888
7. Ibid., 30 September 1888
8. Ibid.
9. Ibid.
10. *New York Times*, 11 October 1888.
11. *North American Review*, August 1883, 124.
12. *AEGT*, vol. 19, no. 7, 15 January 1901, 309.
13. *New York Times*, 17 December 1897.
14. Leech and Carroll, *Armour and His Times*, 310.
15. *Chicago Tribune*, 17 December 1897.
16. Ibid.
17. *AEGT*,vol. 19, no. 7, 15 January 1901, 309.
18. Leech and Carroll, op. cit., 316.
19. *Chicago Tribune*, 26 March 1898.
20. Ibid.
21. *Chicago InterOcean*, 26 April 1898.
22. *New York Times*, 13 December 1914.
23. *AEGT* vol. 19, no. 7, 15 January 1901, 309.
24. *Chicago Tribune*, 1 June 1898.

25. *New York Times*, 15 June 1898.
26. Ibid.
27. *Chicago Tribune*, 15 June 1898.
28. *New York Times*, 15 June 1898.
29. AEGT, vol. 19, no. 7, 15 January 1901, 309.
30. *Chicago Tribune*, 15 December 1914.
31. Ibid.
32. Ibid.
33. *New York Times*, June 1898.

CHAPTER EIGHT

It's Fun, but
Is It Legal?

Neither the urban nor the rural attacks upon grain futures trading had been successful, but during the 1890s and the 1900s, yet another type of attack developed. It came from establishments that actually benefited from grain futures trading, although in a dubious way, and made its approach through the nation's court system.

These establishments were known as bucketshops. Initially, they were viewed as small grain or stock exchanges, similar to the New York Stock Exchange or the Chicago Board of Trade.

Several theories exist as to the origin of the term "bucketshop." Simplest is that the phrase "to bucket" was a colloquialism meaning "to cheat." Bucketshop might have derived from that, meaning a place where one was cheated. A more romantic theory claimed that beer scavengers from London's slums in the early nineteenth century walked the streets with buckets, draining every beer keg they came across. Returning to their haunts, they then enjoyed a social evening together, passing the buckets from one to the other, each taking a swill as the beer swashed by. These rendezvous were called bucketshops. The word came to mean any place of low repute.

Another version was based on the fact that trading in grain futures in Calhoun Place ("Gamblers Alley") was possible in 1,000 bushel lots in contrast to the minimum 5,000 bushels on the Board of Trade. When dealings on the Board grew slack, some traders would say they'd send down a bucket to get a bucketful of orders from the dealers in the alley. Hence, the word bucketshop came to be applied to small time operators in grain and then to firms which accepted customers' orders but did not execute them.

In appearance the bucketshops were not much different from regular stock and grain commission houses. What they lacked was membership on the Chicago Board of Trade, the New York Stock Exchange or some similar institution. The all-essential difference between a regular commission house and a bucketshop was this: when a transaction was made at a regular commission house, the transaction resulted in a purchase or sale of stock or grain for future delivery on an exchange. It was real. When a transaction was made at a bucketshop, nothing happened on any exchange. When the customer won, the house lost; when the customer lost, the house won.

Legally, a bucketshop was "a place where wagers are made on the fluctuations of the market price of grains and other commodities."[1] A purchase or sale of a commodity is a contract between an individual and a broker—a contract to deliver or to accept a delivery of a commodity. The true validity of the contract is whether the selling party can tender and compel the delivery of the commodity purchased.

While the bucketshops in stocks flourished in the East, the most vigorous growth occurred in the less financially sophisticated Midwest. At the height of the bucketshop boom, 25 such firms operated in the immediate vicinity of the Board of Trade; more than 100 were in the city. One firm sent a salesman to drum up business in the country.

In the later years of the nineteenth century, the bucketshops seemed quite respectable when compared with other forms of entertainment offered Chicagoans. The city stewed in vice, gambling and corruption.

Mike McDonald, the most powerful gambler in the city's lurid history, operated a place called "The Store," a four-story, brick, gambling edifice. From here, he ran the city. Billy Fagin owned the "House of David," a gambling establishment which had a room set aside exclusively for prayer. One could use it either before or after playing. Theodore Cameron, Ed Wagner and Pat Sheedy were other gambling kings.

Along with the gambling establishments were the red light districts of Little Cheyenne, Coon Hollow, Satan's Mile, Black Hole and a dozen others, mostly on the south side. (Cheyenne, retaliating, called its red light district, "Little Chicago.") Micky Finn held forth in his Lone Star saloon, where he came up with his celebrated knock-out drink—raw alcohol, water in which snuff had been soaked and hydrate of chloral.

As the bucketshops expanded, they alternated with pool shops and faro banks; sometimes all three were combined in one establishment. The pool shops in a later era would be called "bookies," places where bets on horse races were made. Faro became an extremely popular game in the years when the West was won. Bets were placed upon the manner in which a banker drew cards from a deck. Some faro terms are now part of the stock market terminology—"whipsawed," "split," "spread," and "calling the turn."

Money could be made in bucketshops, but only against substantial odds. Most bettors took the "long" side of the market, just as the average man entering the market through regular commission houses usually bought securities or grains rather than selling short. When the market declined, bucketshops cleaned up on their customers. This encouraged the bucketshops to join in "bear" raids—concerted efforts to force prices down—on the Board of Trade. To do this, they of course had to place their orders through firms which were members of the Board, an indication that the quest for commissions left some of the member firms lacking in scruples.

Even when the customer was right on the market, he had only a marginal chance of collecting. When numerous customers were owed money, which could happen in an advancing market, the bucketshop simply "failed." After a respectable interval for mourning, the failed promoter could open another shop under a different name. This peculiarity of bucketshops became more apparent each year, but it did not snuff the citizens' urge to do a bit of gambling in grains.

As the years progressed, the Board of Trade grew more incensed with bucketshops. There were several good moral reasons, including the fact that this type of outright gambling discredited all futures trading, but probably the most potent cause of the Board's concern was financial: the bucketshops took away trade which would otherwise have gone to a member commission house. Regular commission houses, seeing their business flowing to bucketshops, secretly cut commission rates below the official level.

The Board's fight against bucketshops centered around quotations. If the shops could be kept from obtaining these figures, there would be nothing on which customers could bet. For 10 years, from 1882 to 1892, the Board tried to keep quotations out of bucketshops. The results were hilarious.

With the cooperation of the telegraph companies (which the Board did not think were as enthusiastic as they should have been), the bucket-shops were cut off from all quotations. But they had other means, aside from occasionally tapping a wire, of obtaining them. At one time a buck-etshop stationed two men in the street. From the window of a commis-sion house allied with the bucketshop, a board was hung. When the mar-ket declined, so did the board; when the market rose, the board followed. One man stationed under the board signaled the fluctuations to another man in front of the bucketshop, who relayed them to the clerks in the shop.

Other members of the Board of Trade, not immune to picking up some extra income, were caught standing before windows and giving signals by stroking their chins or raising cards. Some bucketshops employed run-ners, or messengers, to bring them the vital figures. Quotations could be copied from the blackboards of regular commission firms and hurried to the bucketshops, and consequently the Board asked all firms to stop marking up quotations. With equal perspicacity, all grain tickers were removed from saloons.

In 1887 the Board of Trade's president, Abner "Charlie" Wright, a former school teacher and boys' school headmaster, gave this fight a slight touch of the ridiculous. One night a cable of wires in the basement of the Board of Trade building was cut with an axe. Among other places, these wires connected with the police and fire departments. Board officials at first denied all knowledge of the axe chopping, but later Wright admitted that he was responsible. He wanted to make sure the bucketshops did not get quotations, he explained. The cable was quickly repaired.

The Board decided to stop sending out any quotations—to bucket-shops, commission houses and everyone else. In order to prevent leaks all entrances except one were barred, an act which so infuriated one trader that he battered down a closed door to gain entrance. Bucketshops got quotations. Use of all telephones on the exchange floor was prohibited. Bucketshops got quotations. All the windows of the Board's building were soaped to prevent signaling. Bucketshops got quotations.

The Board gave up in 1892. Back came the telegraph companies; the quotations were sent out to all who wanted them.

John Hill, Jr., a member of the Board of Trade and also of the Civic Federation, an organization formed to cleanse the town, then took up the Board's fight against bucketshops. Something of a moralist in a dissolute world, Hill left his imprint on the Board's history as its most aggressive, persistent and successful reformer. In 1896 he found a way to attack the bucketshops: he drove them into the courts, claiming they were merely gambling houses. That year 87 bucketshops were indicted.

Bucketshops spread over the farm regions and Hill followed them. He noted that the shops had a happy habit of "working" a town. They would land in a small farming community, encourage betting, get as much money as they could from the restless natives, and move to another town as soon as they had cleaned up all the loose money in the first one.

A step further from reality than the bucketshop was the tape game. The game was played with a tape similar to that used to report transactions on the Board of Trade and the New York Stock Exchange. Each evening quotations were printed on the tape, which was rewound and placed in a box. These quotations were entirely imaginary; they did not pretend to be anything other than figures in a game. The next day the tape was drawn out of the box at the rate of one quotation every thirty seconds. The quotations were posted on a blackboard under such head-lines as "May Wheat," "September Corn" or "December Oats." Customers "bought" and "sold" grains, guessing the trend of the figures on the tape. Bets of $1 and up were accepted.

This game became extremely popular. For the promoter it had some advantages over bucketshops. For one thing, the frequency of quotations created a continuously active "market." There were no dull periods without price changes. It could be, and was, played morning, noon and night. Long after the Board of Trade had closed each day, (thereby closing the bucketshops) the tape game "market" continued to function. And finally, the promoter had complete control over prices; it was he who established them. There was no need to worry about a run-away bull market bankrupting the house.

From March, 1896 through the autumn of 1898, Hill led raids on 30 offices in which the tape game was played. There never was any question about the fact that this was gambling. In Criminal Court one of the customers of William Shakel, leading tape game firm, testified:

Customer: I am a grocer. I engaged in transaction at Shakel's place of business for the last three or four years.

Attorney: How many times?

Customer: Well every day I used to go in, I used to buy as I had money to spend. I saw a machine there with tape running out which showed quotation. I used to put up as much as I

	wanted on a $200 trade, and if it used to go against me, I
	would re-margin up to $100, not to let it freeze me out,
	but it froze me all the same, even if I did re-margin.
Attorney:	Did it freeze you?
Customer:	Every time.
Attorney:	How much did you lose in the freezing business?
Customer:	Between $5,000 and $6,000.[2]

Hill made an impressive record in his anti-bucketshop campaign until he ran up against C. C. Christie of Kansas City, who at one time had been a regular commission house broker in Missouri, possessed of a virtuous contempt for the bucketshop men. In 1887 he made a speech before the Missouri legislature in which he declared:

> The exchange is a huge piece of time and labor saving machinery. Its benefits are universal in their spread. While its privileges are valuable, they have been rendered so by hard work. Its members are entitled to the protection of the state against thieves, and the bucketshop is only a thief.[3]

A few years later, however, virtue had succumbed to the blandishment of profits. Christie was operating the Christie-Street Commission Company, an outright bucketshop with headquarters in Kansas City, Missouri. He had 4 private wires going as far west as Denver and as far south as Fort Worth. In 15 cities and towns along these lines, branch offices poured the public's money into Kansas City. The public called him "King of the Bucketshops."

Christie proclaimed his services in newspaper advertisements: "We buy or sell for immediate or future delivery, grain and provisions for delivery on the Board of Trade in Chicago."[4] That was not true. Christie was not a member of the Board. No grain was ever delivered or received through his firm.

An example of how Christie operated was given in later court testimony by a client:

> I went to the man at the counter, named Mason, and I said I would buy a thousand July corn. Mason said, "All right." He took the price off the board—the latest quotation that came in [from the Chicago Board of Trade]. There was nothing said about agreeing on a price, except that he took the price off the board and I paid him $10, and that was the understood price— one cent margin.[5]

Mason testified as to how difficult it might be for a customer to get his money if he were ahead on the market:

> If a customer wants to close a purchase, he would step up to me at the counter and signify his desire. I would look at the last quotation on the blackboard. . . . and from that derive a closing price. . . . It is optional with me whether I will close the trade or not. . . . When a man gets in on a deal, he cannot get out without our consent. . . . The Christie Company reserves the right to keep a man in until it wants to let him out.[6]

Hearing rumors that the Board of Trade would make another effort at refusing to distribute its quotations to bucketshops in 1900, Christie reacted vehemently—and that reaction produced a U.S. Supreme Court decision which became the basis for the legitimacy of trading in all commodity futures. On February 23, 1900, Christie secured a temporary injunction from Judge Murray Tuley in the Circuit Court of Appeals of Cook County, Illinois, enjoining the Board from discontinuing the telegraphic reports. The Board thereupon filed a cross bill against Christie and Western Union Telegraph Company, which distributed the quotations. Before a master-in-chancery at Kansas City, employees and customers gave testimony which indisputably proved the firm was an outright bucketshop.

After studying the testimony, Judge Tuley ruled:

> . . . so prevalent has this [bucketshop] evil become that the betting upon the price of grain without the intention of delivery may be said to have become the national mode of gambling. . . . The evidence shows that the Christie-Street Commission Company never purchased or sold a bushel of grain, although it made trades amounting to 157 million bushels in a year. The evidence shows that bucketshopping or gambling in prices on the Chicago Board of Trade of grain and other products was the main business of complainants so far as the dealing in said grain and other products was concerned. The printed contract was a mere pretense, it was one of the instruments used in carrying on the gambling, the quotations being used as dice are used, to determine the result of a bet. The assertion in the contract that it would accept business only on the agreement that the property was to be delivered or received, as the case might be, and they would not accept business under any other condition, was a pretense of virtue calculated to arouse suspicion in itself.[7]

Judge Tuley granted an injunction restraining Christie-Street Commission Company from receiving quotations and the Western Union Telegraph Company from sending them to the Christie firm.

Christie made another effort. He secured a stay of proceedings from the Appellate Court on June 29. Subsequently, he endeavored to secure a continuance of the original injunction against the Board. This was denied by the Appellate Court on July 19. A few days later, Christie sent out letters to his customers advising them to close out their trades by July 31 as after that date the firm would be unable to furnish customers with Chicago market quotations.

One of the large Chicago bucketshops was named the Phoenix. Perhaps the name was chosen with wry humor. It seemed typical of all bucketshop proprietors; they had a remarkable facility to rise from the ashes. Christie was one of this resilient breed. He found the road to fortune via the bucketshops and was not one to be easily detoured. After a quiet interval he reorganized in 1901 under the name of Christie Grain & Stock Company. He opened a new office, obtaining quotations from the Chicago Board of Trade, although how he got them was a mystery. Hill decided to investigate this phenomenon.

Hill and his retinue descended upon Kansas City. Spying on Christie's office, which was located about a block from the Kansas City Board of Trade, they noted a man with a telephone headset on his ears. This, they reasoned, was the man obtaining the quotations. They decided to trace the telephone wire. It led along the roofs of several buildings, down an air shaft and through an attic, under the visitors gallery at the Board of Trade and finally into the office of a reputable commission house through a hole bored in the sash of a window opening in the hallway. A large blackboard inside the firm obstructed the window.

Hill tapped this wire. Coming over it were the Morse Code signals giving Board of Trade quotations. The clerk in Christie's office at the other end of the wire translated the Morse Code telegraph signals into quotations for marking up prices on the Christie blackboard.

Later, Christie was to write, "The charge that I was detected stealing quotations by means of a delicately adjusted telephone receiver placed behind the partition of a legitimate broker's office and connected with my own hidden wires is absolutely untrue."[8]

With its evidence the Board of Trade asked for an injunction in 1902 restraining Christie from obtaining and using the Board's quotations. But this time Christie decided to fight back along a new line—one which would lead to a memorable Supreme Court decision. In addition to claiming that the quotations had a "public use" and therefore could not be considered the property of the Board, he charged that the Board itself was a bucketshop.

Christie based his contention on the well known fact—now as well as then—that only a very minuscule proportion of the futures contracts to buy and sell grain were consummated by actual delivery of grain from the seller to the buyer.

The latter charge was of extreme importance; it raised the yet unanswered question, are transactions in commodity futures legal or illegal? Were the Boards of Trade and Produce Exchanges in Chicago, New York, Kansas City, Minneapolis and other cities legitimate enterprises or simply elaborate structures offering a more sophisticated type of gambling than "The Store" or the "House of David?"

Thus what started as a routine move against a bucketshop had become something of far greater significance, a question as to whether commodity futures trading should be permitted anywhere.

On July 5, 1902, Judge William Hook, district judge for the western district of Missouri, granted the Board an injunction, asserting:

> The Board performs a most important function in the internal commerce of the country; in fact, of such importance and of such magnitude have its operations become that defendants are brought to the earnest contention that it is no longer a wholly private concern, but is a quasi-public corporation, and that its property has become affected with a public interest. It is obvious that this contention is not wholly consonant with the claim that it is maintaining what the law denounces as a bucketshop.[9]

Promptly, Christie appealed. The case came before the U.S. Circuit Court of Appeals for the Eighth Circuit at St. Louis. The outcome, announced in a unanimous decision on October 8, 1903, constituted a severe setback for the Board of Trade.

The Court dissolved the injunction, basing its decision on an Illinois statute of 1887 which defined as unlawful places where occurs:

> . . . the pretended buying or selling of the shares or bonds of any corporation, or petroleum, cotton, grain, provisions or other produce, either on margins or otherwise, without any intention of receiving and paying for the property so bought, or of delivering the property so sold. . . .[10]

The statute had been enacted with approval of the Board, which had urged its adoption in Hill's bucketshop war. It was being turned against the Board itself.

The Circuit Court of Appeals decision, written by Judge Oliver Shira, said:

> It is thus proven beyond all reasonable question that the Chicago Board of Trade . . . members . . . engage in making and carrying through deals in grains and provisions, in which it is not intended to make a future delivery of the article dealt in, but which are to be settled by payment of money only according to the fluctuations of the market and which are in all essentials gambling transactions. . . . In seeking the aid of the Court, under the circumstances developed in the evidence introduced in this case, the Board of Trade does not come with clean hands, nor for a lawful purpose, and for these reasons its prayer must be denied.[11]

Meanwhile, the Board had undergone an equally distressing experience, although in a lower court, in the Seventh Circuit at Indianapolis. The Board had brought charges against L. A. Kinsey Company of Indianapolis of practically the same nature as those brought against Christie: that Kinsey, too, was running a bucketshop and therefore an injunction should be issued against his utilizing the Board's "continuous quotation"—that is, the quotations coming over the ticker. Albert Albertson, district judge in Indianapolis, had ruled against the Board on July 14, 1903, stating:

> . . . the evidence in this case shows that almost the entire bulk of the transactions in the pits . . . are transactions in which no delivery is made, and which are closed out by the direct or ring method of settlement. . . .
>
> Instead of real contracts for future delivery of property, they are pretend contracts for immediate settlement upon differences. If this be the case, they are gambling transactions. . . .
>
> I think that the proportion of these transactions which are illegal is so large as to characterize and taint them as a whole, and that whatever property rights complainant may have in the 'continuous quotations' in question is so infected with illegality as to preclude resort to court of equity for its protection.[12]

Fortunately for the Board, it found an appellate court that looked favorably upon futures transactions. Judge Francis Baker of the U.S. Circuit Court of Appeals for the Seventh Circuit delivered an opinion on April 12, 1904, reversing Judge Anderson's decision and giving the Board the injunction it wanted. In so doing, Judge Baker said he regretted he could not agree with the conclusions of the Circuit Court of Appeals for the Eighth Circuit. His decision was based solely on the Board's property rights in its own quotations. He said:

> It seems to us immaterial what proportion of transactions are wagers, since the prices made in the transactions are the prices that farmers and shippers can get, and since the news of the prices and the dissemination thereof are valuable to the community. News may be an object of lawful ownership though nine-tenths of the things reported be unlawful.[13]

But, even though he did not base his opinion on the question of whether futures trading was or was not gambling, Judge Baker had something to say on the subject:

> An indeterminate number [of contracts on which there was no delivery] were "hedging contracts." If we felt called upon by the necessities of this decision to give a definite opinion of hedging, the record might well lead us to find that hedging is a manufacturer's or merchant's insurance against price fluctuations on materials, and no more damnatory than insurance on property and life, which in one sense are wagers that the property will not be destroyed during the term, and the life will not fail in less than the expectancy in the actuaries' tables. The remainder of the no-delivery contracts were "speculative." But speculation is not unlawful.[14]

All was now confusion. Two courts of equal authority, confronted with very similar cases, had reached opposing conclusions. In this situation the U.S. Supreme Court, issuing writs of certiorari, called both the Christie and Kinsey cases before it.

The Chief Justice of the Supreme Court then was Melville Fuller, who was not unknown to the Chicago grain men. In 1856, after an education at Bowdoin and Harvard Law, and a year of practice in Georgia, Fuller moved to the booming city on Lake Michigan's shore. He threw in his lot with the Democratic Party, becoming an ardent admirer of Stephen Douglas. During much of the war years, he served as a Democrat in the Illinois legislature, where he criticized Abraham Lincoln with unrelenting bitterness.

Fuller entered into Chicago life with gusto. All his ties with his New England ancestry—he could trace his line straight to Edward Fuller, who came over on the Mayflower—were severed. Fuller married a Chicago girl, and two years after she died another Chicago girl—Mary Ellen Coolbaugh, a daughter of the President of the Union National Bank, W. F. Coolbaugh, who was a member of the Board of Trade. Fuller's practice boomed among the city's wealthy men. At one time he counted P. D. Armour as a client.

When President Cleveland had the Chief Justice spot to fill on the Court in 1888, he turned to the Illinois Democrat, Fuller. Some opposition developed in the Senate, but Fuller was confirmed, 41 to 20. He was 55 at the time. A gala dinner, attended by all political, business and financial leaders of Chicago, sent him off to Washington. One of the many laudatory speeches was made by Charles Hutchinson, the Board's President.

Another Cleveland appointee, and another justice whose opinion on commodity futures trading was well known, was Edward White. This was the same White who, as a senator from Louisiana, had opposed the Hatch Anti-Futures Bill and generally was regarded as the man who gave the best senatorial argument against it. White was an impressive man with a scholarly background who spoke French, Italian, Spanish and Latin. Later in life, he acquired a reading knowledge of German. During the Civil War he fought in the Confederate Army, and after the war became a Louisiana judge, giving up that post to join the reform element in that state's politics. His reward was the senate seat.

Neither Fuller nor White disqualified himself from the Board of Trade case.

The remainder of the court consisted of one man noted for his dissents (John Harlan), another who eventually would be (Oliver Wendell Holmes) and a rather routine group of competent but uninspired conservatives—David Brewer, Henry Brown, Rufas Peckham, William Day and Joseph McKenna.

The case was heard on April 20, and again on April 24 and 25, 1905. Justice Holmes handed down the majority opinion 13 days later. It upheld the Board of Trade 6 to 3. The dissenters were Justices Harlan, Brewer and Day.

In his opinion, Justice Holmes said:

> The fact that contracts are satisfied by set-off and the payment of differences detracts in no degree from the good faith of the parties, and if the parties know when they make such contracts that they are very likely to have a chance to satisfy them in that way and intend to make use of it, that fact is perfectly consistent with a serious business purpose and an intent that the contract shall mean what it says.

And further:

> In the view we take, the proportion of dealings in the pit which are settled this way [by off-set instead of delivery] throws no light on the question of the proportion of serious dealings for legitimate purposes to those which fairly can be classed as wagers or pretend contracts. No more does the fact that the contracts thus disposed of call for many times the total receipts of grain in Chicago. The fact that they can be and are set-off sufficiently explains the possibility, which is no more wonderful than the enormous disproportion between the currency of the country and contracts for payment of money, many of which in like manner are set off in clearing houses without anyone dreaming that they are not paid. . . .

And further:

> The plaintiff does not lose its rights by communicating the results to persons, even if many, in confidential relations to itself, under a contract not to make it public, and strangers to the trust will be restrained from getting at the knowledge by inducing a breach of trust and using knowledge obtained by such a breach.

And further:

> Time is of the essence in matters like this, and it fairly may be said that, if the contracts with the plaintiff are kept, the information will not become public property until the plaintiff has gained its reward. A priority of a few minutes is enough.[15]

The Supreme Court reversed the Circuit Court's ruling in the Christie case and affirmed it in the Kinsey case. Thus, in both cases, the Board achieved the injunctions it sought to restrain the bucketshops from using Board quotations.

But Justice Holmes went a step further than necessary, and further than other courts had done. He made these comments on the subject of speculation:

> As has appeared, the plaintiff's chamber of commerce is, in the first place, a great market, where, through its eighteen hundred members, is transacted a large part of the grain and provisions business of the world.
>
> Of course in a modern market contracts are not confined to sales for immediate delivery. People will endeavor to forecast the future and to make arrangements according to their prophecy. Speculation of this kind is the self-adjustment of society to the probable. Its value is well known as a means of avoiding or mitigating catastrophes, equalizing prices and providing for periods of want.

It is true that the success of the strong induces imitation by the weak, and that incompetent persons bring themselves to ruin by undertaking to speculate in their turn.

But legislatures and courts generally have recognized that the natural evolutions of a complex society are to be touched only with a very cautious hand, and that such coarse attempts at a remedy for the waste incident to every social function as a simple prohibition and laws to stop its being are harmful and vain.[16]

Thus, a case which had started out as a crusade to wipe out gambling establishments wound up giving legitimacy to trading in commodity futures.

But it did not immediately eradicate bucketshops. Christie himself established an elaborate trading edifice, named the "National Board of Trade of Kansas City," which made a pretense of trading in grains. Critics called it a "quotation factory" for Christie's bucketshops. Eventually, however, the bucketshops disappeared, outlawed by state and local statutes, badgered by the press and abandoned by the public.

NOTES

1. Charles M. Mills, *Fraudulent Practices In Respect To Securities and Commodities* (Albany, NY 1925), 220–221.
2. John Hill Jr., *Gold Bricks of Speculation* (Chicago 1904), 455.
3. Ibid., 69.
4. *Kansas City Star,* 1–30 January 1900.
5. *Gold Bricks of Speculation,* 57.
6. Ibid.
7. Christie-Street Commission Co. vs. Board of Trade and Western Union Telegraph Co. no. 204543 Circuit Court, Cook County, Ill. 1900.
8. *Everybody's Magazine,* vol. 15, no. 5, November 1906, 713.
9. 116 Federal Reports 944.
10. 125 Federal Reports 161.
11. Ibid.
12. 125 Federal Reports 72.
13. 130 Federal Reports 507.
14. Ibid.
15. U.S. Supreme Court decision 198 U.S. 236.
16. Ibid.

CHAPTER NINE

A Reward for "Common Sense"

Some minor skirmishes erupted in the grain pits in the early years of the 20th century as the fight over bucketshops neared the Supreme Court. While the Board establishment vigorously fought the bucketshops, it did nothing to suppress efforts to manipulate prices on its own exchange. Criticism of the "grain gamblers" was left to the press, a few Congressmen and a powerless Federal executive branch.

A man who was something of an outsider to the Chicago grain and provisions fraternity became active during these years. His name was John "Bet-a-million" Gates, almost the complete opposite in personality from that other New Yorker, Jim Keene. Gates was a bluff, hearty man around whom stories gathered. Mostly they concerned his propensity for wagering. A popular story on the origin of his nickname was that he once drew a line across a pane of glass on which a fly was crawling, proclaiming to friends, "I'll bet a million that fly crosses that line."[1]

On one occasion he traveled to San Antonio to look over some property. The Texans, aware of Gates' reputation, and anxious to make an impression upon him, raised a fund of $60,000 for a game of poker. When Gates arrived he was put up at the leading club and asked if he would care for a little game.

"Fine!" Gates responded. "How much have you got?"

"We have $60,000," said the spokesman, with pride and pleasure.

"All right," said Gates, pulling out a silver dollar. "Which do you call—heads or tails?"[2]

One time a son of a friend, fresh out of college, visited Gates at his office and said, "I want to make an honest living in business, and I have decided to start on Wall Street. What do you think of my chances?"

"You couldn't start in a better place!," Gates replied. "You won't have any competition."[3]

In 1902 Harris, Gates & Co. became a big buyer of July corn. At one point the July future ran up 13 cents in two days, an impressive advance for that period. Cynics noted that Isaac L. Ellwood, a special partner of Harris, Gates & Co., was one of the three members of the Illinois Warehouse Commission. Through its inspectors, the commission decided whether or not corn was of sufficiently high quality to be deliverable on futures contracts.

As part of its plan, the Harris, Gates & Co. group made extraordinary efforts to move corn out of Chicago, even bringing into use some Great Lakes boats that had not been employed for 15 or 20 years in carrying grain. Such boats could transport only 25,000 bushels each trip and required two weeks to reach Buffalo.

Harris, Gates & Co. began buying corn in February when the price was as low as 59 cents. On July 9 the July future hit 90 cents, the peak for the contract. Then, on July 15, the Gates firm made a private settlement with the shorts. The settlement price, never officially disclosed, was said to be 80 or 81 cents—that is, the shorts who had contracted to deliver grain to the Gates group, but could not do it, had to pay 80 or 81 cents for each bushel they could not deliver. After news of the settlement leaked on July 15, the July contract promptly fell from 80 to 65¼ cents.

Gates asserted that he, personally, was not involved in the deal, but was simply acting for his customers.

There then emerged in the pits a man who was to be the great bull leader throughout all the years of the twentieth century leading up to World War I—James A. Patten. He linked the buccaneering speculators of the early days with those who played the market in the 1920s. Patten was on the Board when Old Hutch traded there, and he could recall Arthur Cutten, the great speculator of the post-World War I years, standing daily on the rim of the wheat pit and scalping the market for fractions of a cent.

Patten called Old Hutch, "Mr. Hutch." In the later years, he referred to the great speculator as a "crochety old fellow," thereby agreeing with many others. Patten said that once, carrying a piece of paper in his hand, he approached Old Hutch on the floor. Old Hutch, noting the paper, waved Patten away.

"Don't want to sign any petition," Old Hutch said.

"This is not a petition," Patten explained. "It's a subscription list of contributors to bury the old doorkeeper who died last night."

"Take it away," Old Hutch said, scowling.

Patten, angered, asked, "Wouldn't you like your old friends to look after your remains?"

"They can take me out and lay me in the fields when the time comes. Good enough for anybody."[4]

Patten did not get any money from Old Hutch.

Patten was born in 1852 in Somonauk, a little hamlet about five miles from Sandwich, west and slightly north of Chicago in the southern end of De Kalb County, Illinois. He descended from William Patten, who arrived in the United States in 1794. The family settled in New York State. Patten's father, Alexander, moved to Illinois in the 1840s. His father and mother, Agnes Beveridge, neglected to bestow a middle name on son James. He himself inserted the "A," apparently for euphonic reasons.

Patten's father kept the general store at Sandwich, and the family lived in a farm house which served as a station on the Underground Railroad. Patten's grandfather, George Beveridge, was a strong abolitionist.

Patten had more education than the old giants in the grain pits. He attended the preparatory department of Northwestern University for two years. Later the university became the beneficiary of several Patten gifts. The Patten home on Ridge Avenue, Evanston, entertained Northwestern students once a year.

Upon his graduation, Patten worked as a clerk in a store and, for a year, as a farmer's helper. From there he went to the state grain inspection department as a grain inspection clerk at $100 a month. The job represented pure nepotism: the governor, John Beveridge, was Patten's uncle, and the family connection was responsible for starting young James in the grain trade.

In those days Patten enjoyed living in a boarding house with some comrades who also worked in the inspection department. They had good times together, going to the theatre, playing cards and drinking beer. But, according to Patten's later recollections, this easy life was not for Patten. "I found I was spending all the money I earned," he said, "and so I determined to find another place to board."[5]

Patten heard of an old couple—ardent Presbyterians like himself—who wanted to take in a boarder. He went to see them, and recalled this sanctimonious conversational exchange. "We'll take you in," the husband told him, "on one condition: if you are not in the house by ten o'clock at night, mother and I must know where you are."

"This is just the place I've been looking for," Patten replied.[6]

He remained with the couple for four years, and he always got in before ten o'clock. And he saved half his income, or so he later said.

Patten did not remain within the comfortable security of government bureaucracy for very long. His friends called him crazy when he quit in 1880 for a $6 a week job as an errand boy for G. P. Comstock Co., a cash grain firm. Two years later Comstock failed and Patten, with his older brother George and H. J. Coon, formed the grain firm of Coon and Patten Brothers. This did not last long and the Patten boys, after doing business for themselves for a while, joined up with Bartlett and Frazier.

Patten quietly accumulated capital over the years, moved to Evanston and indulged his favorite avocation—politics. He was more fortunate in the north shore suburb than he had been in Chicago, where he had run unsuccessfully for alderman. He became a member of the Evanston City Council and in 1901 was elected mayor for a four-year term. It was in the following year that he engaged in one of his most significant buying campaigns.

In 1902 Patten claimed that the supply of oats from the previous year's crop was less than the major consumers of this grain—horses—needed. Starting to buy in January, he concentrated initially on the May contract but later shifted his operation into July oats. This latter contract stood at 34 cents a bushel on June 2, from which point the upturn started. By the end of the month, the price had risen to 43½ cents. Large amounts of cash oats were shipped out of Chicago in June and by July 5 only 30,888 bushels remained in store compared with 2,294,393 a year earlier. Patten explained in later years, "I knew how to sell grain as well as how to buy contracts."[7]

Then the sharpest part of the total advance got underway. Accompanied by news of heavy and persistent rains, oats prices raced ahead. An agriculture department weekly crop report on July 15 reported that "lodging"—falling over, which reduces the harvest—had become quite extensive in Nebraska and Iowa and to a more limited extent in Ohio. By July 19, oats brought 65 cents, just about double the early June price.

On July 24 Patten offered all the oats anyone wanted at 70 cents. Newspapers noted that this was only 1 cent below the peak of 1874, which in turn was the highest since the Civil War boom. So Patten pushed up the price to 72 cents at the opening the next day, making it the highest since the Civil War, although a later sell-off resulted in a close at 70⅛.

Patten afterward said, "There was no manipulation by me. A short crop had been indicated at the beginning of the year, and I purchased oats. If it had not been for the rain, I might have been licked,"[8] Patten was to claim later, "I never in my life set out deliberately to corner the market."[9] It may be that he did not deliberately set out to corner July oats in 1902, but there can be no doubt that he did in fact corner that contract.

The leadership of the Board, which had moved so effectively against E. L. Harper, did not take any action to halt Patten. In such an institution as the Board, leadership changes frequently. Strict enforcers of rules are succeeded by loose enforcers, and the cycle can be repeated as long as the institution remains independent from outside regulation.

In the absence of Board enforcement, agitation against some practices in futures trading, as well as against all futures trading, mounted in legislative chambers. Beginning a year after Patten's 1902 deal, numerous bills were introduced in Congress against selling short and other phases of exchange operations. This activity continued in succeeding years; one study placed the number of such bills at 164 up to 1920. They did not result in legislation.

Nevertheless, the time was drawing closer, in this initial decade of the twentieth century, when government restraints on some marginal activities would become a reality.

Two years after Patten's oats deal, Japan flung a challenge to Russia in the Russo-Japanese War, but neither Gates nor Pattern benefited from the wheat price upturn that accompanied that challenge; instead the military developments enriched J. Ogden Armour, son of P. D. Armour. J. Ogden (the initial stood for Jonathon, but he never used that name), became head of the House of Armour upon the death of his father on January 6, 1901. Worn out by numerous ills over a two year span, the older man went to bed for the last time after contracting a cold while playing with his grandchildren.

When he became chief executive of the Armour meat packing, grain and other enterprises, J. Ogden was a thoroughly experienced businessman. He had left Yale's Sheffield Scientific School in 1881, entering the

Armour enterprises for 20 years of grooming designed to lead him to succeed his father; and he was in fact running those enterprises at the time of his father's death. Some people criticized J. Ogden as "cold," a term which never would have been applied to P. D. He had few social diversions, although he showed up at times at Grand Operas—an interest that would have astounded and possibly shamed the old man.

In January of 1904, Armour was credited with having a long line of wheat futures, mostly for May delivery, totaling about 15 million bushels. He had purchased much of it the previous fall, when May wheat was selling as low as 76 cents. At the start of the year it had risen to 87¾. By February 2, two carloads of No. 2 red wheat sold in the cash market at $1, the first time that figure had been reached since the culmination of the Leiter deal. On the same day May wheat brought 94½.

The war started officially on February 8, 1904 and, as usual, prices spurted. As they rose, Armour sold. And it must have been at substantial profits, for by February 20, May wheat had risen to $1.07, by which time Armour had sold most of his line. He got out around the top, as the market slipped off to under $1 in March, April and May. From this experience Armour developed an appreciation for the economic possibilities in wars, which was to lead him to both triumph and disaster in World War I and after.

How much Armour profited is, of course, not known, but two days before closing out his line, he gave one quarter million dollars to Armour Institute, a technical school which his father founded in 1893 with the declaration, "The religion of the Armour Institute will be 16 ounces to the pound, but undenominational, and it makes no difference to me whether its converts are baptized in a soup bowl, a pond or the Chicago River."[10]

The Russo-Japanese War and Armour's success prompted "Bet-a-million" Gates to get back into the market the next year. As usual, Gates put together a group rather than playing the game alone. Unfortunately for him and his group, he picked the wrong year. The Japanese quickly smashed the Russians and the Gates group took a severe beating in the market.

A side effect of the disastrous Gates campaign was development of a run on the First National Bank of Milwaukee. G. G. Bigelow, the bank's president, acknowledged embezzling about $1.5 million. His son, Gordon, had been active on the buying side in the Gates speculation; it was believed the son had involved the father in the deal, and the father robbed the bank to shore up his son's speculative splurges.

With the end of the Russo-Japanese War, Patten and his followers began a series of bull campaigns that were to last four years and to make most of them millionaires several times over. The nucleus of the group, in addition to James Patten, was his brother George, W. H. Bartlett and Frank Frazier. Most of the trading was conducted through the brokerage firm of Bartlett, Frazier & Co., and, later, Bartlett, Patten & Co.

In this period, Patten chewed gum constantly, and fellow traders said that if his big jaw worked fast and furious it was a good time for shorts to get out of the market—Patten, the eternal bull, was about to charge the pit. He drank sparingly, and only in his own home or at a restaurant; he made a point of never entering a saloon—"if you can go in saloons your clerks will see you and think they can do it if you can."[1] About his only diversion was the card game "Bridge," played with old cronies.

Early in 1907 Patten started buying May wheat; later he would buy the July contract. In January, May wheat sold as low as 75¼. There was no strong move until April, when it reached 84. In May it got as high as $1.03½, closing out at 97⅝.

A poor wheat crop, not only in the United States but also in several other producing countries, supported the price advance. Private reports estimated winter wheat outturn in the Southwest at 75 million bushels vs. 150 million a year earlier—a startling reduction of 50% in output. In early July reports of poor crop conditions began to arrive from the northwestern spring wheat belt. By mid-July, the English statistical authority, George Broomhall, forecast a wheat deficit of 104 million bushels in the United States and a world wide shortage of 288 million bushels. At that point Patten left on an inspection trip of northwestern spring wheat fields.

At Fargo, North Dakota, Patten rented an automobile—a new gadget, scorned by the village blacksmith—and drove up the Red River Valley to Grand Forks. What he saw electrified him: all the mammoth wheat fields appeared dirty, as if black soot had been sprinkled over them. Patten hurried back to Minneapolis, where he met a grain dealer. He asked, "Got any word about black rust?"

"Oh, we have a little complaint," was the reply.

"A little complaint? You are sitting on dynamite. I tell you the wheat is gone. You had better tell your station men to leave their elevators and get in to the fields and make an examination."[2]

What Patten had seen was the effect of black stem rust, quite prevalent in that period before development of more resistant wheat varieties. Spoors of black stem rust, carried on the wind, lodged in the upper stem of wheat between the top leaf and the head. This fungus stole the plant food which should have gone to form plump kernels. When the sap for the kernel was completely eliminated, the result was a kernel reaching maturity at half-size. A fully infested field was marked by dirty grey-black color of straw, caused by the congealing of sap.

News of the prevalence of rust reached the grain trade later in July and by the end of the month the July contract, which had sold at 81¾ at the start of May, had spurted to $1.00¼.

Patten operated a cash grain business, much as did the Armours. When he took cash grain on delivery on futures contracts, he marketed this grain locally, in the East, and in Europe. The world-wide shortage of wheat in 1907 sustained the price throughout the year. The United States produced 634 million bushels in 1907 compared with 735 million in the previous year. All North America produced 741 million vs. 872 million in 1906. The grand total for the world was 3,104 million vs. 3,424 million.

The 1907 wheat deal propelled Patten into the spot of leading speculator on the Board. When the year ended, the Board held its annual New Year's Eve party. As part of the entertainment, a mind reader went through his routine. Some one asked him to read Patten's mind to see what wheat would do. Patten interjected somewhat too modestly that he would like to know himself. Later in 1908 he gave $250,000 to the Chicago Art Institute.

Some grain men attributed James Patten's success to his brother George, a statistical wizard of whom James once said, "I wouldn't work that hard."[13]

But James himself unquestionably was of a bullish personality, floating on a tide of strengthening developments for grain prices following the desperate years in the latter part of the nineteenth century. James accurately defined his own personality: "I'm too optimistic to be a bear."[14]

The first two decades of the twentieth century saw an astonishing increase in the growth of American cities, reflecting massive foreign immigration, a movement off farms as a result of mechanization, migration of black people from the Old Confederacy to the North and, of course, the fertility of men and women already located in the cities. Though in the 1880s and 1890s grain production outran the demand, the situation in the 1900s had reversed: many more people were compacted into the cities and needed to be fed by American farms.

During January, 1908, Patten joined battle with Armour in the wheat pit and Armour won, gaining $1 million on a price break at the end of the

month. A minor, internal reorganization of the Bartlett, Frazier firm followed, but Patten remained top man. Underneath the failure in wheat,
Patten accumulated May corn.

In January of that year, May corn sold from 58½ to 62 cents. As the
year progressed, Patten purchased significant amounts of the yellow grain.
A small contribution was made to the cause by William Long, a broker.
One day Long received an order from Patten to buy several hundred thousand bushels—an order which, when executed, automatically would have
pushed the price considerably higher, particularly as other traders would
have surmised that Long must be buying such large amounts for Patten.

Long looked over the pit and, instead of bidding, shouted an offer to
sell at a cent above the market.

Other traders turned to the seemingly foolish man trying to sell corn a
full cent above the market and laughed at him. Then they started to tease
him. "Sell you fifty," "Sell you a hundred," they jeered.

With a nod of his head, Long said, "Take it all"[15]

Thus Patten got the corn he wanted at a much lower average price
than he could have hoped.

By May 28, the last trading day, May corn reached 82¾. In the cash
market a chaotic situation developed. Any contract grade corn not ready
for delivery was sold at a substantial discount. The price depended mainly
upon which railroad the grain came in on. Corn that was received where
it could be put into "regular" public warehouses without delay, and therefore was deliverable on May contracts, sold at the May futures price. But
corn of the same grade that could not be so stored sold at a discount of 7
to 8 cents a bushel, even though it was of contract quality.

During the last days of May, Patten sat eating in a restaurant near the
Board of Trade when A. W. Harris, president of Northwestern University,
entered. Patten waved to Harris, an old friend, motioning to him to sit
down. Then Patten asked the surprised but happy Harris how much
money he wanted for Northwestern.

"I would like $100,000," Harris said.

"Why you ought to raise that," Patten said. "Couldn't you make it at
least $150,000?"

"Of course."

"Well, I will give you $150,000 for a new gymnasium for the university."[16]

The announcement of this generosity was made at the university's con-
vocation on May 29, the day after the conclusion of the corn deal, and
brought the students to their feet, cheering. Northwestern's gymnasium

then in use was 36 years old and the university had been trying for five years to raise funds for a new one.

Early the next morning, shortly after midnight, several hundred students took to the streets of Evanston in celebration of the great event. They marched to the president's home. He obliged by telling them, "It is worthy of excitement. We are all ready to lose a little sleep to celebrate such an event."[17]

The students then marched to Patten's home on Ridge Avenue where they were invited in.

The next year Patten got involved in a deal which brought him into conflict with two members of President William Howard Taft's cabinet, editorial cartoonists, ministers, millers and professional reformers. He received threatening letters, hired an extra bodyguard and skirted closely with nervous exhaustion.

Looking back on this operation many years later, Patten was to say he was initially impelled to buy May, 1909 wheat on the basis of frost damage reports in the spring of 1908 from Argentina. But no mention of the damage in the Argentine was made during the life of the deal, which was based, in Patten's own words at the time, on a shortage that he believed existed in the United States. He was correct, however, when he said, "I made no attempt to conceal my position in the market."[18]

Trading in May, 1909 wheat began June 23, 1908 at 89¾ cents. The price slowly advanced on buying from Patten and his group. Patten himself bought 10 million bushels before the deal was concluded. By the last month of 1908, the May contract sold from $1.04⅜ to $1.11. No great change took place in the first three months of 1909, but in April the price got above $1.25, highest since the Leiter deal, and the press moved Patten and his wheat from the market page to page one. Patten explained, "There is a shortage of winter wheat supplies and much higher prices will be justified."[19]

As prices continued to rise, protests mounted. The White House and Congress were "deluged" with complaining letters. Attorney General Wickersham said he was investigating the situation. Patten retained an air of calm: "I know there are a lot of people sore, but it is merely the old law of supply and demand."[20]

Rep. Charles F. Scott of Kansas introduced yet another bill in Congress to prohibit futures trading, proclaiming, "This business of boosting up the price of wheat after the original producer has sold is a bad thing for the country."[21] Thomas Lawson, an erratic dabbler in financial affairs and author of "Frenzied Finance," sent telegrams to kindred spirits around the country calling for mass meetings of protest in Madison Square Garden, New York, and the Auditorium, Chicago. Bakers cut the size of the loaf of bread in Kansas City. Prices were raised in New York. A bakery in Waterloo, Iowa, closed, blaming Patten. In Rhode Island an act was introduced in the legislature requiring that a loaf of bread weigh exactly two pounds.

Receiving threats, Patten hired a white bodyguard to accompany the black West Indian who alone had been performing this protective function. Somewhat defensively, which was unusual for him, Patten asserted, "I have kept wheat from going out of the country because I knew that we did not have any more than we could use ourselves."[22]

Patten's statement insisting there was a shortage of winter wheat brought a rebuke from Secretary of Agriculture Wilson, who asserted such comments were "to be expected from a gambler whose gains depend in part on the impression he creates in the public mind." And the secretary added, "A fictitious price has been established and the result will be harmful."[23]

Wilson said the government's report of wheat stocks on farms on March 1 totaled 144 million bushels, not much under the 149 million a year earlier, but down rather sharply from the 10 year average of 158 million. Wilson did not think this constituted a scarcity or shortage. Patten called the figures a farce—"most of Mr. Wilson's men are postmasters and small country merchants." He added, "My information is far better than Wilson's"[24]

On Sunday, April 18, one Rev. R. A. White, pastor of the People's Liberal Church in Chicago, referred to Patten as the "God of Get" and said that, in order to enable Patten to add two or three million dollars to his fortune, "thousands of underfed people the country over must eat a bit less, thousands of underfed children who attend Chicago public schools must go a little more unfed, children must die and women must weep. . . ."[25]

The same Monday morning newspaper which printed this doleful and exaggerated analysis also carried a front page cartoon by John McCutcheon, the famous *Chicago Tribune* editorial cartoonist, showing a "Mrs. Hubbard" watched by two woe-begone children opening a bare cupboard while outside a window a figure labelled "Patten" held a loaf of bread. Patten replied to both developments: "Some preachers are a good deal like some newspapers: they are always looking for a chance to stir up a sensation."[26]

Actually, Patten considered himself a highly religious man. He not only attended the First Presbyterian Church in Evanston each Sunday but he also was one of those who passed the collection basket.

In Cincinnati on Monday, April 19, a group of Methodist ministers adopted a resolution offered by the pastor of the Christie Methodist Episcopal Church condemning all gambling, "from gambling at bridge whist to speculations on the Board of Trade."

"We especially," the resolution said, "condemn the action which cornered wheat in Chicago and view with alarm the far reaching effects of such action in raising the price of breadstuffs."[27]

That hit Patten in two places—he not only speculated in grains, but he also loved to play bridge. He responded that there were plenty of ministers in the country "who display but a moderate amount of common sense, to say the least."[28]

And the next day Patten disappeared.

While his secretary insisted she did not know where the speculator had gone, he showed up in Trinidad, Colorado, where he was quoted as saying he had sold his wheat and was out of the deal. Obviously, that was absurd, and it may have been a misquotation—or he may just have been trying to get rid of the reporter.

Observers described him as pale, weak and in a highly nervous state. He said he was going to Bartlett's ranch, Vernejo Park, in New Mexico for a rest. The ranch was 25 miles from a railroad and had no telephone—"no one will follow me there." And he added: "I can only repeat what I have said before. There is a shortage of wheat, and that accounts for the high price."[29]

Despite the press, pulpit and Washington uproar, no specific action—other than arousing the weight of public opinion—was taken against Patten. Officials of the Board remained silent. Congress had passed no restraining legislation. The agriculture department was limited to issuing critical statements.

The market sold off after Patten deserted it for the calming climate of New Mexico, May wheat sinking as low as $1.18 on April 24. Thereafter, it started a slow climb. Patten returned to his Chicago office on May 10, by which time May wheat was back above $1.25.

Actually, not much trading was going on in the May contract. The Patten group was holding to its position and the number of shorts decreased daily, either by delivery of cash grain or closing out contracts at a nice profit to Patten. Newspapers had lost interest in the whole subject and there were no further outcries from ministers or drawings by editorial cartoonists. On May 25 the price rose to the high for the deal at $1.35¼. With only one trading day to go, May wheat eased to $1.33 at the close on May 28.

On the last day Patten could have set the price at almost any level he desired, although there could have been legal repercussions if he had been too avaricious. But the days of the uninhibited pirates in the grain pits had passed. In the same position as Patten, Old Hutch had lifted wheat a full 50 cents. Patten was more compassionate, and more aware of public opinion. He contented himself with a one cent gain.

All day the price stood at $1.34—Patten would either buy or sell at that level. Mostly, of course, he sold, responding to demand from the diehard shorts. Patten explained, "That extra cent was just a tag on the deal to certify that I had been right. It was the confirmation of my judgment."[30] During the day employees of Bartlett, Patten & Co. were called into Patten's office. Each received a check equal to one-tenth a year's salary.

It is not possible to state how much money Patten acquired in this May wheat operation. Although Patten began buying on the opening trading day in 1908, when May was quoted at 89¾, he could have bought only a very limited quantity at that price. Considering the fact that he owned 10 million bushels at one time, an average gain of 10 cents a bushel would have netted him $1 million. His average gain was almost certainly well in excess of 10 cents a bushel. There was only a minor problem with burying the corpse as demand for cash wheat held up well throughout the year. No. 2 red, after a brief dip to 99¼ in August, sold above $1 thereafter, bringing $1.15 to $1.28¼ in the last three months of the year. No. 1 northern never fell under $1, selling from $1.04½ to $1.40 for the remainder of the year.

Looking back, Patten justified his activities with the conclusion, "If it had not been for me and that bull campaign which I led there would have been a much smaller stock of wheat in the United States, and as a consequence much higher prices."[31]

This seems highly debatable. If Patten had not bought in late 1908 and early 1909, prices would have been lower—not higher—during that period. Demand for wheat from Europe, the big consumer of American grain, declined because that continent had an exceptional crop. It totaled 1,943 million bushels compared with 1,679 million a year earlier. Exports of American wheat to Europe fell to 48 million bushels compared with 93 million a year earlier.

Patten never disclosed the specific amounts of his profits in futures operations, although he did say, and indicated in the saying that he was aware of public criticism, "What money I have derived from speculation has been a reward for common sense. It may be that the reward was too large, but what I know of the law of supply and demand impels me to believe that this is not so."[32]

NOTES

1. *Munsey's Magazine*, vol. 49, no. 1, April 1913, 12.
2. Ibid.
3. Ibid.
4. James Patten and Boyden Sparkes, "In the Wheat Pit." *Saturday Evening Post* (hereafter cited as *SEP*) 3 September 1927, 97.
5. *SEP*, 3 September 1927, 91.
6. Ibid.
7. Ibid., 11 September 1927, 205.
8. *Chicago Tribune*, 26 July 1902.
9. *SEP*, 3 September 1927, 3.
10. Harper Leech and John C. Carroll, *Armour and His Times* (New York and London 1938), 213.
11. *SEP*, 1 October 1927, 29.
12. Ibid., 22.
13. Ibid., 3 September 1927, 91.
14. Ibid.
15. *SEP*, 5 November 1927, 180.
16. *Chicago Tribune*, 29 May 1908.
17. Ibid., 30 May 1908.
18. *SEP*, 3 September 1927, 3.
19. *Chicago Tribune*, 13 April 1909.
20. Ibid., 15 April 1909.
21. Ibid., 16 April 1909.
22. Ibid., 15 April 1909.
23. *New York Times*, 18 April 1909.
24. *Chicago Tribune*, 17 April 1909.
25. Ibid., 19 April 1909.
26. Ibid., 20 April 1909.
27. Ibid.
28. Ibid.
29. Ibid.
30. Patten and Sparkes, op. cit., 3 September 1927, 3.
31. Ibid., 5 November 1927, 28.
32. Ibid. 1 October 1927, 23.

CHAPTER TEN

"Patriots . . . Should Sell at Once"

With the end of the 1909 wheat deal, the Patten crowd split. James and George Patten, as well as Bartlett and Frazier, walked out of the Bartlett, Frazier firm together, obviously satisfied with their bundles.

George Patten died of tuberculosis in 1910, an event which may well have been responsible for James' decision to continue in the grain market as only a trader and not a man who ran corners. Many felt George was the "brains" behind the Patten deals, and James himself once said, "George was always working. That helped to kill him. He was a careful student of the market, watched every factor and kept track of every detail of the business. . . . I could not have stood to work as he did."[1] James thereupon put up money to found the Chicago Fresh Air Hospital.

Bartlett retired to his ranch in New Mexico. Frazier went to New York, where he made the social register. The name came back to the newspaper front pages in 1938 when his granddaughter, Brenda Frazier, still possessing luscious sums of Frazier money in trust funds, bowed to society at the Ritz-Carlton as the most famous debutante of that depression decade. A New York newspaper, the *Daily News*, headlined, "Bow's a Wow!"[2]

There then came a new figure to the forefront of trading—a Canadian, Arthur Cutten.

Cutten was born in Guelph, Ontario, in 1870. His father was a reasonably successful farmer and Arthur, one of six boys in the family (there were also two girls), attended Trinity College School.

Six or seven miles outside the hamlet of Guelph lived a black-whiskered farmer named Alec Hill. He was a brother of Jim Hill, who had gone to America and had become a famous railroad and empire builder. Cutten often visited the farmer Hill to talk about his fabulous brother and equally fabulous America.

Fascinated with America's possibilities, Cutten got a job at $4 a week with the American consulate in Guelph. He worked six months and saved enough money to go to "the States." Arriving in Chicago in 1890 with $90, he landed a job at Marshall Field's, keeping stock in order, at $7 a week.

During his first year Cutten tried several jobs, batting around like any unsettled and irresponsible youth. He lived in a boarding house at Dearborn and Ontario streets and on Saturday afternoons played baseball in the City League for the Hyde Parks.

In 1891 Cutten joined the provisions firm of A. Stamford White, the distinguished-looking head of the "English Crowd" on the Board of Trade. Part of his job at the White firm was writing foreign invoices, figuring up sterling and the different monies of the world. He was also required, each morning, to visit the floor of the Board of Trade to copy opening quotations which were wired to the firm's headquarters in Liverpool.

For Jim Hill, Cutten substituted other heroes—the men he saw down on the trading floor, the Cudahy brothers, Jim Patten, occasionally P. D. Armour and even Old Hutch himself, then well into his decline. Cutten remembered seeing Hutchinson sitting on a stool in a restaurant near the Board, "spooning his food; hawk-nosed, fierce-eyed, wearing a wide-brimmed slouch hat, his doeskin pants never reaching his ankle bones."[3]

After five clerical years, Cutten persuaded the firm to make him a broker. The membership cost Cutten $800, White loaning him the money. Cutten's first order for the firm was to buy 100,000 bushels of corn. He got it in 25,000 bushel lots from four different traders and remembered the names of three until the day he died. Five years after this debut—in 1901—he resigned as a broker for the White firm to speculate for himself.

It was a fateful move not only for Cutten, but also for the grain trade. In the years ahead, Cutten would become the leading speculator in grain history, and in one historic year the leading stock market speculator, too.

He would also become a sort of personification of all that reformers of futures trading wanted to eliminate; he was wealthy, daring, egotistical, suspicious, devious, uncooperative, conservative and defiant. It could be said of Cutten, more than of any of the great speculators who preceded him, that his actions were responsible for increasing supervision by the Federal government of the market.

Initially, Cutten was a scalper. He bought one minute and sold the next, always feeling the market—"I became skillful in stepping in and out of the market, changing my position from short to long and back again with every fluctuation." He dealt in small quantities, but they added up— "Although I was rarely long or short more than 10,000 bushels at a time, I used to scalp 200,000 or 300,000 bushels a day."[4]

Slowly, the money accumulated and by 1904, he took a position in the corn market and held it long enough to make some real money out of it. Things were going fine for him, but he was to note that not all young men who came to the big city fared as well: his brother Charles, who lived with him, worked at the Union Stock Yards. One day when Charles was learning some meat cuts, the knife slipped and cut him. A doctor dressed the wound but the knife had been tainted with the flesh of a tubercular hog. Within a year Charles died.

As the money rolled up, Cutten remained a solitary figure. "My way," he explained, "was to feel out the market. I took no one into my confidence. I had no employees." To hide his net position he operated through several brokerage houses, establishing long positions in some and short positions in others. "There are too many small-salaried people in brokerage houses," he explained.[5] He did not keep any books until 1913, when Congress passed the first income tax law and he had to monitor his transactions to satisfy the enforcement agencies.

By 1912 Cutten had attained some prominence in the market, a figure to watch but not necessarily to follow. Few did when he started buying July corn that year. He was the only impotent bull in the market. Both J. Ogden Armour and Patten took the bear side. Cutten recalled standing in the pit and hearing an Armour broker yell, "Sell one hundred!" [That is, 100,000 bushels.]

"Take it," Cutten said, paying 60½ cents a bushel and saying to the broker, "You tell Armour I'll take all the corn he'll sell."

With no further offer coming from the Armour forces, Cutten surveyed the pit, whose shouting occupants watched him closely, and bid for another hundred. Emil Garneau, often a Patten broker, sold it to him.

"Two," Cutten said.

"Sold," Garneau replied.

"You tell Patten I'll take all he'll sell me. Three."

"Sold."

"Four."

"No."

Over in his office, his feet on a desk, watching the boy chalk up the figures, Patten inquired, "Who's buying my corn?" Told, Patten responded, "Sell him three hundred more."[6]

Cutten took it, altogether buying 900,000 bushels of Patten's corn. The market climbed slowly and in August cash corn sold at 83 cents, the height of the advance. Cutten not only made a spectacular profit but also made a mark for himself among the high-stakes speculators. He used part of his accumulating capital to buy a farm near Glen Ellyn, west of Chicago.

Then as later, Cutten's most persistent reading was of the daily weather map issued each morning by the Chicago Weather Bureau. "It is in those weather maps during the six growing months from April to September that I have usually discovered the first news of that which has caused me to take positions in the grain market," he explained.[7]

Cutten, Patten, J. Ogden Armour and a dozen lesser lights formed the trading fraternity in the grain pits on that fatal day in June, 1914 when an utterly inconspicuous youth sent two bullets crashing into the car carrying Archduke Francis Ferdinand, heir to the resplendent throne of Austria-Hungary, and his wife. One bullet killed the archduke and the other his wife.

The grain market's reaction to this moment in the history of Gavrilo Princip, the assassin, was completely apathetic. On June 27, September wheat sold in the range of 77⅝–78⅝ cents. The market was closed June 28, the assassination day. On June 29, September wheat sold in a 77½–78¾ range. Of much more interest to the grain trade than Princip's action were reports of black rust in the Northwest, as well as hot, dry weather in the corn belt.

Lack of response to the assassinations did not indicate a narrow provincialism. The grain trade was international in scope and traders were attuned to international conditions, and followed them as closely as any group in the country. It simply did not seem to the grain men, nor to many others, that such an incident would provoke the extraordinary events that followed.

As late as July 22, wheat could be bought in the low 70s. Then ominous news of impending mobilizations startled the grain trade. Big export sales on July 25 and July 26 caused a buying movement. Then, on July 28, Austria-Hungary declared war on Serbia, and the shorts, now thoroughly alarmed at what Europe might do, covered their positions at advancing prices. July wheat jumped 8 1/4 cents and May 9 1/2 cents in a hysterical market.

The excitement prompted C. H. Canby, the Board president, to issue one of those soothing statements that market presidents always seem to issue in such circumstances and no one seems to believe.

"I haven't the slightest doubt," Canby said, "that the powers of Europe will localize the strife with the result that wheat prices here will be little affected. Things in Chicago ought to settle down within a few days."[8]

Within a few days Russia had declared war on Austria-Hungary, Germany on Russia, and France and England on Germany. And dollar wheat returned on July 30, when the May future sold at $1.02 1/4.

While the 1914 wheat crop was very large, enormous exports created a sharp price run-up in the last four months of that year and the first two months of 1915. In contrast with a price of 85 1/4 cents for May on the day before Princip fired his shots, the May contract reached a high of $1.65 in February, 1915.

As a result of the price upturn, the White House—presumably President Wilson—instructed the U.S. Attorney General at Chicago to conduct an inquiry into trading practices. Charles F. Cline, the attorney general, ran up against solid opposition. This was still an era when markets operated freely and inquisitive government bureaucrats could be spurned. The commission firms on the Board simply refused to open their books to Cline, holding that this might be prejudicial to the interest of their customers. Cline retreated and the inquiry foundered.

Clearly, if there was going to be an investigation, there would have to be legislation to support it. In the hectic war years, Congress had little inclination to get involved in a hassle over grain prices, and particularly so when high prices were favorable to farmers.

Nevertheless, this minor incident indicated that the inclination toward some sort of government control over free markets persisted.

In the spring of 1915, the nation harvested an enormous spring wheat crop and prices headed sharply downward, a fact which may have restrained any government attempts at control. By the time August came, and the nation was in the process of harvesting one billion bushels, cash wheat at Chicago had dipped under $1.

In July, 1916, a near disaster hit the wheat crop. Weather, plant disease and insects cut estimated production by more than 100 million bushels. The agriculture department predicted a 654 million bushel crop, down drastically from the previous years. However, there was an unusually large carryover of 75 million bushels from the 1915 crop—unusual, that is, for that period. About 600 to 620 million bushels were consumed domestically at this time.

Wheat responded to this official forecast the next day by surging ahead 11 to 11⅜ cents, the biggest advance of the year. May closed at $1.53.

The higher prices inspired caustic comment from English newspapers, the *London Daily Telegraph* asserting the advance constituted a conspiracy on the part of German-Americans in Chicago to force prices up and embarrass the allies while the *London Daily Express* screamed:

> Undeterred by the war the wheat gamblers of Chicago are sending skyward the prices of grain from which mankind derives its daily bread, amassing their gains with as little compunction as the Bourbons used to gather taxes. . . . That a nation which has been described by its president as too proud to fight in the cause of liberty should comprise a body of so-called businessmen willing to add to the sum of human suffering in this day of Armageddon, actuated solely by the greed of gold, bodes ill for the verdict of the future.[9]

The *New York Times*, a pro-British newspaper, was not impressed by these remarks. "It is too commonplace," it editorialized, "to suggest that the taking of 345 million bushels out of the supply has anything to do with the case."[10] But the Berlin Post found a germ of an idea in what the Daily Express contended was an existing fact:

> If England buys Rumanian grain to let it rot rather than allow us to have it, we can do the same thing by manipulating the grain markets where our enemies buy and which are accessible to us. If corners in Chicago and New York markets are possible in peace times they are more so now, when the demand for grain is so keen and the crops in America and enemy countries are so poor.[11]

But the Berlin Vorwarts called this suggestion "a wild cat scheme" certain to cost Germany more money than it would be worth.

The two big gainers in the price run up were Patten, who usually got his information from reporters in the field, and Cutten, who arrived at his conclusion by studying weather maps. On September 15, they both let go of a little wheat they had bought earlier when the price was down around $1.00. The closing price for September wheat that day was $1.46½. Patten was believed to have cleared $1 million but Cutten topped that with $1.25 million. On October 19, Cutten added to his growing fortune by taking a profit of 50 cents a bushel on over one million bushels. He started building a home on the farm he had purchased near Glen Ellyn. Probably the most distinctive feature of a war is that it can make one man a corpse and another man a millionaire.

America was drawn slowly into the fiery blood-letting in Europe. The trigger for the final, fatal move came at midnight, February 1, 1917, when Germany sent the United States a note saying that, beginning at midnight, February 4, submarines would sink without warning any merchant vessel, neutral as well as enemy, entering a prescribed zone surrounding the British Isles and also Mediterranean Sea waters around Greece.

The note caused panicky selling in grains during early trading on the following day. May wheat dropped 15¼ cents early, touching $1.56. But a recovery set in later and it closed at $1.63¼.

Two days later President Wilson, in an address to Congress, announced breaking of diplomatic relations with Germany. War seemed certain and patriotism swept all before it. Following the President's action, an American flag was draped over the balcony from the visitors gallery at the Board; trading stopped and brokers, visitors and employees stood at attention and sang "America."

Wheat seemed strengthened by the general euphoria. By February 5 it had recovered to $1.68 for May. Not until April 5 did the United States declare war, by which time May wheat was at $2.05⅝, the highest price since the Civil War.

A few days later, the Agriculture Department, in its monthly crop summary, reported that the condition of winter wheat was the lowest on record. Although the crop had been planted on the largest acreage ever, it had been decimated by severe winter weather. The department predicted a winter wheat production of only 430 million bushels. No estimate was made for spring wheat.

Fear gripped the allied and neutral worlds. They rushed to get grain and they concentrated their buying on the May future, the last of the 1916 crop wheat. But if the situation was bad in early April, it became intolerable a month later. On May 8 the Agriculture Department said 64 million bushels had been cut from the crop during the previous 30 days. It forecast a winter wheat production of only 366 million bushels, the smallest in 13 years.

The department did not make any forecast at such an early date on the spring wheat crop, but anyone associated with grain markets could figure out the situation: if the spring wheat crop totaled 250 million bushels, a little higher than average at that time, the total of only 616 million bushels for both spring and winter wheat would be for all practical purposes equivalent only to the normal yearly American consumption. Furthermore, it was believed that the wheat requirement of the allies during the coming crop year would mount to 500 million bushels, of which the United States was expected to furnish one-half. Where was the wheat to come from?

There was still an undetermined amount of wheat carried over from the 1916 crop and a world-wide rush to get some of this grain erupted. Demand centered in the May contract. On the day following the Agriculture Department report, May wheat soared 17 cents, hitting $3 and closing at $2.97. July wheat rose 6 cents. The next day May wheat jumped 14 cents, July 13½ and September 12½. May rose to $3.15 the following day, up 4 cents. July gained 6⅞ and September 5½. There were no sales of cash wheat.

The climax came the next day. May wheat sold at $3.25, highest on record up to that time, and closed at $3.18. Millers managed to get some wheat on the cash market at $3.30 to $3.40.

While the price soared, a group of important grain men and government officials met at the Chicago Club. Among them were A. D. Anderson, vice-chairman of the Royal Food Commission of England; Herbert Robson, purchasing agent of the British government in the United States; U.S. District Attorney Charles Cline, who had been asked by President Wilson to investigate the cause of high prices; and two well-known grain men—Patten and J. Ogden Armour.

None of the principals talked about the conference at the time but, years later, Patten described it. He made himself the hero.

Patten said he asked Anderson, "How much May wheat are you long?"

"Twenty-nine million bushels," Anderson answered.

"Did you buy any more today?"

"None today."

Patten turned to Armour: "Are you long wheat?"

"No," Armour replied.

"Well, neither am I," Patten said.[12]

It developed that the big buyer on this particular day—when wheat sold up to $3.25—was a Duluth grain firm. They had sold grain to

Portugal but, not having it and not knowing where to get it, they had gone into the Chicago wheat pit and bought the May future. That, Patten said, showed how the European countries were competing against one another and running up the price.

"What price do you think wheat will go to?" Patten asked Cline.

"I think it will go to $8," Cline answered.

"It will go higher than that if we do not take some action. We have got to do something or else somebody will come and do it for us."[13]

Regardless of whether this self-praising rendition of events is correct or not, there is no doubt that action was taken. It was provoked by Joseph Griffin, the Board's president, who appointed a committee of three to see what could be done. The committee consisted of Hiram Singer, a former president, A. Stamford White, the British broker, and Patten. It met after the market closed May 11 and decided to halt all trading in the May future and set a settlement price of $3.18, the closing price.

But the action did not stop the wild buying. A great rush developed to buy new crop wheat. On the day after trading in May was halted, July raced up 22¾ to 25¼ cents to close at $2.73 to $2.75; September soared 26 to 29 cents to close at $2.44 to $2.46.

The next day the price committee of the Board restricted trading in all wheat futures as well as May corn and May oats. Trading could be conducted at $2.75 or less for July wheat and $2.45 or less for September wheat. On May corn the ceiling was $1.61½ and on May oats 73½.

After this announcement, Charles Pierce, chairman of the price committee, returned to his brokerage house, an important one at that time, and chalked on a blackboard where price fluctuations were being watched carefully by traders, "Patriots who are long of wheat should sell at once."[14] July fell 16 cents and September 18 cents. Two days later trading was limited to liquidation—no new positions could be taken on either the long or short side of the market. Also, directors set a ceiling of $1.65 for all corn futures.

The Board's efforts to control its trading may have been stimulated in part by indications that Congress was planning to pass legislation which would put control of food production, consumption and marketing in the hands of President Wilson for the duration of the war. Officials of the Board may have reasoned that, if the Board could demonstrate its own ability to sustain an orderly market, it might avoid Federal constraint.

Griffin laid the blame for the price surge on world-wide buying, but there were others who felt a good deal of speculation was involved, too.

"There is plenty of grain in the country to carry us through," Griffin said. "If it were not for this wild frenzy which has seized the allied governments, in fact the whole world, there would be no such prices paid for wheat as at present."[15]

One of those who disagreed with Griffin's explanation was Carl Vrooman, assistant secretary of agriculture, who made several speeches lambasting "food gamblers" and "economic parasites."[16] And the *New York Sun* proclaimed, "Those who undertake to corner the market in any staple should be put in the same class with the spy and the traitor and share their fate."[17]

As Congress worked on a food control act, it became apparent that Herbert Hoover was the most likely choice to administer the law. Hoover was an engineer and promoter who had spent most of his life outside the United States, chiefly in England, but had returned at the war's outset and headed a vast program of relief for Belgium. He was much esteemed and honored, collecting enthusiastic endorsements from high ranking Democrats and Republicans alike and being tapped for honorary degrees by such prestigious Northeast institutions as Princeton, Brown and Williams.

Hoover was not as vehement in his opposition to speculation as Vrooman, but, in mid-May, he declared, "What this nation must have immediately is control of food prices. If the output of wheat is taken over by the government the present price, which is high enough, can be reduced 40 to 50 percent."[18]

Elaborating on this idea of food price control, Hoover spoke in early July like a man who had already been appointed. "It is not the intention," he said, "of the Food Administration to fix the price of wheat, nor is it expected that it will have any such power. If the food bill passes Congress, however, we certainly shall not stand for the speculative buying of wheat."[19]

Hoover followed this up the next day with a letter to Wilson which included the statement, ". . . the speculator, legitimate or vicious, has taken a large part of the money now being paid by the consumer." He advocated government buying of wheat "at some reasonable minimum price."[20]

The Food Control Law, known as the Lever Act, passed Congress on August 10. It placed in President Wilson's hands powers never before granted the Federal government. Among them, President Wilson had the right to limit, regulate or prevent speculation or manipulation of prices, and to prescribe the limits within which various grain exchanges might act. As expected, Wilson named Hoover to administer the law. Hoover chose as his assistant Julius Barnes of Barnes, Ames & Co., wheat exporters doing business in New York, Duluth and Winnipeg. Barnes became president of the Food Administration Grain Corp.

Hoover messaged the various grain exchanges that beginning September 1, the government would buy wheat at interior terminals; he asked the exchanges to suspend all dealings in wheat futures. Promptly, they did so. There would be no repetition of the wild days of the Civil War and the Spanish-American War; no Old Hutch garnering a fortune in flour, grain and whiskey; no Joseph Leiter running a corner in the world's wheat supply. At least during war times, the Boards of Trade in Chicago and other cities submitted meekly to those government restrictions which they had always opposed—provided, of course, that it was understood the restrictions would end with the war's end.

An immediate problem was fixing a price on the 1917 wheat crop. This was not a question upon which agreement could be readily expected. Labor and consumer groups contended the support should be $2 or less while farm organizations insisted on a price of $3 or more. The gap was wide. It was bridged mostly in favor of the consumer, a support price of $2.20 being set for No. 1 northern spring wheat or its equivalent in Chicago. Support prices in other cities were a premium or discount of the Chicago price. In Kansas City it was $2.15, in Minneapolis, $2.17, in New York, $2.30. Hoover said he expected these prices would enable bakers to sell a 16 ounce loaf of bread for 10 cents.

Voluntary cooperation keynoted Hoover's efforts. Adopting the slogan, "Food will win the War—don't waste it," he hammered hard at the public conscience.

Some queer incidents occurred. The government investigated a religious sect which advocated hoarding, believing that the end of the world was near. What they intended to do with wheat after the end was not clear. Hoarding by pro-German farmers was suspected and the Food Administration ordered its deputies to seize grain in such cases. The passengers and cargo of the Holland American SS Nieuw Amsterdam underwent an examination by government officials upon arrival in New York, following a report of a German plot to bring in poisonous pollen or fungus to destroy wheat.

Hoover called upon the public to conserve wheat, decreeing a "Wheatless Monday." Later, there would also be a "Wheatless Wednesday." But the most effective conservation measure was a rule requiring millers to use a larger portion of cereals other than wheat in the manufacture of flour. The result was "Victory Bread," a darker loaf than the ordinary white bread. It would contain a maximum of 80 percent wheat flour, later reduced to 75 percent.

Public opinion responded to the call for support of the conservation drive through such actions as a mob in Birmingham wrecking a restaurant because it refused to eliminate wheat products from its menus. Scores of small bakers, restaurant owners, and macaroni and spaghetti manufacturers were hauled into court. The penalties in some of these cases seemed rather odd: the culprits escaped prison sentences by donating a specified sum, set by the judge, to the Red Cross.

One individual who threw himself into the conservation program with gusto was J. Ogden Armour, who was making millions out of the meat and grain sales to the allied governments. He told reporters:

> Mrs. Armour has adopted measures that prevent any waste of food. If the menu includes rice, we dispense with potatoes and save for later just the amount of potatoes that would have been on the table. If we don't use the potatoes, someone else can.[21]

But not only that. He himself wore old suits and shoes and directed that additional acreage on his magnificent Lake Forest estate be put into cultivation. The estate, known as Melody Farm, totaled 1,200 acres, of which 40 acres consisted of a home and garden. The house was an enormous mansion in what was called the "Italian Villa" style. Included in the remainder of the acreage was an artificial lake of about 20 acres with two islands. Armour had built up the estate over a period of years and it was designed to be a working farm as much as a millionaire's showplace.

With trading in wheat halted, restrictions were placed on dealings in futures of other cereals. These included no trades in excess of 200,000 bushels by any single interest and no dealings in contracts calling for delivery more than four months in the future. These were removed within a month after the war ended.

Cash prices for all cereals soared. Cash wheat at Chicago hit a peak of $3.45 in May, 1917 and $2.34 in August, 1918. Cash corn sold at $2.36 per bushel in August, 1917. Cash corn's best price in 1918 was $1.85, made in January. Cash oats reached a peak of 85 cents in July, 1917 and 99 cents in February, 1918. Cash rye sold for $2.45 in June, 1917 and $2.25 in March, 1918.

Enormous quantities of American grain were shipped overseas during the war years. Food itself did not win the war but it obviously made a vital contribution to victory. As in the Civil War, the side which controlled the larger food supply, in this case the allies, triumphed over the side where hunger obsessed the mind and weakened the will.

Farmers made substantial profits, climaxing the steady improvement in their fortune which began with the Joseph Leiter attempted corner. Using irrigation and dry farming to overcome inadequate rainfall, marginal and submarginal lands were opened to farming. Not only did the farmer reap a reward in the prices of commodities he sold, but he also enjoyed a boom in the value of the land he tilled.

The farmer's isolation diminished. He installed a telephone and, in the case of a few adventuresome souls, bought an automobile. His home was electrified, as was his barn. National and state agriculture departments developed new services to aid him in his work, and state and local governments started to build new roads to take the place of the old dirt paths of the horse and buggy days.

As the war approached its end in the closing days of 1918, grain prices weakened but remained well above their pre-war levels. On the Saturday before the November 11 armistice, November corn was at $1.25, November rye $1.62 and November oats 71½.

The war years had provided flush times for agriculture but disaster—both for the farmer and the speculator—lay ahead.

NOTES

1. *SEP,* 1 October 1927, 22.
2. *New York Times,* 28 December 1938.
3. Arthur Cutten and Boyden Sparkes, *The Story of a Speculator.* Privately printed (New York 1936), 6.
4. Ibid., 14.
5. Ibid., 21.
6. Cutten and Sparkes, *SEP,* 19 November 1932, 3.
7. Ibid., 3 December 1932, 12.
8. *Chicago Tribune,* 29 July 1914.
9. *New York Times,* 14 August 1916.
10. Ibid., 17 August 1916.
11. Ibid., 27 August 1916.
12. *SEP,* 15 October 1927, 175.
13. Ibid.
14. *New York Times,* 15 May 1917.
15. Ibid., 14 May 1917.

16. Ibid., 13 May 1917.
17. *Literary Digest*, 26 May 1917, 1583.
18. *New York Times*, 11 May 1917.
19. Ibid., 10 July 1917.
20. Ibid., 11 July 1917.
21. Harper Leech and John C. Carroll, *Armour and His Times* (New York and London 1938), 354.

CHAPTER ELEVEN

Washington
Makes Its Move

The war ended but the hunger did not. Throughout 1919 huge quantities of wheat were shipped to a shattered and starving Europe—or that part of it that had joined the allied cause. The Federal government guaranteed a price of $2.26 at Chicago for the 1919 crop, but the market held well above that level for much of the year.

In the period from July 1, 1920, to June 30, 1921, exports of wheat reached an astounding 366 million bushels, more than any war year and equivalent to 43.9 per cent of the harvest. In May No. 1 dark northern spring wheat sold at $3.45 in Chicago, $1.19 above the government support price.

These war and immediate post-war years were not normal for the farm community but it was natural enough for farmers who lived through them to wish that they were. Fading into a forgotten past were the bitter years of the nineteenth century. Many of the leaders of the Populist battles had passed away and many of the farmers in the 1910s had reached maturity with only a child or adolescent's view of that ragged time. To them farming had been, thus far in the twentieth century, a reasonably rewarding occupation, financially as well as emotionally.

Nevertheless, the 1920–30 decade would be a depressing period for agriculture and chaotic for the grain trade. It would also produce the first successful attempt by the Federal government to regulate trading in grain futures.

With an easing in world hunger and the prospect of adequate crops, the U.S. Grain Corporation terminated its life, paving the way for a resumption of trading in wheat futures. On the first day of trading, July 15, 1920, December wheat opened at $2.72 and March at $2.75.

A more propitious moment to encourage farmer discontent with futures trading could not have been found. As heavy supplies of wheat came off farms during the summer, and as demand for American grain to feed Europe slumped, wheat prices spun downward with sickening speed. With the government no longer supporting the market, wheat fell below the previous guarantee level without a pause and kept right on falling. By October both December and March wheat had dropped under $2. The year's low was $1.48½ on November 26 for March wheat.

A sense of outrage swept the West, centered as usual in Kansas. The heads of various farm groups called upon farmers to "strike"—that is, not send their grain to elevators—until wheat reached $3. O. G. Smith, president of the Farmers National Congress, echoed the rhetoric of the Populists when he blamed the decline on a "well organized conspiracy on the part of grain gamblers and some captains of finance."[1] The governor of Kansas, Henry Allen, asked President Wilson to conduct an investigation and threatened dramatically: "If it is shown that these price fluctuations were due to speculation—cold, deliberate gambling—and not conditions of supply and demand, I will urge abolition of the Board of Trade."[2]

On the following day, the Federal Trade Commission, in response to a senate resolution, began an inquiry which would result in the eventual publication of seven volumes on grain production, marketing and consumption.

But by December the commission had come to some conclusions even before it had made its investigation, notably, "It appears that there is a large volume of futures trading that is mere gambling and involves a great deal of economic waste. The remedy lies in Congressional action to prevent trading which is essentially gambling."[3]

Two investigations, one in the House and the other in the Senate, had already started, seeking to achieve precisely what the commission recommended. The leading force in these actions was Senator Arthur Capper of Kansas, a man of very considerable influence in the agricultural west. Born and reared in Kansas, he was publisher of "Capper's Farmer," "The Homestead," and several smaller farm publications. He owned two Kansas radio stations and was owner and publisher of the *Topeka Daily Capital*. Over in the House, Capper's efforts were aided by Representative Jasper

Tincher, a fellow Kansan. After a brief career as a school teacher, Tincher worked and studied in a law office and was admitted to the bar in 1892. He practiced law in Medicine Lodge, Kansas, and was elected to Congress in 1918.

It was not unusual for bills seeking to restrain or eliminate futures trading to be introduced in Congress. Almost any senator or representative from a farm area could come up with a bill of this type when he wanted to appeal to his rural constituents. Prior to 1920, a total of 164 bills pertaining to regulation of futures trading in agricultural products had been introduced into one branch or the other of Congress. Twenty such bills were introduced in the 60th Congress after the panic of 1907. In the 61st Congress the fervor for reform slackened a bit, but nevertheless 13 bills were introduced.

The desire for reform was not limited to proposed legislation routinely placed in Congress. Agitation for such reform sputtered regularly in farm areas. In the Democratic convention of 1912, which nominated Woodrow Wilson, the adopted platform included the statement, ". . . we favor the enactment by Congress of legislation that will suppress the pernicious practice of gambling in agricultural products by organized exchanges or others."[4]

Most efforts to control speculation came from the farm areas and, of course, reached a crescendo whenever the prices of farm products declined. None succeeded before 1915, when a Cotton Futures Act imposing Federal regulation upon cotton futures took effect. But grain trading remained unregulated.

As was the case in the Populist era, hearings before the Senate and House agricultural committees on a proposal to regulate futures trading permitted both those who favored such regulation and those who opposed it to appear and present their views. The arguments were the same in each hearing.

One element of trading which puzzled the senate committee was the relationship between speculation and what some witnesses referred to as "legitimate trading." Senator Capper asked Julius Barnes, head of the U.S. Grain Corporation during the war, "Unrestricted and unlimited speculations do not tend to stabilize the market in any way, but the tendency is just the opposite, is it not?" To which Barnes replied, "No. I think unlimited speculation could fairly be said to stabilize the market."[5]

However, when pressed by Capper citing a possible sale of five to ten million bushels in one day from one source and asking, "Does that assist in stabilizing the market or maintaining a steady market?" Barnes replied, "No, because it is a matter which the exchange authorities ought to govern and regulate themselves."[6]

As during the Hatch hearings, members of the grain trade stressed the need for speculation if they were to be able to hedge their transactions. Typical was the statement of T. B. King, treasurer of T. B. Howard Grain Company of Central City, Nebraska:

> I believe that any legislation which is aimed at or results in the curtailing of the speculative, we will say, or the hedging market, would react detrimentally to our business and so detrimentally to the interests of the producer and consumer and miller and everybody concerned in the handling of the grain business.[7]

George T. McDermott, a lawyer from Topeka representing the Kansas Grain Dealers Assn., said, "I believe it is mathematically true that hedging cannot exist without some speculation, at least if the farmers continue to market the grain as they have in the past."[8]

This was a significant statement. Farmers had little or no storage capacity and were forced to market their grain as soon after harvest as possible. As this grain was purchased by the various elements in the trade it was hedged by sales in futures markets. These hedges could be absorbed, and were, primarily by speculators. In some cases the speculators had sold short prior to the harvest and when harvest time arrived and as prices declined, they got out of their short position and transferred to the long side of the market in anticipation of a price rise later in the crop year. While this grain deluge hit the market, speculators were necessary. But what if farmers could withhold their grain for months or years? McDermott did not mention it, but this was an idea which had intrigued farmers and agriculture economists and propagandists for decades.

As far back as 1889, a man named Harry Skinner, writing in Frank Leslie's newspaper of November 30, had advocated that the farmer should receive assistance from the Federal government in the form of warehouses to deposit his product and government loans secured by the deposited farm product. Skinner, a North Carolinian, referred to cotton, not grain; he ruled out grain because he thought it was perishable. The next month, at a meeting of the Southern Alliance, C. W. Macune, a former president of the Alliance, presented a report advocating a variation of Skinner's proposal and including grain. The convention adopted this report. Thereafter, much publicity and discussion followed, including ridicule from the urban press, about Macune's plan—known as the Sub-Treasury Plan—but the interest subsided with improvement in agriculture's economy.

Another witness before the Senate Agriculture Committee was Samuel Taton, who appeared on behalf of the American Farm Bureau Federation and presented statistics showing the enormous disparity, actually well known to anyone familiar with the market, between the number of futures bought and sold each year and the production of grain. Taton was a former professor of accounting and economics at the University of Pennsylvania.

"Three times as much wheat is sold in the futures pit at Chicago in an average year as is grown in the entire world. . . . [and] 51 times as much grain as is shipped into Chicago . . . in a year," Taton said.[9]

In his testimony, McDermott referred to these statistics, noting,

> The actual grain may be handled 6 or 8 times; if each transaction is hedged by a purchase or a sale, then the actual grain and its hedge account for the handling of 32 times as many bushels as there is actual grain. Many times a man will transfer his hedge from one option to another, from one month to another, or from one market to another . . .[10]

McDermott castigated the big "wire house" brokers, who, he claimed, stirred up interest in trading among poorly informed people throughout the country.

The question of intent came to the fore during the testimony of F. C. VanDusen, director of the Minneapolis Chamber of Commerce. Buyers and sellers of grain futures were required to sign a statement that they would indeed accept delivery of the actual grain if they had bought, or would indeed deliver it if they had sold. But, obviously, many of those who bought and sold had no intention of handling the actual grain.

VanDusen, Senator Ellison Smith of South Carolina and Senator William Kenyon of Iowa engaged in this exchange:

VanDusen: If you make a purchase you must stand ready to take the actual grain on that purchase.

Smith: Of course.

VanDusen: If it is not delivered to you at the close of the market, or the last day of the month, then it will be settled by the payment of the difference.

Smith: But the great percentage of it—not the great volume but a considerable per cent of the trades never contemplate either the delivery or the demand for the delivery.

VanDusen: It must be made in contemplation of the delivery.

Smith: That is ostensible in the contract.

VanDusen: It is in the contract.

Smith: It is in the contract.

VanDusen: It is printed there.

Smith: It is in the contract.

VanDusen: Yes sir.

Kenyon: With a mental reservation.[11]

The testimony provoked Senator Capper to assert to newsmen that the Board of Trade ran "the most wanton and the most destructive game of chance in the world." He expressed some sympathy for the little man out to make a cheap dollar: "The small gambler in futures has no more chance to win than the small gamester in a gambling house where they use marked cards and loaded dice."[12]

What most concerned Capper appeared to be speculating in grain by people not connected in any manner with the grain trade. He saw the grain commission houses, the so-called "wire houses," as the sinister culprits in this situation: "The private wire houses reap fortunes from gambling in futures. A single house will in three days sell as much grain as can be delivered on the futures market in a year."[13]

Out of these hearings came the Grain Futures Act of 1921 which passed both the Senate and the House and was signed by President Harding on August 21. It was a profound effort at regulating grain futures well in excess of anything previously attempted by the Federal government. Its descriptive title, very apt, said, "An Act Taxing Contracts for the Sale of Grain for Future Delivery, and Options for Such Contracts, and Providing for the Regulation of the Board of Trade and for Other Purposes."[14]

The core of the bill was imposition of a tax of 20 cents a bushel on every bushel of grain sold for future delivery, with the seller paying the tax.

The tax could be avoided if:

1) The seller owned the grain at the time of sale or was owner or renter of the lands on which the grain was to be grown, or was a member of an association made up of such owners and renters.

2) The sale was made by or through a member of a Board of Trade designated by the agriculture secretary as a "contract market." Failure to comply subjected the offender to a fine of $10,000 and/or a year in prison.[15]

For a board of trade to be designated as a "contract market," and thus permit those who traded through it to avoid the tax, certain very rigorous rules were imposed.

Boards of trade could be designated as contract markets:

1) When located at a terminal market where cash grain was sold in sufficient amount and under such conditions as to reflect the value of the grain in its different grades, and where there was recognized official weighing and inspection service.

2) When the governing body of the board adopted rules requiring members to make and keep records of all transactions in grain, whether cash or for future delivery, as directed by the secretary. These records were to be kept for at least three years and be open to official inspection [i.e., by the Agriculture Department].

3) When the governing body prevented the dissemination by the board or any member thereof of false, misleading or inaccurate reports concerning crop or market information or conditions that affect, or tend to affect, the price of commodities.

4) When the governing board provided for the prevention of manipulation of prices, or the cornering of any grain by the dealers or operators upon such board.

5) When the governing body admitted to membership on the board . . . any authorized representative of any lawfully formed and conducted cooperative of producers having adequate financial responsibility.

6) When the governing body made effective the orders and decisions of a commission appointed by the secretary of agriculture. This was to consist of the secretary plus the attorney general and the secretary of commerce. They were given the authority to suspend or revoke the designation of any board as a contract market if it did not comply with all the regulations outlined above.[16]

There were really two main sections to the act, each equally distasteful to the brokers. The first promoted the welfare of farmer cooperative associations: the tax did not apply to them. Furthermore, a board of trade that wanted to be designated a "contract market," (and no board could operate without that designation), would have to admit cooperatives to membership. This would enable the cooperatives themselves to buy and sell without going through a broker, thereby eliminating commissions. The second section would enforce various rules against price manipulation by requiring the keeping of records and making such records available to the agriculture department, which could (through the three man enforcement commission), suspend or revoke the contract market designation. All this would be enforced by a 20 cents a bushel tax on futures in case of noncompliance.

As expected, the provisions of the act produced a sense of outrage upon the part of members of various boards of trade, particularly Chicago. John Hill, Jr., who had fought so strenuously against bucketshops, and seven other members of the Board filed a brief to restrain enforcement of the act. On the matter of options (puts and calls), however, a surge of reform swept the beleaguered membership and trading in these instruments was brought to an end by an overwhelming 545 to 41 vote.

Hill and the other plaintiffs filed their brief against Henry Wallace, the secretary of agriculture, and several others, including the directors of the Board of Trade. The plaintiffs claimed they had applied to the directors to institute the suit but the directors had declined, announcing they intended to comply with the act. Hill claimed that the directors turned down his application because they feared antagonizing public officials whose duty it was to enforce the act. Possibly this was an elaborate ruse, for the directors could not have been any happier over the act than Hill and his colleagues. The plaintiffs claimed that, if the act were upheld, it would cause irreparable damage to them and all other members of the Board of Trade.

The case first came before the District Court of Northern Illinois, which upheld the act. Hill and the seven other members appealed to the U.S. Supreme Court, which heard the arguments January 11 and 12 and handed down a decision on May 18, 1922. It was unanimous in favor of Hill, basing the decision on the tax feature. Chief Justice Taft wrote the opinion:

> The imposition of 20 cents a bushel on the various grains affected by the tax is most burdensome. . . . this tax varies, according to the price and character of the grain, from 15 per cent of its value to 50 per cent. The manifest purpose of the tax is to compel boards of trade to comply with regulations, many of which have no relevancy to the collection of the tax at all. . . . The act is in essence on its face a complete regulation of boards of trade, with a penalty of 20 cents a bushel on all 'futures' to coerce boards of trade and their members into compliance. . . . The provisions of the act . . . cannot be sustained as an exercise of the taxing power of Congress.[17]

While it seemed that almost everybody connected with the grain trade was deeply involved in the battles over futures trading, one person was not—Arthur Cutten. He was doing what he knew best how to do: speculate in grain. Late in 1921, after the sharp price break of 1920–21, Cutten started to buy May, 1922 wheat. He continued to accumulate it throughout the early months of 1922. Wheat prices climbed rather slowly and Cutten's activities did not attract much attention outside the grain trade until April 15 when May wheat jumped to $1.43.

The following day wheat advanced early and then eased off. Each time May wheat reached $1.44, heavy selling developed. There were reports of cash wheat being purchased by J. Rosenbaum Company and Armour Grain Company at Missouri river markets for shipment to Chicago. Cutten said he would pay cash for all wheat delivered to him. Grown cautious, Patten said he was afraid to trade May wheat.

Cutten seemed to have control of the market on April 21 when May pushed through the $1.44 barrier, sailing to a new high at $1.47 3/4 before easing off to close at $1.45 1/2. This day *Modern Miller*, a trade publication, estimated the wheat crop in Kansas, Oklahoma, Nebraska and Texas at 174 million bushels compared with 235 million a year earlier, an encouraging sign for Cutten.

The market held quiet and steady for a week, but, on April 29, the Board's directors provided additional storage room for delivery of grain on May futures by declaring a part of the Keystone elevator, heretofore not an elevator where grain could be delivered on futures contracts, as "regular." Hence, any grain in that section of the elevator could be delivered to Cutten. The action was an ominous tip on what the directors might do if it appeared Cutten was set to run a full-fledged corner. Two major elevator firms were involved in selling May wheat—Armour Grain Company and J. Rosenbaum Company. George Marcy, president of Armour Grain, advised no one to sell May wheat futures unless he had the cash grain to make delivery.

At the start of May, May wheat was still selling in the $1.43 to $1.44 range. E. F. Rosenbaum, president of J. Rosenbaum Company, met with Board directors and urged them to permit him and other shorts in the May contract to make delivery of wheat in railroad cars on track in the Chicago area. This recalled the E. L. Harper attempted corner, when the threat that directors would take such action broke the corner and eventually sent Harper to jail. (The car delivery rule was adopted in 1918; it could be applied only on a vote of the directors.)

Directors acted on May 5. Declaring that Chicago elevators were full and that an emergency existed, they took the action that Rosenbaum, Marcy and other shorts wanted. In effect, wheat held in railroad cars within 50 miles of Chicago was declared "regular" for delivery on May contracts. Two days later May wheat sank to $1.36 1/2 on a report that 400,000 bushels of wheat had been purchased in Kansas City and Omaha to come to Chicago. Further, reports from Kansas City claimed that 2½ to 3 million bushels would be shipped to Chicago before the end of the month.

On May 9 the price collapsed rapidly in the afternoon and finished at $1.32¼. The corner, obviously, would not materialize. Everyone could see that Cutten was licked. Close to 8,000 cars of wheat stood on track around Chicago, all of it deliverable to Cutten. On three successive trading days after May 25, the close was $1.28, $1.18½ and $1.16, the last price of the disastrous affair.

Possibly stimulated by the congressional agitation against manipulation, the directors of the Board had prevented a corner. But the prevention created some problems of its own, as was pointed out to the Board of Trade in a letter by Julius Barnes, the former head of the U.S. Grain Corporation: "Present conditions lay an economic burden on distribution cost by drawing wheat to Chicago out of its accustomed channels, and from points of supply needed shortly for actual consumption elsewhere."[18]

At a later investigation by the Federal Trade Commission, Cutten claimed that he would have made a profit if the directors had not declared railroad cars "regular" for delivery purposes. He charged that "certain parties," which he did not name but were obviously Rosenbaum and Marcy, caused the directors to make the delivery ruling.

"I lost plenty," Cutten grumbled and recalled:

> What made me furious at the time was that plenty of storage space was being found for coarse grains. With 7,800 cars bearing 8 or 10 million bushels of wheat standing on track at a demurrage cost of $39,000 a day, there were only 800 cars of oats, corn, rye and barley standing on track. These grains were being received in elevators.[19]

In short, he felt that the elevatormen, particularly Rosenbaum and Marcy, had conspired to defraud him.

The Federal Trade Commission also wanted to hear from Barnes, and he elaborated upon the charge he had made in his letter to the Board of Trade:

> ... by the end of the month [May] there was accumulated in Chicago a stock of 10 or 12 million bushels of wheat, which was beyond the normal absorbing capacity of the consumption trade that rests in Chicago, and that wheat had been lifted ... from centers where it should have remained for the consumption which normally overtakes it from those centers—Omaha, Kansas City, Minneapolis, all these other points.[20]

Barnes made a significant suggestion on a method to control manipulation. He noted that the varieties and grades of wheat that could be delivered on futures contracts had been increased over the years and he said he had suggested in 1917 to the Board that it make wheat stored in Omaha, Kansas City and Minneapolis, and not just Chicago, deliverable on futures traded in Chicago. "I stand today," he told the Federal Trade Commission, "for that as being the one real constructive thing left for the Chicago market if Chicago is to be the liquid grain futures market of America."[21] (Today, Toledo is also designated a city for "regular" warehouses for corn, wheat and soybeans; St. Louis for corn; and Minneapolis for oats.)

Barnes noted that, if this rule had been in effect during the Cutten manipulation, ". . . that wheat would have been delivered but the wheat itself would have physically been in Omaha and Kansas City and available for milling in June and July, when it was needed, and it would not have been in Chicago . . ."[22]

While Cutten was conducting his campaign in May wheat, Senator Capper, nursing his wounds after his rebuff by the Supreme Court, was trying to frame a law which would prevent Cutten—and others like him—from any manipulation. Once again the two sides—those for regulation and those against—presented their cases before the Congressional agriculture committees. In reporting to the Senate, its agriculture committee noted:

> Every member of a grain exchange who testifies before this committee acknowledged that there is at times excessive speculation and undesirable speculation in the futures market. Furthermore, it was brought out that a few big traders at times influence—manipulate the market—by the great volume of their operations.[23]

Charging that speculation caused a continuously fluctuating market, the committee argued:

> A market without wide and frequent price fluctuations would greatly benefit the producer. The reason for this is that rapidly fluctuating prices cannot be fully reflected in the prices paid at country stations, so an additional margin must be allowed for buying in the country.[24]

The bill which Capper and Tincher came up with on the second time around, known as the Grain Futures Act of 1922, eliminated completely the 20 cents per bushel tax on futures transactions. Instead, the bill was based upon the power of Congress to regulate interstate commerce and use of the mails. Otherwise, the bill was similar to that of 1921 which the U.S. Supreme Court had declared unconstitutional. The formal title of the new act showed its difference from the 1921 act. The new act was "For the Prevention of Obstructions and Burdens upon Interstate Commerce in Grain by Regulating Transactions on Grain Futures Exchanges and for Other Purposes." It quickly passed Congress and was signed by President Harding on September 21, 1922.

The Board of Trade, along with John Hill, Jr., and others filed a brief against it, naming Henry Wallace, Edwin A. Olsen, U.S. attorney for the Northern District of Illinois, and Arthur C. Lueder, U.S. Postmaster at Chicago, as defendants. (The case is known as Board of Trade v Olsen.) The plaintiffs submitted a large number of affidavits in support of a motion for a temporary injunction. These contained opinions of many professors of political economy in colleges throughout the country to the effect that trading in futures in the long run did not depress prices but stabilized them.

The District Court of Northern Illinois ruled against the Board of Trade and it appealed to the U.S. Supreme Court, which in an opinion handed down on April 16, 1923 upheld the act. The vote was 7 to 2 and Chief Justice Taft again wrote the opinion. He said:

> Manipulations of grain futures for speculative profit, though not carried to the extent of a corner or complete monopoly, exert a vicious influence and produce abnormal and disturbing temporary fluctuations of prices that are not responsive to actual supply and demand and discourage not only this justifiable hedging, but disturb the normal flow of actual consignments. A futures market lends itself to such manipulation much more readily than a cash market. . . .
>
> If a corner and the enhancement of prices produced by buying futures directly burden interstate commerce in the article whose price is enhanced, it would seem to follow that manipulations of futures which unduly depress prices of grain in interstate commerce and directly influence consignment in that commerce are equally direct. . . .
>
> By reason and authority, therefore, in determining the validity of this act we are prevented from questioning the conclusion of Congress that manipulation of the market for futures on the Chicago Board of Trade may, and from time to time does, directly burden and obstruct commerce between the states in grain, and that it recurs and is a constantly possible danger. . . .
>
> For this reason, Congress has the power to provide the appropriate means adopted in this act by which this abuse may be restrained and avoided.[25]

Thus it was that, 75 years after the Board of Trade was officially founded, a combination of Senator Capper, Arthur Cutten, J. Rosenbaum and Armour Grain companies, and Julius Barnes had, somewhat inadvertently in most cases, produced the first Federal regulation of grain futures trading.

Happy with his triumph, Senator Capper enthusiastically stated, "It's a great victory. I believe the law will eliminate the vicious practices which have been at the bottom of grain gambling and will make it impossible for speculators and manipulators to bring about conditions which produce violent fluctuations in the market."[26] But this was not a universally shared opinion. The *New York Commercial* asserted, "Our opinion is that the law is largely political buncombe, or bunk."[27]

The new Grain Futures Act, quickly implemented by a Grain Futures Administration, may have restricted speculation but it did not help the price of wheat.

The American Farm Bureau Federation appealed to President Harding to use his influence to induce farmers to hold wheat off the market until the price stabilized. Bernard Baruch, an economic advisor to presidents and other political leaders, suggested that farmers should market their crops through cooperative associations. He mentioned this to J. Ogden Armour and George Marcy and was told by them that they would be willing to sell their elevator facilities to farmers. F. Edison White of Armour & Co., the meat packing firm, urged farmers to feed their surplus wheat to livestock—"hogs and poultry thrive on wheat," he said.[28] Senator Royal S. Copeland of New York advocated eating more bread, asserting that if everyone ate an extra slice at every meal for a year the surplus would be consumed.

On July 11, 1923, for the first time since World War I started in 1914, July wheat sold below $1. It hit a low of 99⅛ cents, closing at 99¾. Brokers thought they knew one reason. If speculators were the culprits to the farmers, the Grain Futures Act served the same purpose for brokers. They said the act had dried up speculation, which they asserted was needed to maintain prices at harvest time.

On the same day that wheat sank below $1 in Chicago and the country wondered what to do with its surplus grain, food riots broke out in Potsdam, Germany. Unemployed metal workers marched in the city, converged on the open market, and demanded the food dealers sell food at cost. The dealers refused and the market was wrecked before militia arrived. Five days later all wheat futures in Chicago sold below $1 for the first time on the crop.

Topeka clothing stores accepted wheat warehouse receipts at $1 a bushel (higher than the current market value for wheat) in exchange for merchandise. Agriculture college economists in Missouri and Kansas joined White in urging farmers to feed wheat to livestock in place of corn. Omaha bakers endorsed a suggestion that bakers should pay more for wheat, but there was no indication that they raised their own payments. Farmers in Oregon sat down to a meal totaling 16 cents a plate, the cost being computed on the price the farmers obtained for their products. The same meal, the farmers said, cost $1.50 in Portland restaurants.

Governor Jonathon Davis of Kansas urged that "The Farm Loan Board, or, let us say, perhaps Henry Ford, take over 150 million bushels of wheat at $1 a bushel and hold it for a year. Whoever did that would lose nothing, for he would control prices absolutely."[29] There was no response from Ford, who stuck to his cars.

The grain trade seized upon the price downturn to argue that the Grain Futures Act, by stifling speculation, was at fault and should be repealed. This dubious point of view received support from the New York Times, which asserted, "If the iniquities of grain exchanges have anything to do with the low price of wheat, regulation has only increased this maleficent work."[30] The Chicago Board of Trade hosted a meeting of the executive committees of the nation's grain exchanges at which a call was made for elimination of the daily reports on traders' activities and open positions. The Agriculture Department insisted that the required reports be made.

Reluctantly, without stopping their rhetorical opposition, the grain men made the reports. And they found a way to get around the purpose of those reports.

NOTES

1. New York Times, 17 November 1920.
2. Ibid., 6 October 1920.
3. Ibid., 21 December 1920.
4. Arthur Peterson, "Futures Trading with Particular Reference to Agricultural Commodities" Agricultural History, vol. 7, no. 2 (April 1933), 74.
5. Hearings of the Senate Committee on Agriculture, Future Trading Act of 1921. no. 212. 67th Congress, 1st session. Washington D.C., 1921, 90.
6. Ibid.
7. Ibid., 144.
8. Ibid., 207.
9. Ibid., 156.

10. Ibid., 208.
11. Ibid., 291.
12. *New York Times,* 10 August 1921.
13. Ibid.
14. *The Statutes at Large of the United States of America,* vol. 42, part 1, 187–91.
15. Ibid.
16. Ibid.
17. 259 US 44 (Hill v Wallace).
18. 262 US 1 (Board of Trade v Olsen) Lawyer's Edition. Cases argued and Decided in the Supreme Court of the United States, October term, 1922. Book 67:844–5.
19. *SEP,* 26 November 1932, 33.
20. 262 US 1 (Board of Trade v Olsen).
21. Ibid.
22. Ibid., 843.
23. Ibid.
24. Ibid.
25. Ibid., 844.
26. *New York Times,* 17 April 1922.
27. *Literary Digest,* 3 May 1923, 16.
28. *New York Times,* 23 June 1923.
29. Ibid., 4 August 1923.
30. Ibid., 10 August 1923.

CHAPTER TWELVE

The Man Who Liked to Make Money

"I never was much of a hand to mix," Cutten said."[1] He was talking about his social life, but his description applied equally well to his operations in grain. In the latter area he noted, "I have little faith . . . in the ability or disposition of other people to keep their mouths shut. For that reason I have been a lone trader."[2]

In the mid-1920s, after his failure to corner May 1922 wheat, Cutten conducted an extraordinary series of one man campaigns in wheat, corn and rye. These were the years when he bought, owned and sold more grain than any man who ever operated in the grain pits.

During this period he used a small office near the Board of Trade building. It did not have his name on the door. He was a slight, wiry man, his hair turning grey. He wore glasses, dressed conservatively and more closely resembled a bureaucratic clerk than a wildly daring speculator. He had long ago given up sand lot baseball, but liked a game of golf with friends of his early days on the Board of Trade. One of his gifts to Guelph, Canada, was a golf course and country club.

Besides the 800 acre farm near Glen Ellyn, he and his wife maintained an apartment on Lake Shore Drive. Neither of them appeared at Chicago social functions although Mrs. Cutten, childless, developed an interest in child welfare and contributed liberally to homes for destitute children. They lived a very quiet life outside the market place, protected by walls of money.

Cutten's campaigns in the mid-1920s started in 1924 in corn. Studying the government weather maps, he noted that the corn belt suffered from excessive rainfall throughout the spring. This delayed planting, which raised the possibility that the crop would be damaged by frost before it could be harvested. Cutten started to buy corn at the depressed price of 40 cents a bushel.

The speculator continued to accumulate the grain as the price slowly climbed; when May arrived he took delivery of four million bushels. By late June the price reached 85 cents and Cutten, enthused with his own prescience, predicted it would go to $1. At this time he exchanged his cash corn for July futures. By mid-July the price hit $1.10 and Cutten sold much of this July corn to a glucose factory at that price.

Late that month the agriculture department, in its official crop summary, stated what Cutten had been claiming all along: "A large portion [of the corn crop] is so far behind on development that grain will be matured only in the event of frost holding off unusually late in the fall."[3] As it turned out, corn production that year totaled 2,312,745,000 bushels compared with 3,053,557,000 in 1923. This corn deal was one of the most successful and rewarding ever run by Cutten, or by anyone else. And it did not arouse public protests that less spectacular deals had done.

"Most of my success had been due to my hanging on while the profits mounted," Cutten explained. "This is the big secret. Do with it what you will."[4]

The story in rye was quite similar. Cutten started to accumulate this grain at 72 cents, and in all he bought between seven and eight million bushels. The price moved above $1.50 late in the year and Cutten again came out with an impressive capital gain.

But it was Cutten's wheat campaign—he started buying the bread grain at $1.05—which aroused the most interest in this and the next year.

Discontent still gripped the western grain states at the time Cutten initiated his buying. As a result a third party was formed, the Progressive Party, and Robert La Follette of Wisconsin was nominated for the presidency. One of the reforms he advocated was prohibition of "gambling" in grain futures. He expected to make a strong showing in the plains states.

On July 17, two weeks after La Follette's nomination, July wheat closed at $1.30½, up 26¾ cents in seven weeks. July corn was $1.12¾, up 36⅝, and July rye 85⅞, up 19⅛. Cutten had accumulated approximately 15 million bushels of wheat and predicted the grain would go to $1.50. Many other traders, including Patten, followed Cutten onto the buy side.

Out in Kansas joy swelled in the hearts of farmers, bankers and trades people as the price advanced. The Kansas Daily Newspaper Advertising Association took a full page advertisement in the *New York Times* to proclaim in big, bold type, "Prosperity Has Come to Kansas!" Not only were there big crops, the association exulted, but, "Grain prices are the highest in years—and going up, up, up!"[5]

Dark trickery was uncovered by the La Follette campaigners, who saw a prime issue slipping away from them. The *Milwaukee Leader*, socialist newspaper and ardent supporter of La Follette, said the price gain was "inspired by the rich folks" and "intended to head off the candidacy of La Follette and Wheeler." It was, the paper said, "a cunning way to campaign," but any voter taken in by it was "a far gone boob."[6] Senator Henril Shipstead of Minnesota cried, "A small group of financiers in control of the farm products market have inflated prices during the past two months in an attempt to fool the farmer into believing prosperity is at hand. The farmer can't be fooled."[7]

On October 2 wheat roared through the $1.50 barrier, the May contract closing at $1.51¼, up 15 cents in a week. Even that was mild compared with rye's action—it advanced 25½ cents in the same period, May closing at $1.35. Accompanying this surge were reports that wet weather at harvest time had lessened the yield from European farms, already suffering from a cold and wet summer. Cables from Germany said that country was experiencing an acute shortage of food and feed grains.

Among the frustrated supporters of La Follette was Senator Burton K. Wheeler. Campaigning in Kansas, he charged the big financial interests, anxious to see President Coolidge elected, had aided in creating an artificial price for wheat and would desert the farmer and permit the price to drop after the election.

Whatever threat to futures trading may have existed in La Follette's campaign subsided quickly when he carried only one state—his own Wisconsin. Coolidge, of course, won.

Contrary to Senator Wheeler's prediction, the election did not stop wheat. It kept right on going up. Cutten accepted for December delivery five million bushels of wheat. His wheat jammed elevators at Chicago and Baltimore, the big Atlantic coast exporting center. Dealers estimated it was costing him $100,000 a month in storage costs and insurance to carry the grain.

By the end of January, 1925, wheat had risen above $2.05, the highest price in more than 60 years except for the World War I period. Wheat on

January 29 gained 5¾ cents in Chicago, 9 cents in Winnipeg and 8 cents in Buenos Aires. In London, a speculative panic swept through the grain trade. Brokers bought and sold grain cargoes by telephone all night long.

An example of the effect of the buying by Cutten and those who followed his lead on the international trade was provided by the Lisbeth, a cargo ship that left Adelaide, Australia on January 19 with 3,000 tons of wheat for England. The cargo that day sold at 66 shillings and 7 pence a quarter. Four days later it sold again for 67 shillings. Thereafter it changed hands half a dozen times and when word came through of the advance of wheat to $2.05 at Chicago, the Lisbeth's cargo sold at 70 shillings 3 pence a quarter.

William Nicholls, governing director of the Spillers Milling & Associated Industries, told the worried Royal Commission on Food Services:

> In this country we follow U.S. markets, whatever they do. We cannot help ourselves. The Chicago market rules the world and fixes the price for all other markets. We cannot get away from it. What Chicago prices were last night is known today throughout the world and the prices of all other wheat markets follow. It matters not where they are trading, whether in the Antipodes or the Azores. That is the power of Chicago.[8]

The International Institute of Agriculture, located in Rome, inadvertently helped the advance by stating that the outlook for the summer crop in Hungary and Rumania was bad, Russia had become an importer and the crop in the Argentine had fallen 50 million bushels short.

Russia had been buying flour all through January from the United States, Canada, Germany and France. Exporters believed Russia would have to import between 25 and 50 million bushels of American wheat plus some rye.

But, at $2, wheat looked mighty high to some old timers. Patten, now 72, his mustache turned white, his brown hat still tipped back on his head, smiled when asked if he were sorry he had sold out: "Sorry? Not at all. Can't be sorry in this game."[9] He said he did not see where Russia would get the $50 or $100 million needed to buy all that American wheat. (Russia's imports from the United States in 1925 totaled only 16,000 bushels of wheat and 4,372,501 bushels of rye, plus 294,919 barrels of wheat flour and 1,400 of rye flour.)

E. F. Rosenbaum—no friend of Cutten's—said Argentina was offering wheat at 10 to 15 cents a bushel under the American price, and added, "Unless our price comes down to the world level, and we dispose of some of our wheat, the surplus in this country is going to be a very depressing price factor when the new harvest comes in."[10]

And B. F. Eckhart, the flour miller, who had been bullish for months, stated flatly that the price rise had been overdone and a reaction was due.

Cutten, owning much of the wheat, went to Florida for a vacation.

Prices weakened materially during February. On February 6, May wheat fell 9¾ cents from its early top in a break which uncovered many "stop-loss" orders. At its low May was off 20⅛ cents from the high on January 28, but that was less than the tumble in Winnipeg—there, May plunged 28⅞ cents.

Then came Friday, March 13, Black Friday. May wheat dropped more than 15 cents to $1.66¼. At that price it was off 38⅝ cents from the January high. During the same time period, Winnipeg May fell 48⅝ cents. Needed heavy rains in Kansas and Nebraska had something to do with the decline, but obviously a market honeycombed with "stop-loss" orders had collapsed under the weight of professional selling.

Cutten was in Baltimore that day, inspecting his wheat in the city's elevators on his way from Florida to Chicago. One of his brokers called him and requested $1½ million as additional margin. Cutten supplied it. Then another broker called him, demanding more money. Again, Cutten supplied it.

Three days later Cutten arrived in Chicago, still talking bullish on wheat when May closed at $1.64½. It was a natural public attitude for a trader who, long on the market, found it necessary to liquidate his holdings: the report that he was bullish might stir up some demand from the public to meet his selling orders.

The next day May wheat broke 14 cents in Chicago, 13 cents in Buenos Aires, 18 cents in Winnipeg and 10 cents in Liverpool. Two weeks earlier May had sold at $2.02 in Chicago; this day it sank to a low of $1.51. In Winnipeg the earlier high of $2.09 compared with this day's $1.53½. Two brokerage houses which often operated for Cutten admitted to reporters that he had been selling wheat for some time.

Looking back on this adventure later, Cutten said he had overstayed the market: "I had believed wheat would go to $2.50, but I was mistaken."[11]

Over the next week wheat rallied, making the normal recovery after its plunge. Late in the month Cutten sold another 10 to 15 million bushels through Jackson Brothers and Bartlett, Frazier & Co., his favorite brokerage houses at the time. At the month's end he announced, "I am not interested in wheat."[12]

He meant May wheat. By the end of July he had engineered a slight squeeze in the July contract. The price advanced 17 cents in the last few days of the month, gaining 9 cents the last trading day. Cutten sold one million bushels at the top, but also took 2.3 million bushels of grain on delivery. He explained, "I have not bought any July wheat for two months. A grain merchant like me must have a little stock on hand to do business with."[13]

The wild gyrations annoyed W. M. Jardine, successor to Wallace as agriculture secretary. "It has gotten so that a great many people believe the Board of Trade is a nuisance," he said. He insisted that the "gambling" be eliminated.[14]

Initially, the Board's directors ignored Jardine's statement but he kept repeating, over a period of months, that the Board should "clean its own house." He warned that if the Board's directors did not take some action, he would ask Congress for additional laws to regulate "abuses." He put a time limit for the Board action: January 1, 1926.

With reluctance, the Board directors backed down. If there was one thing they did not want, it was another and more rigid Grain Futures Act. In September—six months after the March price break—a Business Conduct Committee was formed. Furthermore, a limit could be placed on price changes whenever directors declared an emergency existed. In a burst of propriety, members of the Business Conduct Committee agreed not to speculate while serving. Jardine was happy: it was "one of the most progressive steps ever taken by the Board of Trade."[15]

It did not stop Cutten from buying. Once again he bought May wheat, this time the contract that would expire in May, 1926. And, once again, he bought several million bushels. But times had changed: the Agriculture Department through its Grain Futures Administration was carefully watching his moves.

The Grain Futures Act required that members of contract markets, which included Cutten, report to the Grain Futures Administration their net position in futures owned by them, long or short, by grain and by future, when they had net open commitments in any one future equal to or in excess of one half million bushels of wheat, corn, oats and 200,000 bushels of rye or barley.

Having access to Cutten's trading record, the Grain Futures Administration suggested to the Board of Trade that Cutten's holdings were too large for one person. Cutten did not see it that way: "I was carrying a big line of wheat, but in my opinion not too big. I could pay for what I had."[16]

He had bought most of this wheat around $1.50 but at the time the call came from the Board's Business Conduct Committee for him to appear, the May contract was selling around $1.65.

When Cutten crossed Jackson Boulevard on his way to meet the Business Conduct Committee in the Board of Trade building, he was observed by other grain traders and brokers. They knew where he was heading; guessing what would happen, they began to sell wheat.

At the meeting the committee members told Cutten, "Look, the Grain Futures Administration has made complaint that you are carrying too much open stuff."[17]

Cutten protested that he had bought the wheat for himself, which he had a right to do: "By every right of commerce I was entitled to a profit on my transactions for the position I had taken."[18]

One of the committee members put his arm around Cutten's shoulder. "You ought to sell some wheat for the sake of the Board of Trade. You know, this committee is the device we settled upon to keep the government from taking fuller control of trading in futures. They get the figures and watch the accounts from day to day."

"I know all that. But is there anything criminal in an honest profit? I'm buying and risking my own money. Why should I sell before I'm ready?"

"For the sake of the Board of Trade."[19]

Cutten threw up his hands and agreed to sell part of his line of wheat.

By the time Cutten had returned to his office, wheat had declined 4 cents on selling by those who believed, quite correctly, that at least part of the Cutten wheat was to be dumped on the market. At the close the price was off 7 1/4 cents.

"Before the gong rang for the closing of trading in the pit that day, all the grain in the United States, even that just sprouting in the ground, had become less valuable to its owners," Cutten recalled, somewhat grandiloquently.[20]

Cutten was not a popular man, although he had a group which followed him in his operations in the hope of scurrying up a little money for themselves, and he did not increase his popularity when he asserted, "If I had a son, I would keep him away [from the grain pits]; I wouldn't let him touch the market with a 10 foot pole." He went on to explain why: "There are too many wrecks down in the pit. People call themselves brokers. They're only part of that—the 'broke' part of it. Not more than 10 per cent of the men who go into grain ever remain. Ninety per cent just dwindle away, pass out."[1]

While Cutten accumulated gains in the mid-1920s, another of the great grain traders, J. Ogden Armour, found himself in a far more unfortunate situation.

Armour & Co. was basically a meat packing firm but it owned subsidiaries in other food related areas. It was controlled entirely by members of the Armour family, of whom the most important personage was J. Ogden Armour. He personally held about 80 per cent of the company's preferred and common stocks.

Armour & Co. reported handsome profits ranging from 28½ per cent to 37½ per cent return on capital stock in the years 1912–15. The next year the company declared a 400 per cent stock dividend. Return on capital stock was 20 per cent in 1916, 21 per cent in 1917 and 14 per cent in 1918. At the end of World War I, Armour's fortune was estimated between $100 million and $200 million.

But in 1919 the firm suffered huge losses on its inventories, swollen because Armour believed World War I would continue for some years longer. The next year the company had to borrow from a group of bankers to stay financially afloat. In fiscal 1921 the company suffered an appalling loss of $31,709,817, substantially larger than earnings in any one of the war years. Armour tried to explain in his annual report to stockholders: "A business such as ours must carry many millions of pounds of products in process of cure. Price declines, therefore, mean losses not only in sales but inventory values as well."[22]

In the following year, the bankers had to infuse some more money into the firm, which they did by creating a new company to take over the assets of the old one. By this time Armour personally was in as bad a condition as his company. He received a personal loan of $20 million from the bankers, placing his securities in their hands for administration. Armour paid off the loan in 1925 by selling part of his stockholdings to the bankers, who then sold it at a profit to the public.

One estimate was that, at the peak of the wash-out, Armour lost money at the rate of $1 million a day for 130 days. Armour told a friend, "I lost money so fast I didn't think it was possible."[23]

The Literary Digest, a news and editorial weekly of the era, referred to him as the "World's Biggest Loser."[24] It seemed an appropriate title.

Armour had not just overstayed the market; he had overstayed the war. It had been good to him, just like the Russo-Japanese War. Advancing prices in the war years inflated inventory profits. Higher prices and a 400 per cent stock dividend increased cash pay-outs. At the war's end his firms were loaded with huge inventories because he expected the good times to keep rolling for at least another year. No other major packer suffered so grievously because no other had played so recklessly with beneficent fortune. The war's end was a terrible blow to J. Ogden Armour.

Like all millionaires, Armour had numerous investments other than his major source of wealth. Among these were Armour Leather Company, which slipped into bankruptcy, and the Kansas City Railway Company, forced into receivership. A favorite project was Sutter Basin Land Company of California, where Armour sank $15 million in reclaiming 45,000 acres of land. He was the largest single shareholder in Chicago banks and he sold all of those shares to raise cash. And then there was Armour Grain Company.

For decades, under direction of both J. Ogden and his father P. D., Armour Grain played a powerful part in the marketing of grain both in this country and throughout the world. In 1924 Armour Grain, along with several other grain firms, was taken over by the Grain Marketing Corporation, a gigantic $26 million cooperative incorporated under the Illinois Marketing Act. This was the farmer cooperative initially suggested by Bernard Baruch, agreed to by Armour and George Marcy, Armour Grain's president, and encouraged by the Grain Futures Act. It represented farmer cooperatives, local cooperative elevators and other organizations doing a cooperative marketing grain business. It was the greatest cooperative project, up to that time, ever launched by American farmers. In a year it failed.

An acrimonious dispute developed among the leading principals. Edward E. Brown, an attorney and vice president of the First National Bank of Chicago, was named arbiter. After an investigation he handed down a decision in early 1927: Armour Grain was to pay $3 million to other participants in the dispute.

Brown cited three separate acts of Armour Grain in arriving at his decision:

1) In April, 1924, when anticipating the merger into Grain Marketing, employees of Armour Grain changed the stock books at their elevators in South Chicago in order to show a greater amount of grain than actually was on hand. This was done, Brown found, "so that the changes would somehow result in Armour Grain Co.'s later getting a better price for wheat from some farmers' organizations than would otherwise be possible."[25]

2) George Thompson, general superintendent of Armour Grain, on July 1 or 2, 1924, reclassified all the grain in one elevator by raising the

grades. "The total grades so raised on the stock books aggregated over two million bushels," Brown said.[26]

3) Just before Armour Grain was taken over by Grain Marketing, samples of wheat procured from one Armour Grain elevator by samplers of the Board of Trade were left in the testing room overnight. They were changed so that samples of a better grade of wheat would be shown the next day. It had been agreed that the wheat held by Armour Grain would be taken over by Grain Marketing on the basis of the samples.

Brown said that changing the samples was done:

> . . .either by substituting entirely different wheat, by picking out bin-burned kernels, or by throwing out part of a sample containing damaged wheat and replacing the part thrown out with good wheat. The testimony on this point is overwhelming and conclusive.[27]

The Board of Trade, like other grain, stock and bond exchanges, still operated as a sort of private club, enforcing its own rules. It was shocking indeed that such duplicity had been discovered at Armour Grain. There was, however, no evidence that Armour himself knew what was going on at the elevator. Armour had owned 62½ per cent of the stock of Armour Grain. The rest was held by other members of the Armour family except for 12½ per cent owned by Marcy.

Following these disclosures a special committee of the Board recommended that Armour Grain officials be suspended from membership. Directors promptly took such action and, in addition, found Thompson guilty of "dishonest conduct" and expelled him.

The disgrace of Armour Grain, with its honored tradition in the international grain business, was another blow to Armour. Despite his heavy losses, he still had his yacht, the "Atowana," and traveled around the world in the top rung of society. In July, 1927, while staying at the Carlton Hotel in London, he suffered an attack of typhoid fever. On August 6, with Lord Dawson of Penn, personal physician to the King, and two other doctors in attendance, his heart gave out.*

At the time of Armour's death, Cutten was no longer in Chicago. Unhappy with the rules of the Grain Futures Administration after his 1926 wheat deal, he turned to the stock market at a time when it was taking off on a spectacular surge which would draw millions of unsophisticated speculators into a get-rich-quick ploy. It was not a new area for Cutten; after all, some of his early money had come from the opportune

---

*Armour's estate was closed out in probate court in 1929. It showed an insolvency of nearly $2 million. Mrs. Armour obtained $750,000 on a $1,055,000 claim and Mrs. John Mitchell, Jr., Armour's only child, $500,000 on a $2,000,000 claim. (*New York Times*, 13 November 1929)

purchase of railroad shares. But he had given only minor attention to the stock market during his hectic years in wheat, corn and rye.

Why seek to duplicate in stocks what he had accomplished in grains? Obviously, he did not need the money; speculation is always risky, even for those who are very astute at it, and he might lose much or all of his capital. The answer may lie in Cutten's own comment, made a few years after the stock market venture: "I like to make money. There is a thrill in the actual process unequaled by any emotion a man of my years is apt to experience. . . . I have made it because I like to make it."[28]

There was also the fact that trading in stocks was unregulated: no government agency received a daily record of your trades, no government agency could force you to liquidate if it felt you owned too many shares, no government agency prohibited squeezes or corners. Government regulation in the stock market would come, but it would not come until the same thing happened to stocks as had happened to grains: a vicious bear market.

In New York the great speculator was a member of what newspapers referred to as the "Big Ten" in the wild market of 1927, 1928, and, until October, 1929. The journalists found 10 big speculators from the West, notably associated with the automobile industry, and tagged Cutten as their leader. It is doubtful if Cutten shared knowledge with any of them, but it is possible that he and they knew they were sharing a common market position in the same securities.

A favorite early target of Cutten's was Baldwin Locomotive Works. When discussing the stock market, security analysts and economic professors like to talk about such esoteric matters as call money, rediscount rates, Federal Reserve inventory, money supply and related profundities. None of this interested Cutten. What he saw in Baldwin was a chance to corner the market.

Baldwin was capitalized with 200,000 shares of $100 par value common stock; no other shares existed. Of this, many shares were held by long term officers and directors of the company. It was estimated that the floating supply totaled a mere 100,000 shares. Such a small floating supply made a stock a prime target for aggressive bulls. Cutten bought his Baldwin stock at around $100 per share. As the price advanced, the shorts in the stock had to get out of their position by buying, which sent the price still higher. The stock ran up to $265 per share and Cutten was named a director.

As the stock market boiled upward, Cutten extended his holdings. He became a major holder of Continental Oil. A famous Chicago mail order house, Montgomery Ward & Co., attracted his buying. He also bought into a bakery company, Loose-Wiles Co. And he was among the bulls in the fabulous Radio Corporation of America skyrocket. Cutten owned 40,000 shares of Radio. It went to $500 per share and was split five for one. Cutten's investment in this stock alone had a paper value of $20 million at its peak.

While Cutten busied himself with stocks, the Chicago Board of Trade went through a physical transformation. It moved out of its old building after 43 years and operated in a building on Clark street for 1½ years. Then it moved back to a new building on the old spot on Jackson Boulevard—a building combining the Board's facilities with rental offices and soaring higher than any other edifice in Chicago at that time.

One of the stained glass panels from the old building was given to Patten's widow. Cutten got another. Cutten also took two eight ton draped female statues that had stood in the doorway, one labeled "Commerce" and the other "Labor." He transported them to his Glen Ellyn farm, but never erected them; it was a little too much for his wife and the statues remained prone on the ground in an out-of-the-way portion of the estate.

President Herbert Hoover in Washington pressed a button to signal the start of trading in the new building. Sounds of cheering on the Board's floor were carried by transoceanic telephone to the Liverpool Corn Exchange, where they were distinctly heard. That evening a banquet of celebration was attended by 2,450 members and guests. In this era, with the conservative spirit ascendent, no anarchists or communists repeated the 1885 threats.

A slight hitch developed within a few days, perhaps a harbinger of problems to come in an electronic age. An electric bell system had been installed to lend some modernity to the starting and stopping of trading, replacing the booming gong of the old building. Unfortunately, the jingle of the electric bells could not be heard above the trading uproar at the end of the session. So back came the sturdy 800 pound gong—the gong that had once swung above City Hall. In the Great Fire it had partly melted, but it was recast in 1873 and became the property of the Board of Trade. Doubtless its return gave immense satisfaction to many nostalgic traders.

A hitch had developed, too, in the nation's economic system, and it could not be remedied by bringing back an old gong. By the time the new building was occupied, the Great Depression was getting underway.

The traditional starting point of the Great Depression is the collapse of the bull market in Wall Street in late 1929. It certainly was the most public and dramatic manifestation of the nation's and the world's underlying economic malaise. But well before that shocking event, the already distressingly weak farm economy had sagged further.

At the start of June, 1929, wheat at terminal markets was bringing less than $1 a bushel. May wheat closed out at 93¼ cents in Chicago, within ¼ cent of the 1915 low. It had fallen 24¾ cents in 30 days. July wheat sold at 96 cents, equaling the low of 1923 and with that exception the lowest since 1914. From the highs of February, prices had dropped 37½ to 42⅜ cents. Glutted markets, a huge carryover from the previous year and expectations of a bumper 1929 crop caused the selling.

The highly inflated stock market ignored the spring break in grain prices, but, during September and early October, stocks headed downward with a persistence and speed that puzzled market analysts and annoyed Republican politicians.

By October 14, Cutten, never hesitant to use journalists to manipulate public opinion, was provoked to describe the decline as a typical sharp, short-lived retreat in an upward secular trend. "I used to make money on the short swings," said Cutten, "but I found that it could not be done consistently and I now follow the policy of picking good companies and staying with them." Obviously, he was attempting to forestall nervous selling on the part of the public. "With inventories held to a minimum," Cutten added. "American business is in wonderful shape and no depression can go far."[29]

Only brief rallies interrupted the frightful slide. On Saturday, October 19, the market plunged in the second most active Saturday in history. The *New York Times* noted that Cutten—whom the *Times* described as "the recognized leader of the bull crowd"[30]—spent the day in his suite at an Atlantic City hotel, watching the chattering ticker and telling newsmen that nothing had happened to change his opinion that good stocks would eventually sell higher.

On Thursday, October 24, the market again had to absorb an avalanche of selling, retreating throughout the day, while Winnipeg wheat prices broke 15 cents and it was rumored that Cutten had dumped 10 million bushels of the grain at any price it would bring.

On Monday, October 28, the good people of Guelph, Canada, had reason to wonder if, by following their home town boy into the stock market, they were not following a false prophet. Cutten spoke by phone with the editor of the local newspaper, denying rumors in the worried village that he had been responsible for the price break. He stated truthfully that the stock he himself still held had suffered disastrously.

The next day the market was rocked by the largest one day price break in history.

NOTES

1. Arthur Cutten and Boyden Sparkes, "The Story of a Speculator," SEP, 19 November 1932, 66.
2. Ibid.,26 November 1932, 18.
3. New York Times, 25 July 1924.
4. Cutten and Sparkes, SEP, 3 December 1932, 13.
5. New York Times, 5 August 1925.
6. Ibid., 7 August 1924.
7. Ibid., 11 September 1924.
8. Ibid., 30 January 1925.
9. Chicago Tribune, 31 January 1925.
10. Ibid., 30 January 1925.
11. Cutten and Sparkes, SEP, 3 December 1932, 13.
12. Chicago Tribune, 29 March 1925.
13. Ibid., 28 March 1925.
14. New York Times, 19 March 1925.
15. Ibid., 11 October 1925.
16. Cutten and Sparkes, SEP, 19 November 1932, 3.
17. Ibid.
18. Ibid.
19. Ibid.
20. Ibid.
21. New York Times, 2 January 1927.
22. Ibid., 19 January 1922.
23. Ibid., 17 August 1927.
24. Literary Digest, 10 September 1927, 42.
25. New York Times, 4 March 1927.
26. Ibid.
27. Ibid.
28. Cutten and Sparkes, SEP, 10 December 1932, 25.
29. New York Times, 15 October 1929.
30. Ibid., 20 October 1929.

CHAPTER THIRTEEN

End of an Era

For farmers, prosperity ended well before the stock market crash of 1929. It ended with the termination of World War I. Throughout the 1920s various farm programs, often highly complicated, were trotted out by the farm bloc in Congress to be routinely shot down by either the full Congress or Presidential vetoes. Farming was secondary to business in that boisterous decade.

Upon his inauguration as President in 1929, Herbert Hoover called a special session of Congress to deal with agricultural relief and tariff revenue. No action was taken on the tariff, but Congress attacked the farm problem by passing the Agricultural Marketing Act of 1929.

The act set up a Federal Farm Board, gave the Board a $500 million revolving fund, and authorized it to create "stabilized corporations." These were to control, handle and market the surpluses of their particular commodities. Alexander Legge, president of International Harvester Corporation, was named chairman of the Federal Farm Board, which had two divisions that influenced prices—the Farmer's National Grain Corporation (FNGC) and the Grain Stabilization Corporation (GSC). The FNGC was a cooperative clearing house where farmers might find a ready market for wheat at prices prevailing in the cash market. The GSC supported prices by acquiring large stocks of wheat accumulated by farmer marketing agencies, notably the FNGC.

Wheat prices declined throughout the summer of 1930. In September the dreary slump provided a mirthful moment when Secretary of Agriculture Arthur Hyde uncovered a Russian plot.

The All-Russian Textile Syndicate—which, of course, was an arm of the all-powerful Russian government—sold 7½ million bushels of wheat futures on the Chicago Board of Trade. It was not a monumental amount of grain, but Secretary Hyde asserted the Russian selling was designed to send American wheat prices lower and cause "discontent" among farmers. He telegraphed John Bunnel, Board of Trade president, asking what the exchange would do "for the protection of our American farmers from such activities."[1]

At the time Rep. Hamilton Fish, Jr. of New York was conducting the initial Congressional investigation of Communist influence in the United States. He was delighted at the Russian action, asserting, "Nothing has developed recently that shows better just how far the Soviets are willing to go to carry out their doctrines and injure business and government elsewhere."[2] But Senator Brookhart was not impressed: he saw the Hyde charges as an excuse for the administration's failure to keep up the price of wheat. As for Hyde's reason for the Russian action, Senator Brookhart said, "The farmer already is as discontented as he can get."[3]

Just before World War I, Russia was the world's leading exporting country. During the war and subsequent Bolshevik Revolution her exports practically ceased. In the 1926–27 season, Russia's shipments abroad amounted to 49 million bushels, and after that declined to very small amounts. However, the Communist leaders adopted a policy of obtaining foreign credits for needed imports of capital equipment. To that end wheat production was expanded by the 1929–30 season, helped by a phenomenal per acre yield. Russia's exports for 1930 would total 93 million bushels as compared with 6 million in the previous year.

In 1930 Russia undercut prices of other exporting countries on the European market, selling mostly to England. While no explanation was ever offered for her selling wheat futures in Chicago, the move appeared to be an effort to make money on a declining market. As she sold wheat in Europe, depressing prices, the price of futures could be expected to—and did—decline in Chicago, also. Obviously, there was no intention to deliver cash grain on futures contracts as the United States at this time imposed a tariff of 42 cents a bushel on imported wheat.

The immediate reaction of the grain trade to Secretary Hyde's blast was a combination of amusement and cynicism. James E. Bennet, the head of an important commission firm, asserted, "We gladly receive orders from Canada, Russia or any other country. So-called farm relief is hopelessly ineffective and it looks like somebody is looking for an alibi." President Bunnell replied to Hyde, "It should be remembered that the Chicago Board of Trade is a recognized world market and hedges protecting grain in all positions over the world are customarily placed here."[4]

A telegram to Chicago from the Winnipeg Grain Exchange said some brokers had gone to work wearing red ties, jocularly hoping this display might encourage Russia to send some orders through them at regular commission rates.

Nevertheless, following Hyde's revelation, September wheat dropped to a new low since 1906 at 74½ cents and Bunnell thought better of his initial noncooperative attitude. The Board's directors passed a resolution stating, "The selling of futures on our exchange by any foreign government is a new development of commerce of a seriously objectionable character and must be brought to an end."[5]

A beneficiary of the Russian selling was one of the biggest capitalists and speculators around—Arthur Cutten. Licking his considerable wounds from the stock market crash, Cutten returned to the more hospitable environment of the wheat pit in early 1930 in an effort to recoup.

Cutten jumped in and out of the market but he emphasized short selling in anticipation of making a profit as prices declined and the worldwide depression worsened. A detailed government study of his operations revealed the manner in which a big, active trader plays the market.

On January 25, 1930, Cutten was short 1,050,000 bushels of all futures in wheat. May wheat closed that day at $1.26⅝, July $1.27⅛. Between January 25 and February 25 he sold 2,710,000 bushels, increasing his short position to 3,760,000 as May declined to $1.08½ and July to $1.10⅛.

While these positions involved fairly large amounts of grain, they did not match his buying in the mid-1920s. He was suffering grievously in the stock market decline—"I never want to live through another experience like the last three years," he said in 1932.[6] By now Cutten was 60 years old, and he showed it. He was very hard of hearing, chewed unlighted cigars and spoke in a low voice not much above a whisper.

By April 10 (May $1.14⅛, July $1.15) Cutten had completely covered his short line and gone long 1,800,000 bushels. Then he started selling again, reaching a short position of 1,410,000 bushels by April 26 (May $1.03, July $1.04⅝, Sept. $1.08¼, Dec. $1.13). This was extended to

2,475,000 bushels on June 12 (July $1.03, Sept. $1.06, Dec. $1.10⅞) when the first grain of the new crop was heading toward market. He reached his maximum short position, 7,525,000 bushels, on June 24 (July 88⅝, Sept. 91¾, Dec. 97⅛).

But by August 8 (Sept. 96⅜, Dec. $1.02¼, March $1.06⅞) he was again on the long side of the market—to the extent of 4.1 million bushels. Then, in just six trading days, he sold 5.1 million bushels, winding up with a short position of 1 million bushels (Sept. 91½, Dec. 96⅝, March $1.01⅜). During the year he was short 79 per cent of the time he was in the market.

The Grain Futures Administration still required reporting of positions of 500,000 bushels or more in futures of major grains. But Cutten, possibly remembering how he was obliged to sell some May wheat in 1926 by the Business Conduct Committee of the Board of Trade at the suggestion of the GFA, hit upon a plan to escape repetition of such an annoyance.

Cutten opened 32 different accounts with seven different firms—Bartlett Frazier Co.; Clement, Curtis Co.; Jackson Bros. Bosel & Co.; F. B. Keech & Co.; James Kidston & Co.; C. D. Robbins & Co.; and Uhlmann Grain Co. The accounts were in the names of relatives and friends and usually were carried as numbered accounts, such as Special 57 or Special 57-A (his two accounts with Uhlmann Grain Co.). Not a single account at any time had a net position of as much as 500,000 bushels either on the long or short side. This was the figure at which Cutten would have been required to report to the GFA. A large number of accounts stopped at 495,000 bushels. "The notion that I could buy or sell no more than 500,000 bushels without having my trades subjected to the scrutiny of government clerks was to me galling beyond my powers of expression," Cutten was to write in 1932.[7] (He misquoted the rule slightly. A report had to be made at 500,000 bushels.)

As early as February 25, 1930—the day that Cutten, through his numerous accounts, was short 3,760,000 bushels of wheat—Secretary of Agriculture Hyde telegraphed Cutten concerning his operations in the market:

> It is reported to me that you have been operating on the bear side of the grain market and that these operations have contributed to the collapse of the market. I have no right or authority to suggest any course to any business-man in his own business but just in the public interest if you could abandon such a course it would help many thousands of people in time of distress. If the report is not true then disregard my anxiety in the matter.[8]

To this timorous, deferential and apologetic wire, Cutten's reply was at best evasive; at worst, a lie. He replied:

> Your wire received and your information misleading. I have not been very active in the markets. My activity for the last two weeks consisted of selling about four hundred privileges each way. I don't think I have sold a bushel of wheat during that time except to protect the trades put.[9]

(Privileges were options—rights to purchase or sell at a specific price within a limited period of time—in which trading had been reinstituted by the Board. A put is an option to sell; a call an option to buy.)

Regardless of his telegram, it should be noted that Cutten did abandon his short selling and started buying until he had a long line of 1,800,000 bushels by April 10 (May $1.14⅛, July $1.15). And then he started selling again, reaching a short position of 1,410,000 bushels by April 26 (May $1.03, July $1.04⅝).

If the Russian government could not trade in wheat futures, the American government could. With the price of both cash and December wheat in the 70s, a frightening situation developed with country banks. Many of these little banks, scattered in small towns throughout the grain belt, had made loans to farmers on the basis of dollar wheat. Farmers selling wheat at the market price received less than the banks had loaned on the grain. Because outstanding bank loans could not be collected in full, the banks had to cut down on new loans.

Aware of this disastrous situation, Chairman Legge of the Farm Board authorized the GSC in November, 1930 to step into the wheat market and buy futures at all major exchanges. He made it clear that this was no small deal: "There is no limit to the price or the quantity of wheat which we plan to purchase."[10]

The stabilization price—the price at which the corporation bought—was 73 cents for December wheat in Chicago and 77 and 78 cents for new and old crop May wheat. Later purchases of May were in the low 80s.

During 1931 the May future, representing the last of the 1930 crop, held up as a result of the GSC buying while the July future, on which the new 1931 crop wheat would be available for delivery, declined. May sold above the price in Liverpool from January through May by 15 to 20 cents. Normally, when the United States had an exportable surplus, the Chicago price was below the Liverpool price. The July future, not subject to stabilization, sold below 60 cents in March, April and May.

Despite Chairman Legge's statement that there was no limit to the amount of wheat the GSC would buy, there was a limit to the available funds. Consequently, the Farm Board announced on March 22, 1931 that the GSC would cease its purchases with the conclusion of trading in the 1930 crop, which meant the May future.

Thus at the end of May, the program terminated with the government in possession of more than 200 million bushels of wheat at key markets throughout the country—Minneapolis, Kansas City, Chicago and Duluth-Superior. Grain men estimated that farmers held 43 million bushels back on the farms, an action which had been urged on them by the Farm Board but which would now leave them without government support for this grain.

The final quotation for May wheat in Chicago was 83¾ cents per bushel.

Looking back on his own efforts, George S. Miller, president of the GSC, said:

> Since last November, the price of No. 2 hard wheat has advanced in Chicago from 76 to 84 cents a bushel. These prices have in turn been reflected throughout the entire country, with the result that farmers and others have been able to liquidate their wheat holdings at an average of 20 to 30 cents a bushel above the world price levels, which declined to 42½ cents at Winnipeg, 60½ cents at Liverpool and 45⅛ cents at Buenos Aires.[8]

Yet the government was in the position of so many speculators who accepted delivery of grain: it had to bury the corpse.

Lacking support from the GSC, the price for new 1931 crop wheat plunged as this grain arrived at markets in the southwest. In Chicago, the July future fell to 56⅝ cents by June 4, lowest for any July contract since 1896.

Again in this year, Russia poured wheat into the world market, depressing prices everywhere, as that country pressed forward with its economic plan that would eventually transform it from a nineteenth century rural nation into a growing twentieth century industrial power. Gigantic state farms were established on previously unused land while peasant holdings were gathered together in "collectives" (communes) and the kulaks, the top 5 per cent of the peasantry, were "liquidated." The urban population was placed on short rations and in some cases a shortage of food developed even in rural areas. Many people starved.

Cutten was a more active short in 1931 than in 1930—he was short 89 per cent of the time he was trading. Early in the year—February 10—he assumed a short position of 1,945,000 bushels of all wheat futures. May closed that day at 84 cents and July at 71⅝ cents. He increased this position, getting ready for the new crop deluge, until he reached his top for the year of 6,770,000 bushels sold short on April 10, when May closed at 84 cents and July 62½ cents and September 60⅝ cents.

In this year it was not Secretary Hyde but his superior, President Hoover, who endeavored to exert pressure on Cutten. Harassed and bedeviled by many misfortunes, some of his own making, the President blamed short sellers for the price decline:

> It has come to my attention that certain persons are selling short in our commodity markets, particularly in wheat . . . I refer to a limited number of speculators. . . . It has but one purpose, and that is to depress prices. It tends to destroy returning public confidence. The intent is to take a profit from the losses of other people. Even though the effect may be temporary, it deprives many farmers of their rightful income. If these gentlemen have that sense of patriotism that outruns immediate profit, and a desire to see their country recover, they will close these transactions and desist from their manipulations.[12]

By the middle of July all wheat had gone to new lows with July at 52⅜ cents. In Liverpool the July contract dipped to the lowest level since 1654.

The *Kansas City Star*, which had supported the nomination of President Hoover prior to the start of the 1928 primary campaign, urged the government to impound the leftover 1930 crop. It said this would cost $60 million and contrasted it with President Hoover's declaration of a moratorium on a much greater sum of World War I debts owed this country by European nations.

Within a few days, wheat slipped to 50¼ cents for July, an all time low up to that date for that contract. But the cash price held above the all-time low of 48⅞ cents set in January, 1895.

In Salina, Kansas, new 1931 crop wheat sold at 25 cents a bushel, which, it was noted, was several cents less than the price of two packages of cigarettes. In Guyman, Oklahoma, many farmers refused to harvest their grain; a few plowed it under. In Enid, Oklahoma, the price was 28 cents; in Independence, Kansas, 30. And in Bucklin, Kansas, one Forrest Kennet opened the end gate of his truck and let his wheat spill out on the street rather than sell it at 27 cents a bushel. His truck had two big jackasses painted on the sides. One read, "Kansas Wheat Farmer," the other, "Farm Board."

Wheat became a medium of exchange in Dodge City, Kansas, and as a result, it piled up in vacated buildings and garages. Merchants were willing to take wheat in exchange for goods, offering farmers 15 to 25 cents above the market, because they believed the price would advance later in the year—the merchants became wheat speculators, taking the place of the fearful speculators on the nation's grain exchanges by being willing to "carry the crop."

On the last day of July, the July wheat future closed out at 48 cents—the lowest price for any futures contract in history up to that time. No. 2 hard wheat sold in the cash market at 50 to 50¾ cents. In Liverpool the July future sank to 55⅞ U.S. cents, lowest since the reign of Queen Elizabeth (1558–1603).

It is doubtful if President Hoover's plea had an effect on Cutten, but he did give the market support in the tradition of the professional speculator, covering his short lines as the new crop arrived at terminals. Cutten had completely eliminated his short position and gone long 2,845,000 bushels by November 12, when December sold at 61¼ cents. A few days earlier a delegation from the Board of Trade visited President Hoover and told him the Board had protective regulations against "bear raiding." In view of a substantial price upturn since his July 10 declaration, and also probably because of what he knew from the trading reports to the Grain Futures Administration, President Hoover expressed satisfaction with the situation.

But hardly had President Hoover been mollified when Cutten started selling again. Between November 12 and 25, when December wheat closed at 54⅜ cents, Cutten sold 6,805,000 bushels, putting him on the short side of the market by 3,960,000 bushels. By the end of December, wheat closed out the dismal year in a range of 53⅛ to 56⅞ cents for the various contracts.

Corn performed much better than wheat, selling at a higher price at times and attracting much attention from speculators—and particularly Thomas Howell, something of a rival of Cutten at this time for the dubious distinction of leading commodity speculator in the country.

In the summer of 1930, the country suffered the worst drought on record up to that time. Droughts were not unusual. They had occurred in 1881, 1894, 1901, 1911, 1916 and 1924. And they would become more severe, and more dramatic because of dust storms, within a few years. But the 1930 drought sufficed to cut corn production to 2,060,185,000 bushels, down about 25 per cent from the average harvest of the previous five years.

Heavy losses occurred in the Midwest states surrounding Chicago. In the seven states most severely affected by the drought, yields averaged less than half those usually obtained. Because of the crop damage, much more corn was destined to be used for silage and forage and less in the form of grain.

One of the speculators attracted to corn by this situation was Howell. He justified his buying entirely on the drought: "With the shortest crop in years, if corn is not worth 60 cents a bushel I am willing to lose money buying it."[13]

Howell made his first purchase, 700,000 bushels of July, on April 24, a day on which the July future sold from 59¾ to 61⅛ cents. He kept on buying and by May 28 accumulated 4,995,000 bushels. As with Cutten's activity in wheat, the figure is significant. At this time the supervisor of the Chicago office of the Grain Futures Administration had an unofficial understanding with the Board of Trade that he would notify the Business Conduct Committee when the speculative net position of any individual totaled 5,000,000 bushels, which was viewed by the Grain Futures Administration as the level at which a situation dangerous to market stability could be created. Presumably, the Business Conduct Committee would persuade the speculator to lighten his position, as it had done with Cutten in 1926. Howell stopped buying in his own name at a mere 5,000 bushels under the 5,000,000 figure.

But Howell was not alone in the operation. He had friends, including three members of the Board of Trade, he brought along with him. Two of these members—R. N. and J. R. Meyer—were brothers of Mrs. Howell. Mrs. Howell also had an account, as did Howell's daughter, Helen. Both purchased July corn. So did the Barrington Company, a Delaware corporation directed and controlled by Howell. Once Howell's own holdings reached 4,995,000 bushels, he directed purchases in the names of family and friends.

By June 27 the Howell Group had run up their purchases to 8,310,000 bushels. At that time there were only 1,480,189 bushels of corn of a deliverable grade in "regular" Chicago warehouses. The visible supply of all grains east of the Rocky Mountains, including quantities afloat on the Great Lakes, totaled only 7,197,000 bushels. By July 18 the Howell Group held warehouse receipts for all the corn of deliverable grade in store in Chicago. By July 25 deliverable corn stored in "regular" Chicago elevators totaled 3,688,941 bushels while the Howell Group was long 5,260,000 bushels on the July contract.

To the surprise of many in the grain trade, Howell called for the delivery of grain on maturing July contracts. He also bought large quantities of cash corn arriving in Chicago, shipping it out of the city. From a price of 57½ cents on July 20, the July contract ran up to 72½ cents on July 31, the last trading day, before slipping on a rumor of a private settlement at 68 to 69¼ cents. Howell acquired more than eight million bushels of cash corn.

Nearly three million bushels of the cash grain came to Howell from the FNGC, an action which stirred up much criticism from the anti-government private grain trade. It was claimed that the government agency had sold July corn short, the precise type of activity that the farm bloc progressives had bitterly criticized the grain speculators for doing over the years. Such action, the progressives always claimed, drove down prices. Directors of the Board met with the FNGC. They determined that the selling was not speculative but instead was a hedging operation as the FNGC had the cash corn on hand at the time it sold July futures.

Howell was not successful in disposing of his cash corn profitably throughout the world. The 1931 crop turned out to be a good one at 2,567,306,000 bushels and offered severe competition in the market place for Howell's 1930 crop corn. In the end, Howell claimed he lost $1,250,000 on the deal, and the government did not dispute his contention.

Both Cutten and Howell demonstrated that it was possible to avoid the restrictions of the Grain Futures Act and it is a reasonable assumption that other traders, less conspicuous than those two, followed the same procedure on a smaller scale. Despite many efforts over a long period of years, speculation in grains had not freed itself from duplicity and trickery.

The problem of speculation had worried observers as far back as the Civil War, when Secretary Beaty hoped, in his 1865 annual report, that "this fever of speculation will abate, and trade will be conducted on a more thoroughly legitimate basis."[14] Many, at that time, felt that all trading in futures was gambling—betting on rising and declining prices—and that only dealings in cash grains were legitimate. Thus the *Chicago Tribune* after the Great Fire in 1871, condemned the "gambling spirit" and urged the Board to "expurgate this excresence and keep it banished forever."[15]

The two facets of speculation which aroused the greatest criticism were "corners," which infuriated consumers, and "short selling," which had a similar effect on producers. As far back as 1868, the directors of the Board adopted a resolution calling for the expulsion of any person attempting a corner, but as we have seen this threat had little influence on more adventuresome speculators. Charles Randolph, secretary in 1883, called cornering a "positively pernicious method of conducting business," adding "any device which will tend to hold speculative operations in reasonable check should be hailed."[16]

No really effective device was uncovered until the Grain Futures Act of 1922, although the Board's directors did have sporadic successes in frustrating corners by easing the requirements for "regular" storage. The Grain Futures Administration required large traders to report their positions in the market and restricted the amount of grain they could buy or sell. This was an important step because it meant that the corner or manipulation could be averted before it occurred—provided the large trader complied with the law. It remained possible, however, for a group of traders, each acting within the limitations of the administration's regulations, to act in collusion to manipulate prices.

Short selling baffled and angered producers almost from the start of futures trading, as witness the Illinois law of 1867 which prohibited such activity. (It was repealed the next year.) This type of selling was the main target of Senator Washburn and Representative Hatch in their 1892 crusade. The idea of people selling what they did not own aroused both President Hoover in 1931 and Secretary of Agriculture Arthur Hyde in 1930 to plead with Cutten to desist in that activity.

Critics felt that short selling drove down prices at harvest time, thus injuring the farmer; defenders said the short selling occurred mainly prior to the harvest and when harvest time arrived the shorts supported prices by their buying to cancel out their previous short sales. It was this feature which prompted economic professors to assert, in affidavits submitted in Hill vs. Wallace (1923), that in the long run futures stabilized prices.

The enormous volume of trading in comparison with the amount of grain actually delivered on futures, as noted by Samuel Taton of the American Farm Bureau Federation in his testimony before the Senate Agricultural Committee in 1921 (51 times as much wheat sold in the futures market as actually shipped to Chicago), caused farm legislators to refer to such grain as "wind wheat" and to condemn it. Much of this trading represented hedging—the buying or selling of futures inversely to the buying or selling of cash grain.

Defenders of speculation claimed that if the intent to make or accept delivery existed, that justified the speculation. Brokers required customers, when giving an order, to sign a statement saying they would deliver or accept delivery of the actual grain. But, as Senator Kenyon noted in the 1921 Senate Agricultural Committee hearings, most customers signed "with a mental reservation."

The speculative presence was essential to a liquid market. It was true, as Senator Capper claimed in 1921, that the large brokerage houses eagerly sought customers, thereby encouraging speculation and gaining substantial commissions. But speculation was not unlawful, as Justice Holmes noted, and an active market was essential if the grain trade was to use it for hedging. Hedging transferred the risk in handling grain from elevators, shippers, millers, exporters and others to speculators. Without such transfer of risk, the agribusiness concerns would be compelled to increase their operating profit margins. In a free market speculators were—and are—essential.

Of course, it is possible for an economic system to function without a free market. In the nineteenth century, Chicago was foremost in setting the price of grain around the world, as William Nicholls, governing director of the Spillers Milling & Associated Industries, said in 1925, but there were also futures markets in Liverpool, Buenos Aires and Winnipeg. In England and Argentina, the futures markets were subsequently abolished; so was the wheat market in Canada. Government alone sets the price— precisely what the GSC, on a small scale, had attempted to do in 1930. And the GSC had the same problem that so often confronted large scale speculators: how to bury the corpse?

The GSC made a deal with Brazil in 1931. That country, suffering from a suffocating surplus of coffee, was burning it at the rate of one million bags a month. The GSC traded 25 million bushels of wheat for about one million bags of coffee in a straight commodity transaction with no money involved. The corporation also gave 85 million bushels to the Red Cross, sold 15 million bushels to China on credit for a little over $9 million and 7½ million bushels to Germany for nearly $4 million. For the rest, the grain was sold piecemeal in the domestic and foreign markets with the last sale in the spring of 1933.

Nineteen hundred thirty-two saw the Great Depression reach bottom.

During the dreadful summer of that year, prices of most farm commodities hovered around record lows. Revolt flared in rural communities— farmers blocked shipments of grain to cities, halted farm foreclosures, fought pitched battles with deputy sheriffs and threatened to storm jails to release arrested pickets.

The farmer no longer believed that the "short seller" was responsible for all his woes, nor was the speculator on the Board of Trade the primary culprit. The Grain Futures Act had been enacted to prevent manipulation of prices; but it did not prevent fundamental economic developments from causing a price collapse. All over the world, in industry as well as agriculture, it appeared that an unequal distribution of reward for work had caused production to expand beyond the capacity of consumption to absorb that production. Idle factories stood silently beside bulging grain elevators.

Yet a change blew in the wind. With the 1932 Presidential election looming, it seemed certain that the Republicans would renominate Herbert Hoover and that the Democrats would nominate Franklin Delano Roosevelt, governor of New York. As a governor preparing for the presidency, Roosevelt gathered around himself a group of newsmen, politicians, friends and, most prominently, college professors. The group was dubbed the "Brains Trust," subsequently reduced (without malice) to the singular—Brain Trust.

The governor listened to various recommendations of farm leaders at the Executive Mansion in Albany. With rural America in a state of revolt, Roosevelt considered the farm problem high on his agenda for solution. One solution was offered by John Simpson, president of the small Farmers Union; he urged that the government set the price of grain. Obviously, that would have eliminated the futures market. But there is no indication that this suggestion was taken seriously.

Farm prices clearly fell more drastically than industrial prices during the Great Depression. From August, 1929 to August, 1932, prices of all groups of farm commodities, at the farm, declined nearly 65 per cent. In the same period nonagricultural prices at wholesale declined 24 per cent. The ratio of prices received by farmers to prices paid at retail for commodities used in farm living and production illustrated the disparity between agriculture and industry to an even greater extent. In other words, farm commodity purchasing power was little more than half what it had been in the years—uniquely favorable to agriculture—immediately prior to World War I.

The farmer's actual purchasing power, at one time totaling $16 billion, had shrunk to less than $5 billion. A market for $11 billion in industrial and consumer goods had disappeared, wiped out by the world-wide calamity. That loss was more than twice the nation's annual total retail sales. Besides the 30 million people living on farms who were directly affected, there were at least 50 million more whose fortunes were linked with the farmer.

A good deal of bickering, back-biting and jealousy developed within the Brain Trust, even before the nominating conventions. The academicians were not immune to these human frailties. Henry Morgenthau, Jr., a Dutchess County, New York neighbor of Roosevelt and publisher of the *American Agriculturist*, was suspected of wanting to become Secretary of Agriculture by Rexford Guy Tugwell, a Columbia University economics professor who had joined the group as an agricultural expert at the suggestion of Adolf A. Berle, Jr., a Columbia Law School professor. Tugwell had a somewhat contemptuous attitude toward George Warren and Frank Pearson, professors of agriculture and farm management at Cornell University. He saw them as being aligned with Morgenthau and referred to them as "the Cornellians." Roosevelt acted as an amused and amicable referee.

Nevertheless, from the standpoint of future agriculture policy, the most important man in the group was Tugwell. And from the standpoint of grain traders, he was also the most feared.

Tugwell was an up-state New York boy, born in Sinclairsville in Chautauqua County. Curiously for a professor in a university situated in a densely populated residential area of the nation's largest city, Tugwell's main interest centered in agriculture—"Since my graduate days," he said, "I have always been able to excite myself more about the wrongs of farmers than those of urban workers."[17]

In 1927 Tugwell had visited Russia with several other intellectuals and concluded "the humanly achieved industrial balance of Russia is more likely to attain the objective of 'necessities for all before luxury for any' than is our competitive system."[18]

Speaking in 1931 before the American Economic Association, Tugwell espoused a planned economy concept and asserted it entailed, among other things, controlled prices and elimination of speculative gains—and "an enlarged and nationalized police power of enforcement." The future, he said, was "becoming visible in Russia."[19] (Several years later, before a congressional committee, he displayed his dexterity in answering hostile questions by saying he was just tracing the requirements of a planned economy to show it would not work.)

Tugwell was disdainful of the concept that an "invisible hand" ruled the free market equitably and justly. "The cat is out of the bag," he proclaimed. "There is no invisible hand. There never was." Tugwell wanted a "managed society," calling for "a real and visible guiding hand to do the task that mythical, nonexistent, invisible agency was supposed to perform."[20]

To someone such as Cutten, Tugwell must have appeared as a person with a bomb in one hand and a stick of dynamite in the other, heading for the Board of Trade building.

In July, 1932, while the Republican Party still held the presidency, Cutten called the Washington regulators "bureaucratic lap dogs . . . fed out of the public purse." He reached the conclusion that "farmers are being exploited and the public gouged only to benefit partisans of a political party, in reality a machine of destruction, a steamroller of ruthless violence, crushing all in its greed for waxing fat on public money."[21]

On July 16, following the national conventions (which did the expected) all wheat futures dipped below 50 cents for the first time since futures trading started more than 75 years earlier. No. 2 hard wheat brought a miserable 48 to 48½ cents in the cash market.

Once again, a withholding movement developed in the Northwest, farmers claiming they would not sell their wheat until it reached $1. Participants in the movement who lacked storage space were allowed to haul their grain into elevators and obtain storage. Possibly because of this development, which attracted considerable national publicity, wheat prices advanced slightly in the next month, staying above the 50 cent level. Early in September the GSC announced it would withhold wheat and cotton from the market. Its cash wheat supply had dwindled to a small three million bushels from 250 million in July, 1931. The GSC would not disclose its holdings of futures but did say it would sell no futures prior to January 1, 1933. It was an obvious move to remove some pressure from the market prior to the presidential election.

At the start of November, Canada and Argentina strained to outdo one another in selling wheat in response to private estimates that it would take nearly two years for the world to eat through the stocks it had on hand, not considering production in the years ahead. Russia dumped wheat into Europe through her Black Sea ports. Antwerp, Rotterdam and other European harbors were clogged with grain. In the American farm belt, grain piled up in warehouses and farm politicians warned of revolution.

On November 3 half-dollar wheat—in itself an incredibly low figure— disappeared from the North American continent and virtually all world markets. The Liverpool Corn Exchange was the only major market on

which wheat brought as much as 50 cents; one futures contract reached
50½. The December future at Chicago, Minneapolis and Kansas City
sold at the lowest prices ever. The quotation was 41⅞ cents at Chicago,
43⅞ at Minneapolis and 37¼ at Kansas City. In the Chicago cash market, No. 2 mixed wheat brought a dismal 43 cents. These prices were for
good quality wheat. It was estimated that in some sections of the wheat
belt distant from terminal markets, wheat of lower quality, but nonethe-
less fit for human consumption, had no value at all.

Five days later Franklin Delano Roosevelt was elected President of the
United States.

NOTES

1. *New York Times*, 30 September 1930.
2. Ibid.
3. Ibid.
4. Ibid., 20 September 1930.
5. Ibid., 21 September 1930.
6. Cutten and Sparkes, *SEP,* 3 December 1932, 67.
7. Ibid., 10 December 1932, 24.
8. Secretary of Agriculture v. Arthur Cutten. Transcript before the Commission created by the
   Grain Futures Act. Docket no. 7, 49–50, Record group 180, National Archives.
9. Ibid.
10. *New York Times*, 18 November 1830.
11. Ibid., 30 May 1931.
12. Ibid., 11 July 1931.
13. Ibid., 31 July 1931.
14. Seventh Annual Report. Chicago Board of Trade, Chicago, 1865, vii.
15. *Chicago Tribune*, 15 October 1871.
16. Twenty-fifth Annual Report, Chicago Board of Trade, Chicago, 1883, xii.
17. William E. Leuchtenberg, *Franklin D. Roosevelt and the New Deal, 1932–40* (New York 1963),
    35.
18. Arthur Schlesinger, Jr. *The Crisis of The Old Order, 1919–1933* (Boston 1957), 142.
19. Ibid., 196.
20. Ibid., 194.
21. *New York Times*, 24 July 1932.

Epilogue

I mprovement in the devastated farm economy had a priority in the Roosevelt administration, but reforms in grain trading did not. Such reforms were preceded by the Agricultural Adjustment Act of 1933 which, among many other actions, set up a price support system for farm products, a move obnoxious to the free market advocates in the grain pits.

Three years later Congress got around to the marketing mechanism and passed the Commodity Exchange Act of 1936 as an amendment to the Grain Futures Act of 1922. The new law established rules to protect traders against fraudulent practices by dealers and it applied registration requirements and penal sanctions to individual futures commission merchants and floor brokers.

This was the first enlargement of the original Federal attempts to regulate trading practices and it would be extended in the next several decades. Along with the growth in Federal regulation came, perhaps surprisingly, an enormous expansion in the futures trade based upon inauguration of trading in areas beyond the imagination of the early grain dealers.

The major step toward Federal regulation came in 1974 when Congress passed the Commodity Futures Trading Act. This act created the Commodity Futures Trading Commission and gave it broad powers over futures trading. The act was renewed in 1978, 1982 and 1986, each time strengthening the control of the Federal government over futures market activity.

The commission was an independent agency, not a division of the Department of Agriculture as its predecessor had been, and was created to monitor and police not only agricultural products trading but also trading in metals, rubber, currencies and other nonfarm items.

The exchanges—and particularly the Chicago Board of Trade—gave up their powers grudgingly. Examples:

In March 1979 the commission ordered that all trading in the March wheat contract on the Chicago Board of Trade be prohibited in order to forestall what appeared to be a developing corner in that contract. Promptly, the Board went to the U.S. District Court and obtained a preliminary injunction against the commission's action. The commission appealed to the U.S. Court of Appeals for the seventh district and on September 12 that court unanimously reversed the lower court's opinion.

In 1980 the Chicago Board of Trade and the Chicago Mercantile Exchange acted to expand delivery months in the twenty-year Treasury bond contract and the thirteen-week and one-year Treasury bond contracts without submitting new regulations to the commission for approval. The commission thereupon altered the proposed regulations, emphasizing its authority in such matters.

The most attention-getting action by the commission related to the Hunt family of Dallas, Texas. The commission had set the limits on any individual trader in soybean futures at 3,000,000 bushels in 1971. Reports showed that various members of the Hunt family had a net long position in old crop soybean futures of 22,760,000 bushels on April 27, 1977.

This provoked a long running legal skirmish which ended in 1981 when the Hunts offered to settle and the commission accepted. The Hunts were assessed a civil monetary penalty of $500,000 and each individual was prohibited from trading soybean futures for two years (except for hedging in the case of Nelson Hunt). Previously, a Federal judge had ordered a court supervised, orderly divestiture of all Hunt family holdings in excess of 3,000,000 bushels.

The 1976 act that had established the commission had also authorized the formation of "registered futures associations." Nothing was done along this line until 1981 when the National Futures Association was formed. When fixed commission rates on exchanges were eliminated, many commission firms found it profitable to forego exchange membership. As a result the exchanges—the futures trade's self-regulatory organizations—lost control over the ethics and solvency of these commission firms. But in 1978 Congress authorized mandatory membership for commission firms in registered futures associations, a prerequisite if self-regulation was to work.

The National Futures Association was organized as a nationwide body to police areas of the commodity futures industry and it has taken some duties previously performed by the commission, which had to adjust to budget restrictions at the same time the futures trade was sharply expanding. The association establishes training standards, provides arbitration for futures related disputes, tests and registers futures professionals, and monitors them for financial and general rule compliance. However, the commission can review (and reverse) disciplinary actions and membership applications if it so desires.

In September 1975 the commission took a significant step when it designated the Chicago Board of Trade as a contract market in Government National Mortgage Association certificates (GNMAs), the first financial instrument futures contract. This was quickly followed by designating the Chicago Mercantile Exchange a contract market for 90-day U.S. Treasury bills. Even before these designations, between 1971 and July 1975, the commission approved 44 contract markets to add to the 38 that had existed at the time of the commission's creation. The new contract markets were in metals, forest products, currencies and international commodities.

What was behind such an explosion?

First, the exchanges had a long history of seeking new types of commodities to trade. The reason is obvious: the more commodities to trade, the more transactions—and that results in more brokerage house commissions and greater value for exchange memberships. Commodities which failed to attract a steady following in those pre-commission years ranged all the way from steel scrap to onions.

Second, opposition to futures trading in the past centered in the liberal farm organizations and the farmers they represented. But the farm population had declined steadily for many years and the farmer lost the political clout he once had. Larger grain producers are more likely to use the futures markets for hedging than small farmers and therefore have a less antagonistic attitude toward the markets.

Third, it is in the interest of regulators to have something to regulate. Based upon the record, the exchanges do not appear to have had much difficulty in convincing the commission to permit them to experiment with new commodities and new trading vehicles. In consequence, the commission grew in size and status.

Fourth, the political and social climate was favorable for expansion. Presidents Nixon, Ford, Carter and Reagan set a conservative tone which encouraged businessmen to venture into new areas. The futures exchanges were not unresponsive to this situation. The results were apparent in the number of exchanges handling futures trading and the number of contracts which were traded.

In 1977 four New York exchanges—the New York Cotton Exchange, the Coffee and Sugar Exchange, the New York Mercantile Exchange and Commodity Exchange, Inc.—moved into a joint facility at the Commodity Exchange Center. In Chicago, the Chicago Mercantile Exchange, at one time a relatively obscure butter and egg market, moved into a new structure. The old Open Board of Trade, which traded in odd lots (contracts of 1,000 bushels and not 5,000 bushels as on the Board of Trade) in a little store on a side street off La Salle Street, became the MidAmerica Commodity Exchange, still trading in odd lots in grain but also listing contracts in various metals, foreign currencies, hogs and cattle. The New York and American stock exchanges also set up futures trading. In 1981 the New Orleans Cotton Exchange started with trading in cotton and rice futures but ended trading in New Orleans the next year, transferring its transactions to the floor of the MidAmerican Exchange in Chicago where it became known as the Chicago Rice and Cotton Exchange.

In 1982 the commission approved the first futures contract based upon a stock index: the Value Line average traded on the Kansas City Board of Trade. Three other commodity exchanges also inaugurated trading in market indices, including the Chicago Board of Trade which continued as the largest commodities futures exchange in the world. These stock market futures were viewed by the commission as offering hedging possibilities "for money managers seeking to reduce portfolio market risk."[1]

These contracts were, of course, settled in cash. Other contracts settled in cash included gold bullion on the AMEX in New York, the municipal bond index on the Chicago Board of Trade, the Euro-dollar time deposit on the Philadelphia Board of Trade and the consumer price index composite for wage earners and clerical workers on the Coffee, Sugar and Cocoa Exchange in New York.

Obviously, these contracts were far removed from delivering grain held in a Chicago warehouse from one party to another by means of a warehouse receipt. Indeed. it wasn't clear that the 1905 U.S. Supreme Court decision upholding trading in futures contracts could be applied to these nondelivery contracts. Critics contended they were mere bets on the direction of prices in other markets.

Further, in one sense nondelivery contracts, in the opinion of the critics, enabled speculators to circumvent margin requirements set by the Federal Reserve Board. For example, in October 1987, the margin requirement for trading in stocks was 50 per cent of the market price; a speculator or investor had to place with his broker one half of the stock's price when buying that stock. If the stock purchased had a market value of $100,000, cash of $50,000 was required.

At the same time it was possible for a speculator to buy on the Chicago Mercantile Exchange a futures contract for the Standard & Poor's 500 stock index (the most popular index) on a 20 per cent margin. To purchase the stock market futures index when the underlying stocks had a value of $100,000 required only $20,000. Furthermore, the person who borrowed $50,000 to purchase the stock had to pay interest on the borrowed money. No interest was required for the futures transaction because the buyer did not have possession of the stocks; he had simply agreed to settle in cash by the expiration date of the contract.

The Chicago Board of Trade in its report to the Presidential Task Force on Market Mechanism investigating the October, 1987 stock market crash referred to its margin requirement as "performance bond margins" and said such margins "do not involve any extension of credit nor do they result in any transfer of ownership of the underlying commodity."

The Board noted,

> Once a futures contract has served its purpose—providing temporary price protection for a hedger or offering profit opportunities for a speculator—most market participants make offsetting purchases or sales, thereby eliminating their delivery obligations. Less than three percent of all futures trades result in delivery. Those who wish to make or take delivery must follow a strictly defined procedure set by the exchange.

As we have seen, speculators are essential to a futures market. Without speculators, there could be no hedging, no transfer of risk. Money managers—the high paid men who manage investments for various funds, such as pension funds—can transfer the market risk in their investments by selling futures contracts of various indices; in many cases the buyers are speculators carrying the investment similar to speculators in grain who "carry the crop."

In the October, 1987 crash, much selling in both stocks and indices was based on a mathematical formula. The crash spawned at least a half dozen investigations and planned Congressional hearings.

Another interesting development was approval by the Commodity Futures Trading Commission of trading in options (puts and calls). This trading medium was frequently branded "pure gambling" in the late nineteenth and early twentieth centuries. Approximately 30.5 million option contracts were traded on various exchanges in fiscal 1986.

In 1984 the Chicago Mercantile Exchange's International Money Market set up a trading link with the Singapore International Monetary Exchange. Two years later the Commodity Exchange in New York established a link for trading in identical gold bullion contracts with the Sydney Futures Exchange in Sydney, Australia. And in early 1987 the Chicago Board of Trade linked its financial instrument trading with the London International Financial Exchange.

Behind these moves was an emerging plan to usher in an era of global, around-the-clock trading.

In the 1977 fiscal year slightly more than 41 million futures contracts were traded; the total figure in fiscal 1986 was 183 million, an increase of more than 400 per cent—a remarkable surge for a type of activity that received legal justification in a 1905 U.S. Supreme Court decision because of a combative bucketshop operator in Kansas City.

In 1977 the futures markets were predominantly agricultural; by 1987, trading volume was paced by financial instrument contracts. There were 96,886,878 financial instrument contracts traded in fiscal 1986 compared with 10,315,267 grain contracts, 13,798,988 oilseeds and products contracts, 8,571,157 livestock products contracts and 6,699,770 "other agricultural" contracts—a total of 39,385,182 agricultural contracts, less than half the financial instruments total.

Coming under the authority of the Commodity Futures Trading Commission at the start of 1987 were 388 commodity brokerage firms, 55,151 sales people, 7,070 floor traders, 1,084 commodity pool operators, 2,040 commodity trading advisors and 1,247 introducing brokers.

It's a long, long way from Old Hutch sitting on his throne and telling his broker, "Give them what they want at $1.25."

NOTES

1. "Commodity Futures Trading Commission—The First Ten Years," 50. (A pamphlet published by the Commodity Futures Trading Commission, Washington, D.C., 1984.)

Bibliography

I. Books

Abels, Jules. *In the Time of Silent Cal.* New York, 1969.

Ahern, M.L. *The Great Revolution: A History of the Rise and Fall of the People's Party in the City of Chicago and Cook County.* Chicago, 1874.

Albion, Robert. *The Rise of New York Port, 1815–1860.* New York, 1934.

Andreas, Alfred T. *History of Chicago from the Earliest Period to the Present Time.* 3 vols., Chicago, 1884–86.

Andrews, Wayne. *Battle for Chicago.* New York, 1946.

Angle, Paul M., comp. *Prairie State: Impression of Illinois, 1673–1967, By Travelers and Other Observers.* Chicago and London, 1968.

Arnold, Isaac N. *William B. Ogden and Early Days in Chicago.* Chicago, 1881.

Asbury, Herbert. *Gem of the Prairie.* New York, 1940.

Atkinson, Eleanor. *The Story of Chicago and National Development.* Chicago, 1911.

Baer, Julius B. and Saxon, Olin G. *Commodities Exchanges and Futures Trading.* New York, 1949.

—— and Woodruff, George. *Commodity Exchanges.* New York, 1935.

Baker, Charles. *Life and Character of William Taylor Baker.* New York, 1940.

Benedict, Murray. *Farm Policies of the United States, 1790–1950.* New York, 1953.

Bidwell, Percy W. and Falconer, John I. *History of Agriculture in the Northern United States, 1620–1860.* Washington, D.C., 1925.

Bogue, Allan G. *From Prairie to Cornbelt.* Chicago, 1963. Reprint 1968.

Boyle, James. *Marketing of Agricultural Products.* New York, 1925.

—— *Speculation and the Chicago Board of Trade.* New York, 1931.

Bogart, Ernest L. and Thonpson, Charles M. *Readings in the Economic History of the United States.* New York, 1916.

Brooks, Eugene C. *The Story of Corn and the Westward Migration.* Chicago, 1916.

Buck, Solon J. *The Granger Movement: A Study of Agricultural Organization and its Political, Economic and Social Manifestations, 1870–1880.* Cambridge, Mass., 1913.

Buckingham, J.H. *Illinois as Lincoln Knew It.* Illinois State Historical Society Papers in Illinois History and Transactions. Springfield, 1937.

Buley, Roscoe C. *The Old Northwest.* 2 vols. Indianapolis, 1950.

Candler, John. *A Friendly Mission; John Candler's Letters from America, 1853–54.* Indianapolis, 1951.

Caird, James. *Prairie Farming in America.* New York, 1859.

Carey, Peter B. *The Rise of Exchange Trading.* Chicago, 1933.

Chicago Herald. *Chicago As It Appeared in 1858.* Chicago, 1894.

Clark, John G. *The Grain Trade in the Old Northwest.* Urbana and London, 1966.

Cleaver, Charles. *Early Chicago Reminiscences.* Chicago, 1888.

—— *History of Chicago from 1833 to 1892.* Chicago, 1892.

Colbert, Elias. *Chicago: Historical and Statistical Sketch of the Garden City.* Chicago, 1868.

—— and Chamberlin, Everett. *Chicago and the Great Conflagration.* Chicago and Cincinnati, 1872.

Cooke, Guy W. *The First National Bank of Chicago.* Chicago, 1913.

Cowing, Cedric B. *Populists, Plungers and Progressives.* Princeton, 1965.

Coyne, Frederick E. *In Reminiscence: Highlights and Events in the Life of Chicago.* Chicago, 1941.

Danhof, Clarence H. *Change in Agriculture: The Northern United States, 1820–1870.* Cambridge, Mass., 1969.

Dewey, Thomas. *Legislation Against Speculation and Gambling in Futures.* New York, 1959.

Dicey, Edward. *Six Months in the Federal States.* London and Cambridge, 1863.

Dies, Edward J. *The Wheat Pit.* Chicago, 1925.

—— *The Plunger.* New York, 1929.

—— *Street of Adventure.* Boston, 1935.

Dondlinger, Peter. *The Book of Wheat.* New York, 1908.

Dowrie, George William. *The Development of Banking in Illinois, 1817–63.* University of Illinois Studies in the Social Sciences, vol. 2, no. 4, Urbana, 1913.

Emery, Henry Crosby. *Speculation on the Stock and Provisions Exchanges of the United States.* New York, 1896.

Faulkner, Harold O. *The Decline of Laissez-Faire, 1897–1917.* New York and Toronto, 1951.

Federal Trade Commission. *Report on the Grain Trade.* 7 vols. Washington, D.C., 1920–26.

Fergus Printing Co., *Biographical Sketches of Early Settlers of the City of Chicago.* Chicago, 1879.

Fite, Emerson David. *Social and Industrial Conditions in the North During the Civil War.* rpt, New York, 1963.

Frederick, John H. *Agricultural Markets.* New York, 1937.

Frederick, Justus G. *The Real Truth About Short Selling.* New York, 1932.

Friedman, Lear and Osrael, Fred L. editors, *The Justices of the United States Supreme Court, 1789–1969, Their Lives and Major Opinions.* 4 vols. New York and London, 1969.

Gale, Edwin O. *Reminiscences of Early Chicago.* Chicago, 1902.

Gates, Paul W. *The Farmer's Age: Agriculture, 1815–60.* New York, 1960.

—— *Agriculture and the Civil War.* New York, 1965.

Goldstein, Benjamin. *Marketing: A Farmer's Problem.* New York, 1923.

Goodspeed, Weston A. and Healy, Daniel D. *History of Cook County, Illinois.* 2 vols. Chicago, 1911.

Gregory, John G. *History of Milwaukee, Wisconsin.* 4 vols. Milwaukee, 1931.

Grey, Lewis. *History of Agriculture in the Southern United States to 1860.* 2 vols. New York, 1941.

Hadniger, Don F. *Federal Wheat Commodity Programs.* Ames, 1970.

Hager, Charles B. *Milwaukee Illustrated: Its Trade, Commerce, Manufacturing Interests and Advantages as a Residence City.* Milwaukee, 1877.

Hansen, Marcus Lee. *The Atlantic Migration, 1607–1860.* Cambridge, 1940, pbk, New York, 1961.

Havighurst, Walter. *The Long Ships Passing: The Story of the Great Lakes*. New York, 1961.
—— *The Heartland*. New York, 1956.
Hayes, William E. *Iron Road to Empire*. New York, 1953.
Hicks, John D. *The Populist Revolt: A History of the Farmers Alliance and the Peoples Party*. Minneapolis, pbk, 1931.
Hidy, Ralph W. *The House of Baring in American Trade and Finance: English Merchant Bankers at Work, 1763–1861*. Harvard Studies in Business. Cambridge, 1949
Hill, John G. *Gold Bricks of Speculation*. Chicago, 1904.
Historical Publishing Company. *Origin, Growth and Usefullness of the Chicago Board of Trade*. New York, 1885–86.
Hoffman, G. Wright. *Futures Trading on Organized Commodity Markets in the United States*. Philadelphia and London, 1932.
Hubbart, Henry. *The Older Middle West, 1840–80: Social, Economic, Political Life*. New York, 1936.
Jackson, Donald. *Black Hawk, An Autobiography*. Urbana, 1955.
Kindleberger, Charles P. *The World in Depression, 1929–39*. Berkley and Los Angeles, 1973.
Kirkland, Caroline. *Chicago Yesterdays*. Chicago, 1919.
Kirkland, Edward C. *A History of American Economic Life*. 4th edition. New York, 1969.
Kirwin, Albert. *The Confederacy: A Social and Political History in Documents*. New York, 1959.
Leech, Harper and Carroll, John C. *Armour and His Times*. New York and London, 1938.
Lurie, Jonathon. *The Chicago Board of Trade, 1859–1905: The Dynamics of Self Regulation*. Urbana, 1979.
Marsh, Charles. *Recollection, 1837–1910*. Chicago, 1910.
Martineau, Harriet. *Society in America*. 3 vols. London, 1837, rpt New York, 1966.
McHugh, J.G. *Modern Grain Exchanges*. Minneapolis, 1919.
McMath, J.C. *Speculation and Gambling in Options, Futures and Stocks in Illinois*. Chicago, 1921.
McReynolds, Edwin C. *Missouri: A History of the Crossroads State*. Norman, Oklahoma, 1962.
Mills, Charles H. *Fraudulent Practices in Respect to Securities and Commodities*. Albany, 1925.
Mitchell, Harley B. *Historical Fragments of Early Chicagoland*. Chicago, 1928.
Mitchell, Broadus. *Depression Decade—From New Era Through New Deal, 1925–41*. Vol 9. The Economic History of the United States. New York, pbk, 1947.
Morgan, Dan. *Merchants of Grain*. New York, 1979.
Pease, Theodore C. *The Frontier State, 1818–48*. Centennial History of Illinois. Springfield, 1918.

Pierce, Bessie Louise. *A History of Chicago.* 3 vols. New York and London, 1937–57.

Quaife, Milo M. *The Development of Chicago, 1674–1914.* Chicago, 1916.

Rex, Frederick. *The Mayors of the City of Chicago-From March 4, 1835 to April 12, 1933.* Chicago, 1945.

Saloutos, Theodore and Hicks, John D. *Agricultural Discontent in the Middle West, 1900–1939.* Madison, 1951.

Schlebecker, John T. *Whereby We Thrive; A History of American Farming, 1607–1972.* Ames, Iowa, 1975.

Schlesinger, Arthur M. Jr. *The Crisis of the Old Order, 1919–33.* Boston, pbk, 1957.

Schonberg, James S. *The Grain Trade: How It Works.* New York, 1956.

Shannon, David A., editor. *The Great Depression.* Englewood Cliffs, New Jersey, 1960.

Shepherd, Geoffrey S. *Marketing Farm Products-Economic Analysis.* Ames, Iowa, 1962.

Starr, John W. *Lincoln and the Railroads.* New York, 1927.

Stephens, George Ware. *Some Aspects of Early Intersectional Rivalry for the Commerce of the Upper Mississippi Valley.* Washington University. Humanistic Series. April, 1923.

Still, Bayrd. *Milwaukee: The History of a City.* Madison, 1948.

Surface, Frank M. *The Grain Trade During the War.* New York, 1928.

Swift, Louis F. and Van Vlissimgen, Jr., Arthur. *The Yankee of the Yards.* New York, 1917.

Taylor, Charles. *A History of the Board of Trade of the City of Chicago.* 3 vols. Chicago, 1917.

Touman, F.S. *Stock and Commodity Exchanges.* New York, 1931.

Tugwell, Rexford Guy. *The Brains Trust.* New York, 1968.

Walker, Robert A. *Life in the Age of Enterprise, 1865–1900.* New York, 1967, pbk, 1971.

Warren, Charles. *The Supreme Court in United States History.* 2 vols. revised, Boston, 1925.

Warren, Harris Gaylord. *Herbert Hoover and the Great Depression.* New York, 1967.

Woodham-Smith, Cecil. *The Great Hunger.* New York, 1962.

Wood, David Ward. *Chicago and its Distinguished Citizens.* Chicago, 1881.

II. Articles and Pamphlets

Architectural Record. Description of J. Ogden Armour's Melody Farm. (February 1916).

Bakken, Henry H. "History and Development of the Chicago Board of Trade." Futures Trading Session, Madison (1960).

Belcher, Walter W. "The Economic Rivalry between St. Louis and Chicago, 1850–80." *Columbia University Studies in History,* 529.

Boyle, James E. "The Law of Supply and Demand and the Wheat Market." Ithaca, New York (1921).

—— "Chicago Wheat Prices for Eighty-One Years." Ithaca, New York (1922).

Bross, William. "Chicago and the Source of Her Past and Future Growth." Chicago (1880)

Clark, John G. "The Antebellum Grain Trade of New Orleans: Changing Patterns in the Relation of New Orleans with the Old Northwest." *Agricultural History* 38 (July 1964).

Christie, C.C. "Bucket Shops vs the Chicago Board of Trade." *Everybody's*, (November 1906).

Clutton, F.H. "Provisions Market of the Chicago Board of Trade." *Annals of the American Academy of Political and Social Science.* (May 1931).

Conant, Charles A. "The Uses of Speculation." *Forum* 31 (1901).

Congressional Digest. "Congress Investigates Short Selling Practices." (December 1932).

Cutten, Arthur and Sparkes, Boyden. "The Story of a Speculator." *Saturday Evening Post.* 19 and 25 November, 3 and 10 December 1932.

Dart, Joseph. "The Elevators of Buffalo." Buffalo Historical Society Publications 1 (1879).

Dickerson, Oliver. "The Illinois Constitutional Convention of 1862." *Illinois University Bulletin*, University Series 2, no. 5 (1905).

Dunn, Arthur W. "An Analysis of the Social Structure of a Western Town." Chicago (1896).

Eastman, Zebulia. "Charles Walker." *Chicago* 1 (1857).

Emery, Henry Crosby. "Futures in the Grain Market." *Economic Journal.* (March 1899).

—— "Legislation Against Futures." *Political Science Quarterly.* (March 1899.)

Ferris, William G. "Joseph Built the First Wheat Pit." *Nation's Business.* (April 1948).

—— "Old Hutch—The Wheat King." *Journal of the Illinois State Historical Society.* (September 1948).

—— "The Great Corner." *The Farm Quarterly.* (Spring 1968).

—— "Justice Holmes and the Bucketshops." *The Farm Quarterly.* (Winter 1968–69).

—— "Who Sets the Price of Corn?" *The Farm Quarterly.* (Winter 1950).

—— "The Disgrace of Ira Munn." *Journal of the Illinois State Historical Society.* (June 1975).

Gannon, James H. Jr. "Smith, Debtor: A Bucketshop Idyll." *Everybody's.* (September 1906).

Ginsberg, Eli. "The Economics of British Neutrality During the American Civil War." *Agricultural History* 10 (1936).

Grain and Feed Journal. "Hedging as a Problem of Relative Prices." (12 July 1933).

Hadwiger, Don F. "Federal Wheat Commodity Programs." Ames, Iowa, 1970.

Hardy, Charles O. "The Theory of Hedging." *Journal of Political Economics.* (April 1923).

Historical Publishing Company. "Origin, Growth and Usefulness of the Chicago Board of Trade." New York (1885–86).

Hoffman, G. Wright. "Government Regulation of Exchanges." *Annals of the American Academy of Political and Social Science*. (May 1931).

Huebner, S.S. "The Insurance Service of Commodity Exchanges." *Annals of the American Academy of Political and Social Science*. (May 1931).

Huff, C.E. "In the Grain Pit." *Nation's Agriculture*. (April 1936).

Hutchinson, Benjamin P. "Speculation in Wheat." *North American Review* 153 (1891).

Irwin, H.S. "Impressions Concerning Commodity Futures with Special Reference to Wheat Futures." Washington, D.C. (1936).

Irwin, H.S. "Risk Assumption in Trading on Exchanges." *American Economic Review*. (June 1937).

Kemmerer, Donald L. "The Pre-Civil War South's Leading Crop, Corn." *Agricultural History* 23 (October 1949).

Lee, Guy A. "The Historical Significance of the Chicago Elevator System." *Agricultural History*. (January 1931).

Lee, Judson Fiske. "Transportation: A Factor in the Development of Northern Illinois Previous to 1860." *Journal of the Illinois State Historical Society* 10 (1917)

Lindley, Arthur F. "Essentials of an Effective Futures Market." *Journal of Farm Economics*. (February 1937).

Loman, H.J. "Commodity Exchange Clearing Systems." *Annals of the American Academy of Political and Social Science*. (May 1931).

Lloyd, Henry Demarest. "Making Bread Dear." *North American Review*. (August 1883).

Lurie, Jonathon. "Speculation, Risk and Profits: The Ambivalent Agrarian in the Late Nineteenth Century." *Agricultural History* 46 (1972).

―――― "The Chicago Board of Trade, The Merchants Exchange of St. Louis and the Great Bucket Shop War, 1882–1905." *Bulletin of the Missouri Historical Society* (1973).

―――― "Commodities Exchanges, Agrarian 'Political Power' and the Anti-Options Battle, 1890–1894." *Agricultural History* 28 (1974).

Marcossan, Issac F. "The Perilous Game of Cornering a Crop." *Munsey's*. (August 1909).

Modern Miller. "Early Grain Inspection History." (21 December 1935).

North, Douglas. "International Capital Flows and the Development of the American West," *Journal of Economic History* 16 (December 1956).

Olde, Thomas D. "The American Grain Trade of the Great Lakes, 1825–75." *Inland Seas* 7,8,9 (Winter 1951–Autumn 1953).

―――― "Entrepreneurial Cooperation on the Great Lakes: The Origins of the Methods of American Grain Marketing." *Business History Review* 38 (1964).

Parker, Carl. "Government Regulation of the Exchanges." *Annals of the American Academy of Political and Social Science* 38 (September 1911).

Patten, James and Sparkes, Boyden. "In the Wheat Pit." *Saturday Evening Post*. (3 and 17 September, 1 October 1927).

Payne, Will. "The Chicago Board of Trade." *Century* 65 (1903).

Peterson, Arthur. "Futures Trading with Particular Reference to Agricultural Commodities." *Agricultural History* 7 (April 1933).

Revere, C.T. "Short Selling: Its Function in a Free Market." *Review of Reviews* 85 (April 1932).

Rice, Frank A. "History of Ouary." Typewritten manuscript. Ouray, Colorado Public Library.

Rose, Marc A. "Wheat Madness." *Saturday Evening Post* (12 June 1937).

Rothstein, Morton. "Antebellum Wheat and Cotton Exports—A Contrast in Market Organization and Economic Development." *Agricultural History* 40 (April 1966).

Russell, Dudley J. "A Defense of the Grain Futures Market." *Northwestern Miller* (30 March 1938).

Stevens, Albert Clark. "Futures in Wheat." *Quarterly Journal of Economics* (October 1887).

——— "The Utility of Speculation." *Political Science Quarterly* (1892).

Stewart, Blair. "The Profits of Professional Speculators." *Economic Journal* (September 1934).

Stone, George F. "Board of Trade of the City of Chicago." *Annals of the American Academy of Political and Social Science* 38 (September 1911).

Taylor, Alonzo E. "The Cost of Trading in Wheat Futures." *Wheat Studies of the Food Research Institute*, Stanford University 7 (February 1931).

Treleven, Dale E. "Railroads, Elevators and Grain Dealers." *Wisconsin Magazine of History* 52 (1969).

U.S. Department of Agriculture Circular no. 323: "Trading in Privileges on the Chicago Board of Trade."

Veblen, Thorstein. "The Price of Wheat Since 1867." *Journal of Political Economy* (1892).

Woodman, Harold D. "Chicago Businessmen and the Granger Laws." *Agricultural History* 36 (January 1962).

III. Legal Cases, Congressional Hearings and Transcripts

Board of Trade v. Christie. 198 US 236

Board of Trade v. Christie. 116 Federal Reports 944

Board of Trade v. Kinsey. 125 Federal Reports 72

Board of Trade v. Kinsey. 130 Federal Reports 507

Board of Trade v. United States. 246 US 231

Board of Trade v. United States. 314 US 534

Christie v. Board of Trade. 125 Federal Reports 161.

Munn v. Illinois. 94 US 113

"Options and Futures." Committee on Judiciary, U.S. Senate, 52 Congress, 2 Session, Washington, D.C. 1892.

"Fictitious Dealings in Agricultural Products." 52 Congress, 1 Session, Washington, D.C. 1892.

"Commodity Short Selling." Committee on Agriculture, House of Representatives, 72 Congress, 1 Session, Washington, D.C. 1932.

Complaint of the Secretary of Agriculture vs Thomas Howell before the Commission Created by the Grain Futures Act, Docket 8.

Secretary of Agriculture, plaintiff, vs Arthur Cutten, respondent, Docket 7, United States of America before the Commission Created by the Grain Futures Act.

Arthur W. Cutten, petitioner, vs Henry Wallace, Homer Cummings and Daniel C. Roper in the United States Circuit Court of Appeals for the 7th Circuit, no. 5467.

Hearings of the Senate Committee on Agriculture, Futures Trading Act of 1921, No. 212, 67th Congress, 1st session, Washington, D.C., 1921.

INDEX